Sport, culture and ideology

Sport culture and history

Sport, culture and ideology

Edited by *Jennifer Hargreaves*

Routledge & Kegan Paul

· London, Boston, Melbourne and Henley

First published in 1982
by Routledge & Kegan Paul Ltd
39 Store Street, London WC1E 7DD,
9 Park Street, Boston, Mass. 02108, USA,
296 Beaconsfield Parade, Middle Park,
Melbourne, 3206, Australia, and
Broadway House, Newtown Road,
Henley-on-Thames, Oxon RG9 1EN
Printed in Great Britain by
T.J. Press (Padstow) Ltd, Padstow, Cornwall
Selection and editorial matter © Jennifer Hargreaves 1982
Contributors © Routledge & Kegan Paul 1982

Library of Congress Cataloging in Publication Data

Main entry under title:

Sport, culture and ideology

Includes index.
1. Sports - Social aspects - Addresses, essays, lectures.
I. Hargreaves, Jennifer, 1937 -
GV706.5.S698 1982   306'.483   82-16666
ISBN 0-7100-9242-3

Contents

Notes on contributors

ALAN CLARKE is a Research Assistant in the Department of Sociology at the Open University. He is currently working on the media coverage of politics and he has published articles on General Election television and television crime series. He is involved in the course on Popular Culture at the Open University.

JOHN CLARKE is a Lecturer in Social Policy at the Open University. He has contributed to the work of the Centre for Contemporary Cultural Studies at the University of Birmingham, including 'Resistance through Rituals' (1975), 'Policing the Crisis' (1978) and 'Working Class Culture: Studies in history and theory' (1979). He has also published work on sport in Ingham (ed.) 'Football Hooliganism' (1978).

CHRISTINE GRIFFIN is currently working at the Centre for Contemporary Cultural Studies on an SSRC-funded project on 'Young women and work, with special reference to gender and the family', and she is involved in youth work with girls.

PETER HAIN has worked since 1976 as Assistant Research Officer for the Union of Post Office Workers. Publications include 'Don't Play with Apartheid' (1971); 'Radical Regeneration' (1975); 'Mistaken Identity' (1976); 'Community Politics' (ed.)(1976); 'Policing the Police' (ed.), vol.1. (1979) and vol.2. (1980).

JENNIFER HARGREAVES is a Senior Lecturer in Sports Studies at Roehampton Institute, specialising in the History and Sociology Sociology of Sport. She has contributed articles to the 'Bulletin of Physical Education'. Her present research includes a sociological analysis of women's sport in contemporary British society.

JOHN HARGREAVES teaches Sociology at Goldsmiths' College, University of London, specialising in Political Sociology. He has contributed to several books on culture, leisure and sport, including the OU reader 'Education and the State' volume II. He is currently completing a book on sport and hegemony in Britain.

DOROTHY HOBSON is currently working at the Centre for Contemporary Cultural Studies towards a PhD thesis, The Media and Working Women at Home. She has published Housewives: Isolation as Oppression, in 'Women Take Issue' (1978) and jointly edited 'Culture, Media, Language' (1980).

SUE MACINTOSH is currently working on 'Middle-aged Women at Work and at Home' at the Centre for Contemporary Cultural Studies and Middlesex Polytechnic.

TRISHA McCABE is currently involved in youth work with girls and in editing the 'Working With Girls Newsletter' (National Association of Youth Clubs).

MARTYN LUCKING is currently in general practice in Blackpool, with a special interest in sports medicine.

JAMES RIORDAN is a Senior Lecturer in Russian Studies at the University of Bradford. Publications include 'Sport in Soviet Society' (1971); 'Sport Under Communism: U.S.S.R., Czechoslovakia, G.D.R., China and Cuba' (ed.)(1978); 'Soviet Sport: Background to the Olympics' (1980).

DAVID ROBINS is a research worker at London University's Institute of Education. He is co-author of 'Knuckle Sandwich: Growing Up in the Working Class City' (1978).

IAN TAYLOR is Associate Professor in Sociology at Carleton University, Ottawa. He is co-author of 'The New Criminology: for a social theory of deviance' (1973), co-editor and contributor to 'Critical Criminology' (1975), co-editor of 'Deviance and Control in Europe' (1976) and his book 'Law and Order: Arguments for Socialism' was published in 1981.

PAUL WILLIS is currently a Research Fellow at the Centre for Contemporary Cultural Studies and is the author of 'Learning to Labour' (1977) and 'Profane Culture' (1980).

Acknowledgments

I wish to thank everybody who has helped in the preparation
of this volume and with the conference which gave rise to
it. Special thanks are due to Peter Esrich, my colleague
from Southlands, who planned and organised the conference
with me, to John Birch of the Sports Council who gave his
support to the venture, to Jill Tickner of the Sports
Council for administrative assistance, to Juanita Patrick
for help with typing, and to Lawrence Gresswell for
designing the publicity material. Thanks also to my
husband and to friends and colleagues for their assistance
and encouragement in practical ways and at the level of
ideas - especially Stuart Cosgrove, Tony Green, Sheila
Miles, Peter Weston and David Woodman. Finally, I would
like to acknowledge the support and enthusiasm of the
contributors, and particular thanks to Stuart Hood,
David Lane, and Jock Young, who chaired the sessions so
skilfully.

Chapter 1

Theorising sport: an introduction

Jennifer Hargreaves

In recent years there has developed an increasing interest
in sport as a cultural phenomenon (1) - a trend reflected
by this book, which is the direct product of a conference
organised in 1980 by the Department of Sports Studies of
the Roehampton Institute of Higher Education, in liaison
with the Sports Council (London and South East region).
I wish here to give an account of the specific historical
context for the conference in order to make clear why it
was planned and the ambitions behind it, one important
feature of which is a social analysis of sport within the
physical education and cultural studies traditions.

The theoretical treatment of sport in Britain has in
the past been almost exclusively the preserve of the
physical education profession, which has given minimal
reference to the ways in which sport is socially constructed and has ignored the fact that any analysis
implicitly contains a theory of society. Sport has
traditionally been accorded low academic status in higher
education. Any student wishing to study sport was obliged
to attend a teacher training college, and even the
specialist colleges of physical education, (2) which
provided an elite qualification in the field, reinforced
~~inforced~~ the institutional separation of sport from the
the institutional separation of sport from the 'intellectual' curriculum. For more than sixty years no degree
courses in sports studies were available, after which
time just one university offered sport as an element of
context that various theories of sport were established,
all of which, in different ways, tended towards a
conservative and uncritical assessment of the function of
sport in society.

A traditional influence on the subject has been the
entrenched scientific and positivist bias of much sports
theory, established in the early days by the strongly

concern with the 'problem of leisure' (9) and a feature
of the boom in the leisure industry. Teacher education
is now only a small part of the work of 'physical education
lecturers' - a misnomer for those involved in the study of
sport in a wider context.
The stage has been reached now where most of the new
degree courses in sports studies offered at colleges,
universities and polytechnics throughout Britain typically
include some reference to the social construction of
sport. Course texts which focus exclusively on sports
sociology are mostly American and, although between them
different perspectives are represented, together they
portray a mainly uncritical analysis of sport which has
been characterised as functionalist. (10) There is no
equivalent quantity of British work in the field and most
of what there is implicitly validates the existing
authorities and structures of sport and fails to trace
connections between sport, power, domination and political
control. A critical sociology of sport, broadly speaking
within the Marxist tradition, is a recent development
still in its formative stages. Courses in the sociology
of sport are taught, almost exclusively, by specialists
trained originally in physical education who have acquired
additional qualifications in sociology and other related
fields. Sadly, in spite of its quest for academic respectability, the physical education profession has failed to
extend the social analysis of sport and has produced no
substantial or polemical publication which would challenge
the influence of 'mainstream' sports sociology. (11) In
addition, the predominantly unproblematic treatment of the
relationship between sport and society in professional
journals, courses, and conferences reflects the way in
which physical education theorists identify, and work
closely with, practitioners, organisers, coaches and
administrators of sport. (12) These two groups, the
theorists and the sporting personnel, have had a symbiotic
relationship in the production of sports theory and
practice, a determining feature of which is their shared
vested interest in the development of sporting excellence
and in the burgeoning sports recreation sphere. The
structural position of physical education teachers tends
to constrain them from making a contribution to a critical
analysis of the institution of sport. In no way is a
blanket condemnation of what might be termed the 'sports
establishment' implied here, or of the physical education
profession. Our concern is for a more open, less incomplete
and biased social analysis of sport than is at present being
provided by the major institutionalised source of theory.
The potential for such an intervention has been enhanced

by the recent growth in another area of research - cultural
studies. There is increasing concern amongst theorists
from disciplines outside the physical education tradition
to treat sport seriously as an aspect of culture. Sport
is included as an element of study, although not a pivotal
one, in increasing numbers of courses run by different
faculties under such rubrics as community studies, popular
culture, and sociology of leisure. (13) However, it would
be misleading to imply that sport is receiving the same
attention as other cultural practices: the amount of work
is limited and fragmented and sport remains, overall, a
neglected area of study with many components of a comprehensive analysis completely unresearched. (14) The paucity
of literature in the field directs us to seek out scattered
readings from a wide range of sources, such as social
history, philosophy, political theory and anthropology.
However, the potential for a more sophisticated and
rigorously theoretical grasp of sport, which recognises
its complex characteristics and its specific relation to
the modern capitalist social formation, appears to derive
most directly from this group of apparently 'free-floating'
intellectuals from outside the physical education
profession. Such theorists together contribute to the
emergent and fast-growing field of cultural studies,
which is characterised not so much as 'a "discipline", but
an area where different disciplines intersect in the study
of the cultural aspects of society'. (15)

I have identified two sources of the analysis of sport
in society: the traditional physical education paradigm
with a powerful scientific component and an unmistakable
policy orientation underpinned by predominantly functionalist sociology, and the evolving, multidisciplinary field
of cultural studies whose parameters are much wider and
whose whole history has embodied the social.

Different theoretical approaches have been influential
in the development of cultural studies, and although the
arguments are complex and unresolved and cannot be examined
in detail here, my intention in outlining the dominant
perspectives is to show the position of sport, and its
relationship to other cultural forms. In its institu-
tionalised form, cultural studies has had a very brief
history in Britain. (16) Various accounts locate its
origins in the 'cultural debates' of the mid-1950s which
were articulated in response to economic, social and
political changes in British society. (17) The focus of
attention was the 'lived experience of improvement of a
whole generation of working people' in a post-war,
relatively affluent society, and discourse revolved
around the apparent homogeneity of the accompanying 'mass

consumer culture'. (18)   The so-called early 'culturalist'
stance is associated with certain key texts rooted in a
literary-historical mode, namely, Richard Hoggart's 'The
Uses of Literacy' (1957), Raymond Williams's 'Culture and
Society' (1958) and 'The Long Revolution' (1961), together
with E.P. Thompson's 'The Making of the English Working
Class' (1963), which falls clearly within the Marxist
tradition of historiography. (19)

In common, they were hostile to elitist conceptions of
culture, and especially to the unreserved elitism of
literary critics such as T.S. Eliot and F.R. Leavis who
vehemently opposed the debasement of 'traditional' (or
worthwhile) culture by the desensitising properties of
industrial 'mass' (or worthless) culture which had replaced
it:

> Mass production, standardization, levelling-down -
> these three terms convey succinctly what has happened.
> Machine-technique has produced change in the ways of
> life at such a rate that there has been something
> like a breach in cultural continuity; sanctions have
> decayed; and, in any case, the standards of mass-
> production (for mass-production conditions now govern
> the supply of literature) are not those of tradition....
> It is then vain to hope that standards will somehow
> re-establish themselves in the higgling of the market;
> the machinery of civilisation works increasingly to
> obliterate them. (20)

Leavis took the 'general state of language as a paradigm
of the culture', and he counterposed the texts and
artefacts which constituted minority 'culture' to products
of modern mass culture produced for, and harnessed to,
the entertainments industry. (21)

A similar rejection of mass culture, which had its
roots in a re-examination of Marxism in the late 1920s
and early 1930s, was a feature of the critical theory of
the Frankfurt School. (22)   The term 'mass' signified
the transformed social relations resulting from an
extended division of labour, large-scale commodity
production and consumption, the widespread intervention
of technology and science into industrial and administrative processes, and an increasingly authoritarian state.
It was in the context of a declared commitment to human
emancipation that the Frankfurt School stressed the
repressive effects of bourgeois thought and culture.   No
direct reference was made to sport but the products of
the 'culture industry' generally were viewed as thoroughly
destructive and dehumanising:

> Leisure time, like work, is a 'forced activity' and
> 'amusement ... the prolongation of work', a means

whereby the alienated worker replenishes his
psychological and physical strength to start work
again. (23)

In both these formulations, cultural 'massification'
was counterposed to an idealist, ahistorical notion of an
organic 'folk' culture of the past which, for T.S. Eliot,
encompassed a range of activities which included sport:

all the characteristic activities and interests of a
people. Derby Day, Henley Regatta, Cowes, the 12th
of August, a cup final, the dog races, the pin table,
the dart-board, Wensleydale cheese, boiled cabbage cut
into sections, beetroot in vinegar, 19th Century Gothic
churches, the music of Elgar.... (24)

This nostalgia for a specifically English heritage which
constituted a supposedly coherent, national 'whole way of
life' encompassed, unproblematically, elite upper-class
sports alongside 'plebeian' traditional ones. These
coexisted with, and supported, the sense of culture as the
'active cultivation of the mind' - that which is intellec-
tually and aesthetically valuable in classic forms such as
literature, art and music. (25)   In theories of mass society
the elitist conception of 'high' culture is normally
reinforced by sweeping generalisations and a dismissive
treatment of mass culture. Furthermore, the absence of
references to modern, popular forms of sport amounts to
a double elitism, and compounds the problems of an already
incomplete account of the process of cultural 'massification'. It is a significant silence because, from the
1920s, sport became a highly organised, commercialised,
and increasingly accessible and popular component of
modern culture. It shared many of the characteristics
of the consumer fetishism described graphically by the
Frankfurt School with reference to 'barbaric' forms of
art, literature, and music, and to the cinema and radio.
Sport, presumably, also had a role to play in the incorporation of the working class in the mass society that was
being described. In any case, such theories were thoroughly
pessimistic and determinist in their inability to discover
worthwhile or liberative tendencies in any modern cultural
forms. 'Mass culture' was used interchangeably with
'popular culture' as a pejorative term whose 'distinctive
mark is that it is solely and directly an article for mass
consumption, like chewing gum', parasitic upon the elite,
genre-based 'high culture', and having replaced the
traditional, practically based folk culture of the people.
(26) However, the renewed interest displayed in critical
theory during the 1960s reflects its valuable contribution
to an analysis of the culture of contemporary capitalism.
The recognition of the manipulative function of the media

and an awareness of ideology as a critical category for
explaining why culture cannot be considered as autonomous
are highly significant and polemical issues today. The
concept of culture became inseparable from the categories
of ideology and consciousness.

In different ways, the 'culturalists' in their early
work opposed the view that culture was manipulative and
debasing and that the people were purely passive. Hoggart
did this by insisting upon creative, authentic features of
contemporary working-class life - remnants of an urban
'culture of the people' which could not easily be dismissed as vacuous and outside 'real' culture; Williams,
by emphasising social practices and employing the
generalised definition of culture as a 'whole way of
life';   and Thompson, by showing how human experience
arises from the connection between material circumstances
and different forms of consciousness, historically
specific and linked to class cultures. Williams's and
Thompson's reworked positions retain a unifying opposition
to economism and a unifying stress upon human agency, on
creative, sensuous human activity in its historical
specificity. (27) They share a sense of 'cultural
totality', consisting of interconnected social practices
constituted by 'meanings and values which arise amongst
distinctive social groups and classes'. (28) In spite of
the paramount problem of an analytically viable definition
of culture posed by this position, it characterises the
dominant paradigm in cultural studies. (29) It appears
to have particular relevance to sport, because:

Focus was brought to bear not only on the more 'visible'
areas of working class culture such as popular music,
popular literature, the Hollywood cinema, etc. but on
the audience, and the entire social context in which
this culture was consumed. The main strength of this
position in the case of high cultural assumptions was
its ability to demonstrate the richly faceted cultural
life of the urban masses. (30)

However, although sport undeniably has an enormous
working-class following and logically belongs centrally
in this extended account of culture, it is either treated
peripherally, or it is excluded (as in the previous
quotation). For example, the implication of Hoggart's
concern for organic, working-class culture, centring on
magazines, is that sport is less central to working class
consciousness than is pulp literature. In 'The Uses of
Literacy', sport is given the briefest mention in a
descriptive, superficial, and incomplete way. (31) In
'The Making of the English Working Class', Thompson refers
to some traditional sports as a feature of the systematic

repression of working-class leisure in the nineteenth
century. (32) In 'The Long Revolution', Williams argues
that the quality of culture must be assessed and 'the
problem of bad culture' must not be avoided; 'football',
he declares, 'is indeed a wonderful game' and 'the need for
sport and entertainment is as real as the need for art'.
(33) In some more recent general texts on culture, a range
of cultural practices and experiences, but with the
exception of sport, are drawn upon - dance, drama, the
media, music, song, speech, poetry, literature, country
dancing, opera, fiction, film, visual art, painting,
sculpture, science fiction, horror films.... (34) My
concern here is that, if we identify the inadequate
treatment of sport, a situation may be highlighted which
has important repercussions. First, the absences have
an effect on the readers' consciousnesses to reinforce
the commonsense idea that we all understand about sport,
anyway, and it is, quite simply, something 'different',
'neutral', and therefore less important in an analysis
of culture. Second, by referring to sport with such
brevity and in such undetailed fashion, we imply that
sport is a distinct, homogeneous practice. Thus attention
is withdrawn from its multiple forms and complexities.

More recent developments on the epistemological and
methodological problems of analysing culture are located
within various neo-Marxist perspectives. There is a
parallel with trends in sociology and several of its
sub-disciplines including the sociologies of sport,
leisure, deviance and education. (35)

In the late 1960s and 1970s various kinds of
structuralist analysis, including semiology, entered
the field of cultural studies. Althusser's was a
seminal influence at the time and may be understood as
a reaction against the humanism of the 1950s. The controversial arguments surrounding his 'Ideological State
Apparatuses' essay, in which focus is given to the
structural logic of the way in which human experience is
constituted and the determining role of ideology within
cultural apparatuses, have been thoroughly rehearsed
elsewhere. (36) Althusser, unlike most other major
contemporary social theorists, mentions sport in his
theory of reproduction, though its specific relevance to
a social analysis of sport has been given scant attention,
which contrasts with the manifest impact Althusserianism
has had on the sociology of education, and on general
sociological theory. Althusser views sport as a cultural
apparatus of the state - a structure in which ideology is
secreted and becomes a 'lived condition' which functions
to reproduce unproblematically the social relations of

modern capitalist production. Althusser identifies the
ideologies which characterise modern sport as individual
competitiveness, chauvinism, nationalism and sexism, but
his theory treats them as abstract universals and not in
the context of specific historic and social relationships.
Within such a theory of social determination, institutions
such as sport are understood as channels of efficient
social control which have apparently eliminated consciousness and praxis, so that it is difficult to accomodate
oppositional sporting ideologies (e.g. the Black Power
Salute or the Stop the Seventy Tour Campaign). (37)

   Another 'structuralism' which is influential in
cultural studies derives from semiology but, again, its
relevance to sport has hardly been touched upon - rather
surprisingly, because sport is so rich in symbolism,
ritual, spectacle, and gesture. (38) Semiology has its
roots in Saussure's formulation of a science of signs in
society, founded upon structural linguistics, which Roland
Barthes has applied to signifying practices outside
language. A central premise is that 'myth is a type of
speech' which 'can consist of modes of writing or of
representations; not only written discourse, but also
photography, cinema, reporting, sport, shows, publicity',
which together produce a system of communication with a
common, dominant ideological core. (39) Culture is thus
understood as a 'signifying system through which
necessarily ... a social order is communicated, reproduced,
experienced and explored.'(40) The focus of analysis is
the sign systems within the internal structures of
cultural practices which appear, in a commonsense manner,
as unbiased and natural but are, in fact, part of a
systematic ideological process. Barthes's account of
wrestling in France for example, is that above all it is
meant to portray:

   a purely moral concept: that of Justice. The idea
   of 'paying' is essential to wrestling, and the crowd's
   'Give it to him' means above all else 'Make him pay'.
   This is therefore, needless to say, an immanent
   justice. The baser the action of the 'bastard', the
   more delighted the public is by the blow which he
   justly receives in return. If the villain - who is
   of course a coward - takes refuge behind the ropes,
   claiming unfairly to have a right to do so by a
   brazen mimicry, he is inexorably pursued there and
   caught, and the crowd is jubilant at seeing the rules
   broken for the sake of a deserved punishment.
   Wrestlers know very well how to play up to the
   capacity for indignation of the public by presenting
   the very limit of the concept of Justice.... Naturally,

it is the pattern of Justice which matters here, much
more than its content: wrestling is above all a
quantitative sequence of compensations (an eye for
an eye, a tooth for a tooth).... Justice is therefore
the embodiment of a possible transgression; it is
from the fact that there is a Law that the spectacle
of the passions which infringe it derives its value.
(41)
The theoretical problem here is to show how, specifically,
the 'anonymous ideology' inscribed in the rituals of a
wrestling contest, for example, is connected to ideology
in the other levels of social life, notably the economic
and political signifying systems. Raymond Williams
stresses that it would 'be wrong to suppose that we can
ever usefully discuss a social system without including,
as a central part of its practice, its signifying systems,
on which, as a system, it fundamentally depends.' (42)
This seems to have immediate relevance and exciting
.prospects for an analysis of sport with all its manifest
signifying systems. Williams anticipates that this new
kind of convergence in cultural studies will make it
possible to indicate the complex interrelations between
the means of cultural production and the process of
cultural reproduction. However, it is difficult to
conceive of how this might happen without a great deal
of theoretical reworking - the 'structuralisms' generally,
including semiology in their present formulations, retain
a static, non-historical and anti-humanist quality, with
a view of ideology as functional to capitalist society.
They demonstrate an inability to account for the complexity and contradictory features of the real processes of a
lived culture: the much-acclaimed notion of 'relative
autonomy' is a theoretical abstraction, and not grounded
in specific social relations. However, the contribution
of structuralism to cultural theory has been significant;
it correctly attempts to relate cultural phenomena to
class domination and ideology and, as Johnson points out,
it directs us to suggest that we are 'so obsessed with
literature, artistic production or human creativity in
general that we forget the material conditions from which
such creativity is never free'. (43)
Bourdieu has developed a unified theory, supported by
concrete historical research and classical techniques of
empirical sociology, which is in opposition to variants
of semiology and discourse theory. However, his ideas
are little known in this country outside the fields of
anthropology and sociology of education and the substantial
work he has done in the history and sociology of culture
has, surprisingly, been largely ignored. This is unfortu-

nate since his sense of the concrete and historically
specific is seen to have potential value in understanding
the problems of cultural reproduction left intact by the
other theories. (44) Furthermore, Bourdieu is the only
other major contemporary social theorist to have written
specifically about sport, a fact which appears to be
generally unknown. For him:

> the history of sport is a relatively autonomous
> history which, even when marked by the major events
> of economic and social history, has its own tempo,
> its own evolutionary laws, its own crises, in short,
> its own specific chronology. (45)

However, although sport is 'homologous' to, but not a
direct mirror of, social and economic relations of
production, nevertheless, according to Bourdieu, it
invariably reproduces the dominant social and cultural
relations. Bourdieu addresses the central problem of
reproduction and employs the term 'habitus' to explain
the process. Habitus signifies that which generates a
life-style - a set of beliefs, dispositions and behaviour
patterns which produce a unified phenomenon - and habitus
is thus a regulating mechanism operating according to the
'logic of the practice':

> the habitus is a family, group and especially class
> phenomenon, a logic derived from a set of material
> conditions of existence to regulate the practice of
> a set of individuals in common response to those
> conditions. (46)

Bourdieu observes that there are structural regularities
in patterns of cultural consumption, or appropriation,
of commodities such as sport which are determined by the
'class habitus' and by the possession of 'economic and
cultural capital', and spare time:

> whether someone chooses to acquire and mobilize in
> social intercourse knowledge of the field of football
> or of Western European art, of train spotting or
> avant-garde cinema ... will depend upon the cultural
> and economic endowments with which he or she enters
> the field.... (47)

Thus the 'habitus' encompasses sporting 'tastes' which
are class specific. For example, Bourdieu observes that
the working classes have an instrumental orientation and
prefer sports demanding strength, endurance, and the
propensity to violence, whereas the 'privileged' classes
regard the body as an end in itself for reasons of
appearance or health, and participate in such activities
as running - 'movements without any other aim than
physical exercise and the symbolic appropriation of a
world reduced to the status of a landscape'. (48)

Bourdieu describes such tastes, or manifested preferences, as:

the practical affirmation of an inevitable difference
.... There is no accounting for tastes ... each taste
feels itself to be natural – and so it is, being a
habitus – which amounts to rejecting others as unnatural
and therefore vicious. (49)

Bourdieu notes that the field of sporting practices is
the site of struggles over the definition of the legitimate body and the legitimate use of the body in sport –
'amateurism vs. professionalism, participant sport vs.
spectator sport, distinctive (elite) sport vs. popular
(mass) sport' – which is part of a larger field of
struggle for monopolistic power over the body between the
moral categories of the 'ascetic' and 'hedonistic'
definitions and uses of the body. (50) The relationship
of the individual to his or her body, which is a fundamental aspect of the habitus, varies not only between
social classes but between class fractions. Bourdieu
illustrates this by reference to the historical character
of the field of sport, and argues that the dominant
fraction of the dominant class (heads of private industry)
identifies with the amateur-gentleman or aristocratic
ideal of sport, whereas the dominated fraction of the
dominant class (intellectuals, artists and professors)
associates with the meritocratic sporting values, and the
subordinate classes are altogether more hedonistic in
their appropriation of sport. Furthermore, Bourdieu
asserts that the shift from 'sport as an elite practice
reserved for amateurs' to 'sport as a spectacle produced
by professionals for consumption by the masses' has been
determined by economic processes which have altered the
power relations within the field. The demand for
sensationalism and the urgency to produce a result, which
renders the intricacies and finer points of the game less
significant, divides the experts or professionals from
the laymen or fans. Bourdieu describes this division
as a 'deep structure of the collective consciousness' –
a 'decisive political effect' of the structure of mass
spectator sport. The popularisation of sport has allowed
the privileged classes to maintain political capital by,
for example, the provision and control of a private or
state sports entertainment industry, which caters
especially for the 'problems' of youth, and by the
consumer sports market which has become a surrogate
channel for upward mobility available to children of
the dominated classes. (51)

Bourdieu's treatment of culture and his use of
empirical evidence is particularly valuable and appears

initially to provide a potentially more adequate conceptualisation of cultural specificity and cultural autonomy. However, there are problems in Bourdieu's theory which are similar to those of the 'structuralisms' in general. The logic of the cultural field of sport, for example, operates in such a way as to reproduce with apparent inevitability the dominant social relations. This means that sport cannot be, in any meaningful sense, autonomous, and thus Bourdieu's theory overall entails a form of cultural determinism within which the agents of cultural practices, social classes, and power relations are properties of the system.

The various 'culturalisms' and 'structuralisms' have all been seen to have serious theoretical deficiencies. Recently, Gramsci's work has been used in an effort to establish an alternative analysis which can demonstrate the culture/ideology/class nexus without denying human agency, and which can also cope with the heterogeneous nature of culture – its manifest tensions and changes – in advanced capitalist societies. (52) Gramsci explains ideological domination as a phenomenon which is never total or inevitable so that the concept of autonomy is not an abstract concept but has material substance in identifiable social processes. He uses the concept of 'hegemony' to explain the contradictory features of the connections between culture and ideology and economic and political aspects of the totality. Hegemony defines a specifically historical form of class domination, throughout civil society and the state, which becomes embedded in consciousness as 'commonsense' through the ordinary experiences and relationships of everyday life. Raymond Williams describes the concept thus:

> Hegemony is not only the articulate upper level of
> 'ideology', nor are its forms of control only those
> ordinarily seen as 'manipulation' or 'indoctrination'.
> It is a whole body of practices and expectations, over
> the whole of living: our senses and assignments of
> energy, our shaping perceptions of ourselves and our
> world. It is a lived system of meanings and values –
> constitutive and constituting – which as they are
> experienced as practices appear as reciprocally
> confirming. It thus constitutes a sense of reality
> for most people in the society, a sense of absolute
> because experienced reality beyond which it is very
> difficult for most members of the society to move, in
> most areas of their lives. It is, that is to say, in
> the strongest sense a 'culture', but a culture which
> has also to be seen as the lived dominance and sub-
> ordination of particular classes. (53)

Such a lengthy quotation is included here to identify
the major features of a concept which has played a seminal
role in cultural studies. (54) It has particular relevance
to an analysis of sport, which then may be seen to derive
its meaning from the character of the specific historical
context of which it is a part, and which may be understood
as a significant constituent of the totality of social
relationships by which people produce and make sense of
their world. The concept of hegemony directs us to examine
empirically the ways in which sport is related to other
features of the totality such as the mode of production,
the state, education, the media, the family, ethnic groups,
sexual patterns and other cultural practices. It directs
us, also, to consider the extent to which, and in what ways,
sport is involved in the mediation of ideas and beliefs,
some of which become linked to the interests of classes
and dominant groups, and others of which are concealed.
It also encourages us to ask questions about the specific
nature of dominance and subordination: if cuts in welfare
services close a community swimming pool, for example, or
a notice is erected outside council flats where families
are housed, 'NO BALL GAMES ON THE GRASS', such questions
as 'Who made the decision?' and 'In whose interests?'
direct attention to the relationship between power in
society and the lived experience of ordinary people. The
provision of extensive sporting facilities at public
expense at a time of massive unemployment, in an effort
to cope with inner urban deprivation and the problems of
youth and leisure, compared to the increasing interest in
individual activities such as jogging and the response to
the London marathon, (55) highlights the necessity to
examine the precise nature of autonomy in sport.

Such a systematic and comprehensive analysis of sport
in Britain has not yet occurred. (56) The study of film
and popular literature, for example, are far more
developed, and when we consider the universal appeal of
sport, which extends in one form or another to vast
numbers of people, this appears as a serious gap in our
general understanding of culture. There is increasing
interest in the field, but studies on sport are mainly
isolated productions on discrete topics or by-products
of research with a different prime focus. Cultural
studies implicitly includes sport in the ways in which
culture is defined, and in the theories used for analysis,
but, for the most part, sport remains something like an
epiphenomenon in practice.

In part, this may be explained by the multiplicity of
forms and meanings which characterise sport in modern
society. The amount of time, energy and money devoted to

sport in one form or another by all sections of society is
undoubtedly greater than for any other aspect of culture.
Sport encompasses a whole range of activities, from international competitive sport on a grand scale to tennis in
the local park; it can be an alienating and brutalising
experience for the professional performer and in other ways
it can be dynamic, sensuous and beautiful. Stuart Hall
puts it thus:

> we tend to think of cultural forms as whole and
> coherent: either wholly corrupt or wholly authentic.
> Whereas, they are deeply contradictory; they play on
> contradictions especially when they function in the
> domain of the 'popular'. (57)

Sport, without question, constitutes a central component
of popular culture but it cannot be satisfactorily analysed
as an undifferentiated whole. In addition, many of the
various forms of sport are irrecoverable for analysis:
because sport is immediate and transient it can rarely be
reduced to artefacts for examination.

However, it is the 'commonsense' attitudes to sport
which militate most against a social analysis. The
preferred view of sport is an idealised one. It is
generally seen to be a non-serious, enjoyable activity
which satisfies the innate urge to play and which affirms
basic human values. Reality confirms this view: sport
is a heightened experience for vast numbers of people,
and men and women play and spectate with passion. Sport
offers tensions and a vicarious excitement built upon
unpredictability, and it is a compelling and uniquely
gratifying experience making it possible to forget
'ordinary' life. Furthermore, sport is part of a common
cultural tradition of collective experience and shared,
easily understood meanings and values, internalised by
way of unique ritual and dramatic qualities and powerful
symbolic characteristics. 'Common sense' tells us that
sport is accessible to everyone in some form and hence
belongs to everyone, and in this way sport is posed as
neutral. It is difficult to treat as problematic something
which is taken-for-granted as manifestly apparent and to
identify the hidden ways in which sport embodies social
antagonisms and may be biased and partial.

In addition, it may be that cultural studies reflects
and reproduces, albeit unwittingly, a traditional mind/
body dichotomy which entails a type of cultural elitism.
Historically, the political relevance of the body has been
given scant attention in our society which is dominated
by verbal language. (58) This orthodoxy is a cultural
expression of dualism which conceives of sport as a
physical activity rather than a mental one. An alternative

conception would be of sport as a united physical and
mental process, in which the physical is a genuinely
integral and organic expression of individual and social
experience. It is only then possible to understand
experience as comprising 'the mental and emotional
response, whether of an individual or of a social group,
to many inter-related events and to many repetitions of
the same kind of event'. (59) The case that is claimed
by Swingewood, for example, for the centrality of literacy
to the development of consciousness and selfhood,
automatically relegates non-verbal means of communication,
and the body as a medium of expression, to a position of
lesser importance to human experience. (60)   Cultural
studies refuses this position, and employs an extended
use of the concept of culture, with its underlying
assumption that consciousness and experience are no less
informed by sporting practice than by other cultural
practices. This position is exemplified by Johnson as
follows:

> there is no separate institutional area of social life
> in which forms of consciousness arise: mentalities
> and subjectivities are formed and expressed in every
> sphere of existence. (61)

However, the silences about sport and the comparative
dearth of studies in the field are a form of cultural
chauvinism which in practice support a dominant cultural
order within cultural studies, ranking sport low. This
effectively reinforces the low academic status of the
study of sport and its link to the context of physical
education.

It is hoped, therefore, that this collection will go
some way towards redressing the balance. It is an
intervention which treats sport seriously as an aspect
of culture and, in this respect, in an equivalent manner
to other cultural practices. The view reflected here,
and by the conference rationale, is that sport is as
legitimate an area of study as, for example, literature
or art, and that to leave it out is an outdated notion
of what constitutes culture.

The conference was planned as an interdisciplinary
venture intended to challenge traditional barriers and
provoke dialogue normally absent, particularly between
physical education and sports practitioners and cultural
and social theorists. It was hoped that it would
disseminate ideas and raise controversial issues -
particularly about conventional attitudes surrounding
sport. The inevitable outcome of such an aim is to
expose and bring alive the contradictory positions and
antagonisms of those with different vested interests in

sport. To confront sports practice with theory is
sometimes threatening - even painful - but it is healthy
because it is the only way to begin to understand the
complexities of the subject. In no sense was it the
concern of the conference to attack sport as such: it
was a serious attempt to raise the level of understanding
and social analysis of the subject.

The sport/culture/ideology nexus was the selected
focus for the conference. It was assumed from the start
that sport is a socially mediated phenomenon which arises
from the totality of social relations and that it inter-
penetrates with other aspects of culture and may take
different ideological forms. It is not intended in this
introduction to discuss the problematic concepts of ideology
and culture or to examine the complexities of their
relationship to consciousness because such an attempt at
conceptual clarity is made in the following chapter, which
provided the theoretical underpinning and a starting point
for the conference. This book, however, does not represent
a consistent theoretical position overall - it is a
collection of conference papers which reflects varied modes
of analysis, approaches and styles, indicating something
of the multifaceted nature of sport. Although it is in
no way comprehensive in scope, it aims to give some
directions for a potentially adequate analysis of sport.

The opening paper, 'Sport, Culture and Ideology', raises
key questions about the role of sport in society, and most
importantly, the complex relationship between sport,
ideology and the wielding of power. Here, John Hargreaves
comprehensively outlines the field of the sociology of
sport and the inadequacies of existing analyses which
seriously misconceive both the relation of sport to
culture and the relation of sport as a cultural form to
economic, political and ideological processes. He shows
that it is both sport's dependency on, and autonomy from,
key social processes that have been inadequately characterised. One of the most important consequences of this has
been a failure to get to grips with the problem of how
sport in particular, and by extension, culture in general,
contributes to accommodating opposing social classes and
groups and provides oppositional spaces within given
structures of hegemony. Thus the complex relationships
which constitute sport in society and the way in which the
concept of hegemony is helpful in our understanding of
their articulation becomes an important focus in the
reading of each subsequent paper.

Research on the ideological significance of the media
has centred on 'serious' presentations such as television
news and current affairs programmes which are shown to be

by no means as impartial and objective as they claim to
be. (62) Such work highlights the role of the media in
the production of ideology and the winning of hegemony.
However, there has been no equivalent research into the
ideological significance of the media treatment of 'non-
serious' activities which are normally categorised as
entertainment, such as sport. This is a serious omission
because the coverage of sport by the media has become a
gigantic, global affair, and because more people are
involved in sport, by way of the press and broadcasting,
than through any other means including active participation and spectating at live events. (63) The paper by
Alan Clarke and John Clarke entitled 'Highlights and
Action Replays - ideology, sport and the media' is,
therefore, important in helping us to consider the significance of the media treatment of sport in the hegemonic
process. They oppose the 'naturalising' tendencies of
the media coverage of sport, and, with a focus on
televised sport, they examine some of the ways in which
the character of dominant ideology is revealed in the
media's treatment of sport. It would be to misunderstand
their position to read into it that media sport is
ideologically loaded to the extent that the reader or
viewer is completely manipulated, but rather they argue
that the total effect of media sport is likely to be one
which consolidates taken-for-granted and already
entrenched beliefs about, for example, competitive
individualism, nationalism, sexism and racism which
constitute aspects of dominant ideology. It is in the
sense of a broad conception of politics which includes
the realm of power and domination in which ideology plays
a key role that they view the media treatment of sport
as a political issue. Their contribution signals the
need for analyses of the sports media which take into
account questions of power and domination, ownership,
control and their connections with political processes
and ideology.

The following two papers are concerned, in different
ways, with the participation of women in sport. Since
the social construction of sport, both materially and
ideologically, is based on a long and relentless history
of male domination, and sport is typically presented and
defined in masculine terms of reference, these contributions help to focus upon this social imbalance and reveal
the importance of sport as a site for feminist intervention.
First, 'Women and Leisure', by Christine Griffin, Dorothy
Hobson, Sue MacIntosh and Trisha McCabe is an example of
collective research which is an expression of a
specifically feminist standpoint. They argue that the

systematic exclusion of women from conventional and Marxist
studies of leisure, and the overall limited entry of women
into the leisure sphere, has important implications for the
reconstruction of a theory of leisure in general and for
sport specifically. Evidence from their ethnographic
studies shows how white, working-class women from
Birmingham, at home, in waged work, and at school, do not
simply passively accept, but rather affirm their structural
position and ascribed femininity which militates against
involvement in any type of leisure. But we know that
increasing numbers of women are now involved in increasing
numbers of sports (64) and so this paper, together with
the following one by Paul Willis, raises essential
questions about the patriarchal character of social
institutions such as sport and the extent to which sport
reproduces or breaks down sex-role stereotyping in society.
Paul Willis's contribution, 'Women in Sport in Ideology',
which is a revised version of a paper given to the 'Women
and Sport' conference at Birmingham University in 1974,
aims mainly to clarify what it is that is specific, special
and revealing about the sub-region of women in sport.
Sport is deep in the experience of most men but not of
most women: by examining the specific form of sexual
ideology in sport and the reason why differences between
men and women in sport are treated in the way they are we
can come closer to understanding gender relations in a
broader context. Paul Willis suggests that it could be
possible to create new gender identities in the sports
context.

'Sport and Youth Culture' derives from an ethnographic
study by David Robins, written around oral transcripts,
in which he illustrates the accommodative nature of sports
for young, working-class males with reference to speedway,
road racing (motor cycle racing), boxing, and football.
Football has excited the imaginations of many writers but
the accounts of other sports are sparse and so this paper
extends the picture of the place of organised sport in
the lives and consciousness of working-class youth today.
It illustrates how reality belies the appearance that
sport is the one major area of working-class life where
youth and parent cultures seem to find common ground and
display peaceful co-existence. David Robins illustrates
the class nature of youth sports culture and its inter-
penetration with other factors such as race, sex and
deviance. He recognises the importance of an historical
perspective to an understanding of the complicated
ideological features of youth culture and its relatively
autonomous and oppositional forms which conflict with
dominant ideology.

The contribution by Ian Taylor, 'On the Sports Violence Question: soccer hooliganism revisited', also focuses on young working-class males. Ian Taylor has made a major contribution to the debate about football violence in this country and is one of the few people to examine the phenomenon in a critical manner rather than with a narrow policy orientation. He gives a detailed historical account of the growth of football violence in Britain from its original identification as a serious social problem in the 1960s to its contemporary manifestations with gang warfare and racist connotations. He shows the inadequacies of analyses which view the problem at the level of the individual offender or as an insular sporting phenomenon. The alternative is an understanding of football hooliganism as an integral aspect of the historically specific totality of social relations which have generated it. In the case of the British nation state, therefore, the analysis must necessarily incorporate relevant social, economic, political, and ideological factors. From this perspective, football hooliganism is an expression of antagonistic class relations and cannot be dissociated from the present crisis of working-class experience and the crisis of the British state.

Drug use in our society is ubiquitous and most people believe that drug-induced performance is intrinsic to modern competitive sport and probably a prerequisite for success. The use of drugs in sport goes back a long way – at least to the ancient Greeks – but it has reached such proportions in contemporary sport that it is viewed as a serious problem by the sports authorities. (65) In his paper, 'Sport and Drugs', Martyn Lucking develops this theme. He believes that the perfection of testing techniques and the possibility of the inauguration of tests at random in the national and international contexts has made the detection of banned drugs, and hence the elimination of their use, a real possibility. Drug use in sport embodies controversy. For example, the likelihood of the use of new and more sophisticated drugs and techniques to beat detection tests has led to the argument that bans should be lifted because 'medically prescribed and monitored drug-taking is a physiologically safer practice than the haphazard, indiscriminate taking of drugs'. (66) The arguments surrounding drug use reflect the view that it is a self-contained sporting phenomenon and that none of the athletes are 'deviants' in a broader social perspective. There are, however, anomalies raised here with respect to the concept of deviancy and its application in terms of the rules of sport and the concept of deviancy in terms of the criminal

law. We know that drug-taking in sport is unofficially
protected, and in countries both with, and without,
specific anti-doping laws, the possession of most of the
drugs involved is a state offence, and yet prosecutions
are rare. (67) What is required now is an extended
analysis which would take account of all the different
features of the economic and political imperatives of
drug-taking in professional and top-level amateur sport.

The final two contributions in this collection raise
issues about the relationship between sport and the role
of the state. In Britain state agencies, together with
voluntary bodies and private enterprise, are involved in
the administration, organisation, ownership and control
of sport. With the marked broadening of state intervention
into sport in recent years in the West generally, state
socialist societies such as the USSR, where the state
totally controls the sports system, are used as obvious
models for comparison. The supposedly unqualified
determinist effects of totalitarian sporting forms have
been juxtaposed to the apparent scope for human agency
in sport in liberal democracies. However, in his paper
'Sport and Communism - on the example of the USSR', James
Riordan understands Soviet sport to be an integral
component of a process of social change in a developing
country and views as problematic the degree to which
sport reflects the system of government rather than the
interests of the citizens. There is a lack of, and an
evident need for, systematic work which will situate
sport within a theory of the modern state which can take
account of the different, and highly specific forms of
state involvement in cultural hegemony and of the
politicisation of sport within the contexts of different
nation states. (68) In the case of South Africa, the
political character of sport and its association with
dominant, nationalist ideology is easily recognised.
In 'The Politics of Sports Apartheid', Peter Hain makes
explicit the moral dimension which is always present,
but not normally made apparent, in analyses of the sport/
politics relationship. Because sport is so central to
South African culture it is a major site for social
change. The breaking down of the cultural and social
side of life in South Africa could have radical economic
and political reverberations.

It is appropriate to end the collection with Peter
Hain's contribution because it illustrates, concretely,
two theoretical features which are implicit in several
of the papers - the dynamic aspects of hegemony and the
necessity to analyse sport as an integral aspect of the
social totality. This collection as a whole has identified

the way in which sport is 'constitutive and constituting', recognisable only in a dialectical relationship to political, economic, ideological and other cultural forms. Sport exists as a paradox - it has been shown here how its manipulative manifestations need to be counterposed to its liberating tendencies.

NOTES

1   The complex characteristics of sport make a working definition problematic. The term is employed here to include the many forms of organised physical activity in the educational context and in the wider society. For convenience it is used to include older terminologies such as physical training, physical education and movement, as well as those in contemporary use such as physical recreation and outdoor pursuits.

2   A term used to describe colleges which offered courses exclusively in physical education, such as Dartford (founded 1885), Chelsea (1898), Anstey (1899), Bedford (1903), Carnegie (1933), Loughborough (1935). At the time of two-year teacher training courses a three-year specialist physical education course was available to selected students.

3   Sixty years is the time span between the inauguration of the first full-time course in physical education at Dartford College in 1885 and 1946, the date of the first degree course incorporating the subject at Birmingham University.

4   See, for example, I.M. Webb, Women's physical education in Great Britain 1800-1966, unpublished M.Ed. thesis, University of Leicester, 1966.

5   These are examples of texts in this field: J.N. Barham, 'Mechanical Kinesiology', St Louis, C.V. Mosby, 1978; J.E. Kane, 'Psychological Aspects of Physical Education and Sport', London, Routledge & Kegan Paul, 1972;   D.R. Lamb, 'Physiology of Exercise: Response and Adaptations', London, Collier Macmillan, 1978; R.K. Marteniuk, 'Information Processing in Motor Skills', New York, Holt, Rinehart & Winston, 1976; H.T.A. Whiting et al., 'Personality and Performance in Physical Education', London, Kimpton, 1973.

6   See, for example, B.L. Bennett et al., 'Comparative Physical Education and Sport', Philadelphia, Lea & Febiger, 1975; J. May, 'Madame Bergman-Osterberg', London, Routledge & Kegan Paul, 1969;   Van Dalen and B. Bennett, 'A World History of Physical Education', Englewood Cliffs, N.J., Prentice Hall, 1971.

7   The influence of the work of Rudolph Laban is central
     here. His classification of movement was utilised in
     the fields of dance and gymnastics almost exclusively
     by female lecturers of physical education and related
     mostly to the secondary school context for girls and
     to primary education. For its ideological inflections
     see J.W.T. Hughes, Socialisation of the body within
     educational institutions - an historical view,
     unpublished M.Sc. thesis, University of London
     Institute of Education, 1975. For a sample text see
     M. North, 'Movement Education', London, Temple Smith,
     1973.

8   The Sports Council has produced an information bulletin,
     'Recreation Management Training', 1980, which states:
         During the past decade there has been a minor
         revolution in the provision of facilities for
         leisure in this country. The management and
         administration of this wide variety of facilities
         now involves both National and Local Government,
         promotional organisations and the voluntary sector
         and it is evident that an increasing number of
         people are interested in pursuing a career in
         recreation management.
     There follows a list of 43 institutions of higher
     education offering, between them, a range of courses
     in what is nothing less than a new, boom profession.
     This development is reflected increasingly in sports
     studies degrees which have components focusing on
     leisure and recreation.

9   See, for example, the government white paper 'Sport
     and Recreation', London, HMSO, 1975.

10   A position argued by John Hargreaves who gives a
     comprehensive assessment of the development of the
     sociology of sport in his contribution to this
     volume.

11   It is difficult to cite any contribution by a present
     member of the physical education profession which has
     made a lasting impact on the development of the
     sociology of sport in this country.

12   This position is exemplified by most of the profession-
     al publications and conferences. It is impossible
     here to give more than a few examples of journals -
     'Action: British Journal of Physical Education';
     'Journal of Human Movement Studies'; 'Bulletin of
     Physical Education', and conferences - 'The Pursuit
     of Excellence in Sport and Physical Education'
     (NATFHE, 1977); 'National Recreation Management
     Seminar and Exhibition: Design for Better Management'
     (Facilities Unit, Sports Council, 1981); 'Physical

Preparation for Life, From School – to Work – and
Leisure' (Physical Education Association, 1981).

13 For example, the School of Cultural and Community
Studies at Sussex University offers a course to
undergraduates called, 'Popular Culture, Leisure and
the Social Order'; the School of Education and
Humanities at North East London Polytechnic offers a
B.A. (Hons.) Degree in Cultural Studies.

14 The Centre for Contemporary Cultural Studies, (CCCS),
at Birmingham University, has produced some papers
on sport as one area of its work in cultural studies.
The British Sociological Association has also held
study groups in the areas of sport and leisure.
Odd articles in such journals as 'Screen Education'
and 'Media, Culture and Society' have contributed to
an analysis of sport, but there is no professional
journal in this country which exclusively covers the
sociology of sport, whereas in America there are
several – for example, 'International Review of
Sports Sociology', 'Journal of Sport and Social
Issues'.

15 S. Hall, et al. (eds), 'Culture, Media, Language',
London, Hutchinson, 1980, p.7.

16 The CCCS, established in 1964, remains the only
institution whose exclusive concern is with the
development of cultural studies as a field of enquiry.
A range of degree courses and research programmes
which incorporate cultural studies in different ways
have since been initiated in various institutions.

17 For an account of the development of cultural studies
see, for example, Stuart Hall, Cultural studies: two
paradigms, 'Media, Culture and Society', 1980, vol.2,
no.3; Cultural studies and the centre: some
problematics and problems, in Hall, et al. (eds),
op.cit.; Colin Sparks, The evolution of cultural
studies, 'Screen Education', 1977, no.22.

18 Chas Critcher, Sociology, cultural studies and the
post-war working class, in John Clarke et al. (eds),
'Working Class Culture: Studies in history and theory',
London, Hutchinson, 1979, p.16.

19 S.M. Hall and P. Whannel, 'The Popular Arts', London,
Hutchinson, 1964. Although controversy surrounds the
category 'culturalism', it has been taken up in
accounts of the history of cultural studies and I use
it here to describe a generally recognised orientation.
See Richard Johnson, Against absolutism, and E.P.
Thompson, The politics of theory, in R. Samuel (ed.),
'People's History and Socialist Theory', London,
Routledge & Kegan Paul, 1981.

20 F.R. Leavis, The literary mind, 'Scrutiny', 1932, vol.1, no.1, quoted by Paul Filmer, Literary Study as Liberal Education and as Sociology in the work of F.R. Leavis, in C. Jenks (ed.), 'Rationality, Education and the Social Organization of Knowledge', London, Routledge & Kegan Paul, 1977.

21 See also F.R. Leavis, 'Mass Civilization and Minority Culture', Cambridge, Gordon Fraser, 1930. For an account of Leavis's position refer to Francis Mulhern, 'The Moment of "Scrutiny"', London, New Left Books, 1979; Stuart Hall, Cultural studies and the centre, op.cit., p.18 and Alan Swingewood, 'The Myth of Mass Culture', London, Macmillan, 1977, p.8.

22 For an account of the work of the Frankfurt School refer to Martin Jay, 'The Dialectical Imagination: A History of the Frankfurt School and the Institute of Social Research, 1923-1950', Boston, Little Brown, 1973; David Held, 'Introduction to Critical Theory: Horkheimer to Habermas', London, Hutchinson, 1950; Swingewood, op.cit., pp.13-18.

23 Swingewood, op.cit., p.16. Swingewood is quoting Horkheimer and Adorno in 'Dialectic of Enlightenment'.

24 T.S. Eliot (1948) quoted by D. Hebdige, 'Subculture: The Meaning of Style', London, Methuen, 1979, p.7.

25 Raymond Williams, 'Culture', Glasgow, Fontana, 1981, pp.11-12.

26 Dwight Macdonald, A theory of mass culture, in R. Rosenberg and D. Manning White (eds), 'Mass Culture', London, Collier Macmillan, 1957, p.59.

27 Papers in 'New Left Review' by both these authors give more recent formulations. See also Raymond Williams, 'Marxism and Literature', Oxford University Press, 1977 and 'Culture', op.cit.; E.P. Thompson, The Poverty of Theory, in 'The Poverty of Theory', London, Merlin Press, 1978.

28 S. Hall, Cultural studies: two paradigms, op.cit., p.63.

29 Ibid.

30 J. Grealy, Notes on Popular Culture, in 'Screen Education', 1977, no.22.

31 Richard Hoggart, 'The Uses of Literacy', Harmondsworth, Penguin, 1957, pp.108-110, 328-9.

32 E.P. Thompson, 'The Making of the English Working Class', Harmondsworth, Penguin, 1963, pp.443-51.

33 Raymond Williams, 'The Long Revolution', Harmondsworth, Penguin, 1965, p.364.

34 See, for example, Swingewood, op.cit.; Barrett, et al. (eds), 'Ideology and Cultural Production', London, Croom Helm, 1979, and Williams, 'Culture', op.cit. The notable exception is 'Working Class Culture', op.cit.

35   See John Hargreaves's contribution to this collection
     for the developments in the sociology of sport.

36   Althusser's essay, Ideology and ideological state
     apparatuses, is in 'Lenin and Philosophy and Other
     Essays', London, New Left Books, 1971. With reference
     to the sports context, see John Hargreaves's chapter.

37   The Black Power Salute refers to the demonstrations made
     by the black American athletes (notably John Carlos and
     Tommy Smith), during the medal ceremonies at the
     Mexico Olympics in 1968. For an account of the Stop
     the Seventy Tour Campaign see Peter Hain, 'Don't Play
     with Apartheid: The Background to the Stop the
     Seventy Tour Campaign', London, Allen & Unwin, 1971.

38   For example, Roland Barthes's essay, The world of
     wrestling, in 'Mythologies', St Albans, Paladin, 1972
     and Michel A. Bouet's article, The significance of
     the Olympic phenomenon: a preliminary attempt at a
     systematic and semiotic analysis, in 'International
     Review of Sport Sociology', 1977, vol.III, no.12.

39   Barthes, op.cit., pp.109-10.

40   Williams, 'Culture', op.cit., p.13.

41   Barthes, op.cit., pp.21-3.

42   Williams, 'Culture', op.cit., pp.206-7. In 1976, in
     Developments in the sociology of culture, 'Sociology',
     vol.10, no.2, p.505, Williams stressed the importance
     of a semiological analysis to cultural studies and
     the 'correct emphasis on sign systems as the radical
     elements of all cultural process'.

43   Richard Johnson, Three problematics: elements of a
     theory of working-class culture, in J. Clarke et al.,
     op.cit.

44   Nicholas Garnham and Raymond Williams, Pierre Bourdieu
     and the sociology of culture: an introduction, 'Media,
     Culture and Society', 1980, vol.II, no.3.

45   Pierre Bourdieu, Sport and social class, 'Social
     Science Information', 1978, vol.XVIII, no.6, p.821.

46   Garnham and Williams, op.cit., p.213, drawn from
     Bourdieu, 'Outline of a Theory of Practice',
     Cambridge University Press, 1977. Bourdieu employs
     the term 'class' in an unproblematic fashion and
     does not establish a precise, complete account of
     the class structure throughout society which sport
     is supposed to reproduce.

47   Ibid., p.218.

48   Pierre Bourdieu, Aristocracy of culture, 'Media,
     Culture and Society', 1980, vol.II, no.3, p.252.

49   Ibid., p.253.

50   Bourdieu, Sport and social class, op.cit., pp.826-7.

51   Ibid., pp.830-3.

52 For an account of 'culturalist' and 'structuralist' influences on cultural theory and the relevance of Gramsci see R. Johnson, Histories of culture/theories of ideology: notes on an impasse, in Barrett, et al., op.cit., and S. Hall, Cultural studies and the centre, op.cit.

53 Williams, 'Marxism and Literature', op.cit., p.110.

54 According to Stuart Hall, the concept of 'hegemony', though by no means universally used, has been one of the organising ideas at the Centre for Contemporary Studies - see Cultural studies and the centre, op.cit., p.286.

55 There were 24,000 applications for the London Marathon sponsored by Gillett, and organised by the Recreation Department of the Greater London Council on 29 March 1981. Only 7,500 participants were allowed to compete of whom 7,055 started the course and 6,419 finished.

56 To our knowledge, the forthcoming publication by John Hargreaves, 'Sport and Hegemony in Britain', London, Macmillan, will constitute the only extensive analysis of this sort.

57 Stuart Hall, Notes on deconstructing 'the popular' in R. Samuel (ed.), op.cit., p.233.

58 See Jonathan Benthall, A prospectus, and Ted Polhemus, Social bodies, in J. Benthall and E. Polhemus (eds), 'The Body as a Medium of Expression', London, Allen Lane, 1975. Foucault's diffuse notion of power seems to offer insights and a perspective which could be usefully related to sport. See, in particular, Michel Foucault, 'Body/power', in Colin Gordon (ed.), 'Power/Knowledge', Brighton, Harvester Press, 1980.

59 Thompson, 'The Poverty of Theory', op.cit., p.199.

60 Swingewood, op.cit., pp.96-8.

61 R. Johnson, Three problematics, op.cit., p.232.

62 See, for example, the work of the Glasgow University Media Group - 'Bad News', vol.1, London, Routledge & Kegan Paul, 1976 and 'More Bad News', vol.2, London, Routledge & Kegan Paul, 1980, and the Centre for Contemporary Cultural Studies - S. Hall et al., The unity of current affairs TV, 'Cultural Studies 9', CCCS, Spring 1976.

63 J. Curran and Jeremy Tunstall, Mass media and leisure, in M.A. Smith et al., (eds), 'Leisure and Society in Britain', London, Allen Lane, 1973. Two figures will suffice to indicate the scale of modern spectator sport - it was estimated that some 200 million people world-wide watched a tennis match between Billie Jean King and Bobby Riggs, and that

more than one thousand million viewers tuned into the World Cup Final in 1978 (from Angela Patmore, 'Playing on Their Nerves: The Sport Experiment', London, Stanley Paul, 1979, pp.14-15).

64 Central Council of Physical Recreation, 'Report of the Langham Life 1st International Conference on Women in Sport', London, CCPR, 1978. See also Inside track, 'Sunday Times', 16 March 1980, 'women's infiltration into the male sporting world is so widespread that it is now difficult to find a sport where women either don't compete or aren't succeeding'.

65 The extent of drug abuse and the effect of intake was intimated by Ruicki Bruchs (Swedish discus thrower and Olympic medallist) in an interview on British television in September 1978. In common with '101 per cent' of competitors he had met at the Montreal Olympics, he had taken drugs, notably anabolic steroids, for ten years. He had put on 100 pounds in weight, had 6 knee operations, a fractured vertebra and various internal illnesses. Burst testicles, sexual troubles, internal problems and severe pain, and possibly cancer are some of the supposed results of drug-taking which dramatise what is a widespread phenomenon in competitive sport. It has been estimated that at least thirty athletes have died through causes directly associated with dope and the list of those known to be mentally or physically harmed is enormous. Swingewood, op.cit., pp.198-200; Les Woodland, 'Dope: The Use of Drugs in Sport', Newton Abbot, David & Charles, 1980, p.7.

66 A view expressed by Ron Pickering on a Horizon (BBC television) programme called Sport and Drugs, in February 1980. See 'Action', July and September 1980, vol.XI, nos 4 and 5.

67 Woodland, op.cit., p.178.

68 The Sport Studies Research Group at Queen's University, Kingston, Ontario, Canada, took this as the central problematic at its symposium - 'Sport, Culture and the Modern State' in October 1976. See, especially, Richard Gruneau's paper in the conference proceedings, Sport and the debate on the state.

Chapter 2

Sport, culture and ideology

John Hargreaves

I

With some notable exceptions there has been an extraordinary neglect of sport as a social and cultural
phenomenon among the social science and cultural studies
communities, who have largely ignored what is arguably
one of the central components of popular culture. The
neglect is particularly glaring and perhaps least to be
expected in sociology, a discipline whose practitioners
have tended to pride themselves on their willingness to
explore without fear or favour all aspects of social
life, especially those areas traditionally taken for
granted by other disciplines, and one of whose central
aims has been systematically to investigate and render
a comprehensive account of the main constituent features
of the culture of modern societies. No major social
theorist of the modern era has in fact bothered to make
much more than passing reference to sport and games,
though some recent commentators have been tempted to
seize on the odd passage from figures like Spencer,
Veblen, Sumner, Ross, Cooley, Mead, Freud, Mumford,
Piaget, Mannheim and Huizinga, in order to establish
the existence of bona fidae founding fathers for a
sociology of sport. (1) The neglect is perhaps most
surprising in the case of the English-speaking countries,
where traditionally sports have been embraced more
enthusiastically than elsewhere. One looks almost in
vain in the major English language professional sociology
journals for papers on sport, and for material on sport
in research on related areas. (2)

In Britain, for example, though there are well-
developed sub-disciplines within sociology where one
might expect to find an extended discussion of sport -
the sociology of leisure, sociology of culture, community

studies, the sociology of the family, and the whole area
of working class culture and consciousness – material is
singularly scarce and theoretical discussion is rare.
The subject is either passed over completely, or is
accorded attention in almost exclusively descriptive terms,
as if it were a quaint, but insignificant, tribal practice,
worthy of some note but not of sustained analysis. (3)
For example, one of the most influential sociological
studies of the modern British working class, which
actually took the nature of spare-time activity as one
of its main foci, does not even mention sport. (4)   In
the late 1950s and early 1960s, Williams's and Hoggart's
work in the field of cultural studies, while exercising
a seminal influence on sociological research into the
nature of culture in Britain, managed in the first case to
do without any consideration of the place of sport, and in
the second merely to note some detail in passing. (5)
The tradition of neglect continued in the 1970s with,
for example, the publication of a collection of papers on
leisure in Britain which fails to include any consideration
of sport as a whole, and the appearance of an otherwise
painstaking study of family life and leisure in London,
which, while noting the important place occupied by sport
in people's spare time, none the less, yet again, restricts
itself to merely descriptive detail. (6)

With the unprecedented expansion of sociology in the
1960s and 1970s, though the discipline as a whole ignored
the subject, apart, that is, from a tiny minority of
sociologists, the sociological study of sport did
experience a growth in quantitative terms, judging by
the increased outputs of publications, the proliferation
of journals, and the number of conferences.   But
heightened professional activity is not necessarily
synonymous with intellectual growth.   One clear indication
of a lack here is the failure so far to attract its share
of established sociologists and the consequent over-
reliance on contributions which have little or no basis
in any kind of social theory.   This is evident in most
of the different collections of papers which have
appeared in the last decade claiming to cover the
sociology of sport. (7)   Cross-fertilisation between
different disciplines is in principle always desirable,
often unavoidable and frequently fruitful, but it is
probably not being over-harsh to say that in this case
the results have been somewhat meagre.   In the absence
of interest by sociologists, the initiative in the field
has been taken by others from a motley collection of
backgrounds, and with disparate kinds of interests, with
the result that there seems to be little coherent idea of

what constitutes the field of study. There is still no really adequate text available, and in fact, so far only one sociologist has attempted on his own to write a text which in any way can be said to provide a comprehensive coverage of the field. (8)

However, the neglect of sport is by no means confined to sociology: nowhere in the social sciences and related fields is there more than a small minority of people prepared to take sports seriously as an analytical problem. (9) The most obvious result of neglect is that an underdeveloped continent largely remains to be explored, of which there is as yet a relatively shallow understanding, whichever approach one considers.

The blindness of the academic community to the social significance of sport exhibits at one level the operation of a deeply entrenched common sense about it throughout the culture, which at this particular level gives rise to a species of cultural chauvinism, whereby the content of the traditional curriculum of the university is equated with 'culture' and the culture of the mass of the popula-tion is considered beyond the academic pale. Of course, historically sport has very close semantic and institu-tionalised associations with 'play', 'diversion', 'amusement' and 'recreation' - terms which exist in binary opposition to other, contrasting terms. The usual meaning of work, for example, is the opposite of play; and the 'serious' or 'higher' aspects of life are distinguished from mere amusement. These connotations are usually accounted for as a legacy of puritanism and seventeenth-century rationalism, (10) but the meanings also shade off into others more recently established, such as the nineteenth-century public school doctrine that sports are good for 'character', or the later reaction to this idea, that they are necessarily anti-intellectual and authori-tarian.

It is not surprising then that, on the one hand, sport is easily taken for granted as by definition either an enjoyable, unserious activity, which it would be unbearably pretentious, even self-defeating to subject to analysis (the attitude is often the same to the analysis of jokes), or, on the other hand, as an activity which is unquestionably good for the individual and society. And it can also be taken for granted in the sense that it can be easily dismissed as a rather mindless activity or enjoyment unworthy of academic attention. From such stances therefore, sport presents no real analytical problems and it is therefore usually accorded a relatively low academic status. Given the common assumptions about sport, entry to the field by researchers is less likely to enhance career prospects, there will tend to be less opportunity to publish in professional journals, where the topic is likely to be defined by professional gate-keepers as either peripheral or inappropriate to the discipline. (11) Unless there are strong forces working to define the topic as relevant, or individual pieces of work are well above the average in quality of scholarship, researchers will tend to anticipate rejection and either publish in more accessible outlets, or much more likely perhaps, they will be diverted from the area into more conventional problems.

But there is perhaps a more fundamental reason for the existence of conceptions of sport which render it non-problematic by definition. One cannot begin to understand the structure and the meaning of sport without also appreciating that it is intimately tied up with conceptions and evaluations of the social order. Sport, it would seem for many people, many academics included, is in some unique way symbolic of the social order and an important source of meaning. Or more accurately, it tends to represent idealised versions of that order, and as such it takes on for them an aura of the sacred. Such a symbolic universe is strongly resistant to an analysis that might reduce it to something other than its own terms, because it is intrinsically subversive, not only of the universe of sport as thus conceived, but of the order of society it has come to represent. It is thus not unusual to find accounts of sport which step outside the conventional wisdom interpreted as an attack on society itself. (12)

So the second major repercussion of neglect is that the dominant conventional wisdom concerning the domain has been largely left unchallenged. As it is framed in the education system, constructed in the media and promoted by sports organisations, sport is almost invariably assumed to be intrinsically valuable. To put it rather pungently, perhaps, sport is treated as a separate, quasi-sacred realm where values, difficult if not impossible to realise in the normal course of existence, are indeed capable of realisation. We are supposed to be able to experience fun, relaxation, excitement, comradeship, 'fair-play' and justice, manhood, international understanding, the use of skill, and many more values besides. (13) The institutional spheres mentioned are the major repositories of the dominant ideologies concerning sport and they constitute points where the tacit understandings or the common sense about it are articulated, reproduced and often initiated. But they are not sealed off from the rest of

society, for there is a continual interaction between the
spheres where sport is subject to the dominant modes of
attention and others where sport touches on people's
lives. However, it is in the former that the ideological
charge is particularly powerful and consequential in
specific ways. From this dominant point of view the
intrusion of big business, bureaucracy, politics, class
conflict, violence and other such unpleasant phenomena
is seen as unfortunate, fortuitous, and therefore somehow
avoidable. At best this is a naive and utopian view -
at worst it is dangerously misleading in its simplicity,
for it tends to divert attention away from the social
context of sport.

The third major repercussion of neglect then, is not
only that the relation of sport to society is ignored,
but as part of this there is also a tendency to misconceive
the association between sport and the wielding of power,
and I shall be focusing in particular on this aspect.

In what follows I will outline some major ways sport
has been related to culture, ideology and the wielding
of power in sociological and related work, with a view
to airing the main theoretical issues at stake, rather
than attempting to provide definitive solutions or a
detailed coverage of the whole field. Without intending
to foreclose on debate, I want to point out problems
specific to these major approaches, suggest where wrong
paths may have been taken, and make some suggestions as
to how they may be rectified. In this way, also, points
of divergence as well as convergence between different
approaches can be highlighted and perhaps the besetting
sin of eclecticism avoided. For convenience I have
divided approaches into those lying more within the
mainstream of sociological work and those which have
tended to be influenced more by Marxist theory. To a
limited extent I shall further differentiate within
these broad categories where necessary.

II

The first approach to be considered is, in fact, the
dominant one, i.e. the one with the greatest output and
the longest lineage among attempts to understand sport
in terms of a theory of society, namely the body of work
which is, broadly speaking, functionalist in theoretical
orientation. (14) Functionalist work on sport comes in
a strong version, that is, the theoretical framework is
explicitly functionalist - frequently it is Parsonian
structural-functionalism, as in the work of Loy and

Kenyon, Luschen, Guttman, Edwards, Dumazadier, Mangan,
etc., (15) or alternatively, it comes in a weaker version,
of which there are a wide variety of examples, in the
sense that the functionalist element is mostly implicit
and not spelled out as such, for example, the work of
Page, Snyder and Spreitzer, Roberts and Sutton Smith,
Beisser, Lasch, and Dunning. (16)

In functionalist theory culture is conceived as the
realm or sphere of beliefs, values and norms, which are
related to the different social roles and structural
positions in society. In practice, in empirical studies
culture tends to be treated as a leisure-time activity,
and this is especially notable in the case of studies of
working-class culture. Work and politics, on the other
hand, are seen as different and separate kinds of
activities, which are more or less obligated. (17) The
specific function that is assigned to culture is as a
mode whereby society as a whole, and groups within
society, adapt to societal needs and pressures, arising
from processes of economic and social change, and to the
normal functioning of a modern industrial society,
notably, the demands of work, of a bureaucratically
administered social order, and of a mostly urbanised
existence.

Ideology, in contrast, is conceived of as a type of
belief system which arises and is taken up by individuals in response to the experience of 'social strain'.
It therefore tends also to be regarded as an equilibrating
mechanism, provided it does not go beyond certain normal
limits as a guide map to the social world. Should it do
so, it then becomes a pathological phenomenon which is
dysfunctional for the maintenance of society. Usually
in this approach ideology is heavily and unfavourably
contrasted with scientific knowledge. (18)

The emergence, development and the present pattern of
sport is thus identified in one way or another, depending
on the account, as an adaptive response on the part of
society and/or the part of specific groups within
society, to change, which is worked out within the
cultural realm. It is one of the ways the social system
integrates its increasingly differentiated components
and one of the ways society socialises individuals into
what is expected of them. Sport is thus said, among
other things, to help in the formation of stable
identities or personalities, and provide opportunities
for tension release and for channelling aggression under
socially sanctioned and controlled conditions. It is
also said to be a means of integrating the elements of
single institutions like schools, and of integrating the

different institutions comprising the local community, and
of harmonising potentially disruptive divisions in society.
Note that here the emphasis has shifted away from the
traditional idea of play as the main constitutive element
in sport towards the notion of sport as an activity in
which play is just one among several other defining
features. In fact, the cultural historian and theorist
of play, Huizinga, comes under criticism in much of the
literature for 'unscientifically' deriving games and
sport from the category of play. Instead games are
distinguished from play in that they are said to be, in
contrast, rule-bound and organised, and sport is then
classified as a type of game, usually physical in nature,
and involving a contest between players, and regulated by
formal rules. (19)

The progressive extension of sport to the majority of
the population by a process of diffusion from above is
seen as paralleling the extension of democracy to the
masses, that is, as an integral part of the evolution and
emergence of a pluralist society in which the significance
of social class has diminished. The increasing commerciali-
sation, bureaucratisation and rationalisation of sport,
then, is held to be a functional prerequisite, i.e. the
very condition of its extension to the masses, and
therefore the impingement of these phenomena on sport is
not usually taken as problematic. (20) In other words,
the image of the relation of the individual to his
culture - in this case to sport - is of the 'consumer' of
a service or product turned out by an organisation, in
response to a specific type of demand. The consumer's
cultural needs are seen as being catered for through a
combination of market and state provision, with the
latter filling in where the former will not or cannot.

The perspective tends to be implicitly oriented to
conceptualising problems in a particular prescriptive
manner, which follows from the notion that the existing
structure of society is the 'normal' way modern
societies function. For example, once it is conceded as
a general principle and without further concrete
specification that there is a need to adapt to 'society's
requirements', the whole sphere of leisure easily gets
defined as a problem area: thus increasing leisure time
is seen as a problem, and it is a short step from there
to policy-oriented research on how leisure can be
structured, so that, for example, sport can be made more
readily available to fill people's spare time. And if
sport is seen in terms of being an input to the
maintenance of society, conflict around sport, such as
football violence, easily becomes defined simply as

deviance, or anti-social behaviour, and research becomes pre-occupied with finding measures to eliminate it. (21) In other words, the approach tends to be conceptually related to a social engineering perspective, sometimes very explicitly in policy-inspired research, but mostly implicitly in work which claims to be scientifically neutral.

There is no intention here of indulging in gratuitous, functionalist-bashing which has been a ritual activity in sociology for a long time.   Indeed, some credit is due to those who for a relatively long period have constituted a beleagured minority in sociology or on its fringes, who saw long before many others that sport merits serious attention as a social phenomenon.   Furthermore, some individual pieces of research within this perspective have provided interesting insights into processes of conflict and accommodation between groups as they work out in sport, for example, Edwards's work on racial discrimination in American sports, and Dunning and Sheard's work on the bifurcation of association football and rugby union. (22)   But nevertheless, one basic criticism has to be made, and that concerns the inadequate way power and conflict are in general handled.   The conception of 'social needs' which is employed in strong functionalism confuses the needs and interests of specific groups of people with the needs and interests of all, and in the weak, implied form of functionalism, the characterisation of the constraints, to which groups are supposed to accommodate in cultural terms, is usually much too vague.   The whole idea of the development and functioning of sport as an adaptive response to change, and to the nature of society as it is today, tends to miss the complexities of the play of power.   Specifically, the influence of class power is underplayed and therefore there is little room for raising problems about the relation of culture to what Gramsci called hegemony and of the possible role that sport plays in this relation. (23)   Let me illustrate what is meant here with reference to sport in Britain.

The way of life of the majority of people in Britain was subjected to a more or less concerted attack from above in the transition to industrial capitalism. (24) Festivals with which people's sports and pastimes were associated were banned, often with the use of troops and police. (25)   Pastimes were banned by a Parliament which represented at the time only a minority of the population. (26)   Time and space for recreation were virtually eliminated as far as a large section of the population were concerned. (27)   Traditional and folk sports were

reconstructed, newly regulated and centralised in the mid-
Victorian era under patrician patronage. (28)   Voluntary
organisations of a philanthropic and/or religious turn
promoted sport in the interests of social order and the
encouragement of 'respectability'. (29)   At the end of
the century working-class youths were hounded by authority
from playing games in the streets and other public spaces
and pressured into affiliating themselves to one or other
of the   burgeoning youth organisations, or risk being
defined as deviant and locked up. (30)   At the same time
in the state schools 'drill' was compulsory for working-
class children destined for subordinate positions in
society, while in the private schools games were considered
appropriate for those destined to be the leaders of
society. (31)   Girls and women even now have unequal
opportunities to participate in sport. (32)   Today
football supporters react to the changing relation
between themselves, the club, the local community, and the
older generation in violent terms, and the problem is
treated simply as one of crime and law and order by
authority. (33)   The provision of sport switches increasingly from local voluntary organisations to commercial
provision on a national scale. (34)   Sport becomes big
business to the extent that the TV rights of the Moscow
Olympics were rumoured to cost 87 million dollars or more
and the advertising revenue for TV is estimated at around
150 million dollars.   Governments use international
sport as a political weapon. (35)   To a large extent sport
and recreation facilities are planned for, rather than by,
the people that use them. Is it then justifiable or
adequate to conclude that all this happens on behalf of
society, or to conceive of it as an accommodation to
change? As we shall see, imposition from above is by no
means the whole story, but surely what we have here in
these examples is a pattern which has to be analysed in
terms of the policies and actions of organised interests
with their own particular perceptions of what is required?
Though these policies and actions were and are, no doubt,
sincerely felt to be in keeping with the needs of society
as a whole, they involve the bringing to bear of pressure
on subordinate groups: pressure ranging from outright
coercion and the use of material incentives to moral
exhortation.

Conceptions of what constitute 'social needs' and what
is an acceptable form of accommodation vary: more than
that - they are often matters of dispute in which different
and opposed cultural traditions clash, so that culture
cannot be defined simply as an integrative mechanism.
We have to ask the question 'Functional for whom?' - and

if we ask that question we will not be so ready to accept
that when culture proves not to be a means of integration
or accommodation, but instead a means of expressing social
differences, it can be dismissed as merely 'ideological',
or archaic, or deviant. Such a conception of culture is
far too narrow: culture encompasses far more than the
leisure sphere and it cannot be so neatly cut adrift from
work and politics. Ultimately, such an understanding of
sport itself tends to be ideologically inflected in the
sense that the established arrangements are accepted,
indeed often asserted to be necessary and therefore
unchangeable, and the only acceptable form of change is
then seen as piecemeal, i.e. compatible with the existing
structure of interests. There is a continuity here with
the earlier nineteenth-century ideology of 'rational
recreation' - a middle-class movement concerned with
planning other people's cultural pursuits in order to
ensure they got up to no radical mischief. (36)

III

The second approach within mainstream sociology, namely
interactionism, has not been so evident in the sociology
of sport. Writers like Goffman, Scott, and Ashworth
respectively interpret gambling in sports, the behaviour
surrounding horse racing, and sporting scenes in general
as the creation of actors who are endeavouring to
establish and test out identities for themselves in a
world which severely restricts the opportunities for
doing so. Stone interprets the spectacle of professional
wrestling and such sports in general as providing
individuals with a stable reference point which helps
them confer order on a chaotic reality. Marsh, Rosser
and Harré interpret the violence on the football terraces
as a ritualised battle over territory. (37) There are
two basic points that can be made about the approach in
general. First, at the descriptive level, the fact that
to one or other extent interactionism makes a principle
of taking actors' meanings, or the way participants
define the situation, as the point of departure for social
analysis, makes it well able to accommodate the point
previously made concerning the necessity to recognise
the variety of, and the differences between cultures, as
a fundamental aspect of social life.
    In Marsh, Rosser and Harré's work, for example, it is
correctly pointed out (as indeed Thompson, Hobsbawm and
Rudé have shown previously in their work on crowd
behaviour in the eighteenth and nineteenth centuries) that

crowd behaviour is not necessarily irrational, or completely
spontaneous and unstructured. (38) Marsh et al. show that:
the violence of their teenage subjects is rule-bound; it is
limited in intensity; the targets are highly selective; it
is a passing phase in a teenager's career; subjects can
consciously formulate the rules of their behaviour; and
that most accounts by observers grossly exaggerate the
extent and the significance of the violence. The authors
show that when law enforcement agencies fail to recognise
these features and simply deal with it by coercive means
as 'ordinary' crime', the violence is amplified and
informal controls break down.

The weakness of such an approach, however, is displayed
at the analytic level, when it comes to explaining why
this sort of action-seeking should be sought out at all.
The authors argue, falling back on notions derived from
ethology, that aggression is universally generated at the
biological level, and that at the social level ritualised
practices, whereby aggression is released in opportunities
for more or less structured forms of combat, is a universal
way in which social order is created and sustained. Moving
beyond this into the area of policy recommendation, they
argue that if social order is to be maintained in the face
of pressure on working-class teenagers, ritualised ways
of releasing aggression will have to be maximised. The
fundamental weakness here is that there is no account in
terms of a theory of the nature of the society in question,
i.e. there is no specification of the social sources of
action-seeking behaviour, as such, which give rise to
ritualised displays of aggression. Instead the springs
of such behaviour are assumed to be and are accepted, with
regret, as somehow an inevitable feature of society. No
consideration whatever is given to the rather obvious
alternative thought that if the trouble is generated by
the character of the social order, the solution may lie
in seeking ways to change that order, rather than devoting
all our energies to dealing with what may simply be
symptoms of a more basic condition.

In contrast, other work in the same area, such as that
by Cohen and Robins and by Taylor, avoids the interactionist
trap by placing football violence within the context of
changes in modern Britain. Unlike Marsh, Rosser and Harré,
these authors relate football hooliganism to developments
at the political level, which include, for example, the
mobilisation of economically deprived sections of working-
class youth who form the football 'ends', by organisations
like the National Front. (39)

It is possible to demonstrate the same kind of slide
into what is, in effect, a weak form of functionalism, in

interactionist approaches in general and in Goffman and Scott's work in particular. Since a routinised, administered, frustrating life is taken for granted as the existential fate of most people, the analytical focus shifts in such studies to an exclusive pre-occupation with exploring the strategies people adopt for experiencing action as an antidote to this condition. (40)

IV

I now want to turn in contrast to consider work which shows the influence to one or other extent of the Marxist tradition, and firstly, to a group of writers who have tried to apply to sport some of the insights of the Frankfurt School of critical theory. Concentrating on organised sport for the masses, writers like Jean-Marie Brohm, Paul Hoch and Gerhard Vinnai, among others - mostly French and German writers - argue that sport is a mirror or a microcosm of modern capitalist society, an integral part of a system of class domination and exploitation. (41) Firstly, organised sport is seen as playing a very important part in the training of a docile labour force, that is, in inculcating an acceptance of the kind of work discipline demanded in the modern production process, and in encouraging a positive orientation to hard work as such. In their organisation and functioning the major popular sports are seen as replicating all the fundamental features of modern rationalised industrial production: a high degree of specialisation and standardisation, bureaucratised and hierarchical administration, long-term planning, increased reliance on science and technology, a drive for maximum productivity, a quantification of performance, and, above all, the alienation of both the producer and consumer. Major games like European and American football and the modern Olympics are taken as exemplars of this development.

  Secondly, sport is held to be thoroughly commercialised and dominated by market operations, both nationally and internationally. Players, and now often whole teams, are properties to be bought and sold and written off against tax; sports and the big sporting events are increasingly integrated into the structure of capitalist enterprise - the sports goods manufacturers, advertisers and sponsors, the media, and the manufacturers of plant and facilities - so that sport is produced, packaged and sold like any other commodity on the market for mass consumption at enormous profits. Thirdly, sport is seen as inculcating and expressing the quintessential ideology in capitalist

society: egoistic, aggressive individualism, ruthless
competition, the myth of equality of opportunity, together
with authoritarianism, elitism, chauvinism, sexism,
militarism and imperialism. The sports spectacle
generates aggressive impulses and at the same time
sublimates aggression by allowing its release in sado-
masochistic displays of physical activity, whose effect
is to help induce in their audiences a drugged state of
reconciliation to their alienation.

Fourthly, the state, as the representative of capitalist
interests, is seen as being actively complicit in all
this. Brohm goes on to argue that in the above respects
there is essentially no difference between what he calls
the 'state-capitalist societies' of the Soviet bloc and
the 'monopoly-state capitalist societies' of the west.

The superiority of the Marxist tradition as a whole,
as opposed to any particular version of it, has been its
sensitivity to the association of culture with power, and
specifically to the class basis of hegemony. There is
some truth in Hoch, Vinnai and Brohm's sort of account,
perhaps more than some with a vested interest in sport
would care to admit. The effects of the penetration of
sport by corporate capital and the overwhelming conservative ethos of the commanding heights of sport can hardly
be ignored any longer. But if we go along with them all
the way a number of puzzles arise. Why, if sport is so
debilitating in its effects on political consciousness,
are some of the most politically conscious and traditionally radical parts of this country those in which sport
is fanatically followed as well, such as Clydeside and
South Wales?   If sport so closely resembles work in its
propensity to alienate people, why does it, in marked
contrast to work, continue to be so popular? If people
are so stupified as to be completely unconscious of
their alienation - as Hoch, for example, categorically
asserts - would compensatory mechanisms like sports
spectacles be necessary at all, and would it not be
more likely that whatever was imposed on people from
above would be accepted without demur anyway? If the
bourgeois ideology purveyed in sport is so pervasive,
how is it these authors themselves managed to escape
its influences, and how is it - as Hoch and Brohm note -
that there is an increasing awareness, even within sport
itself, that something is wrong?

What we are presented with here is a pathological
model of human behaviour which is inappropriate for the
analysis of cultural phenomena. The conception of the
role that sport plays in hegemony and of the character
of consciousness and ideology is completely deterministic.

Consciousness is assumed to be an 'all or nothing' phenomenon: it is either completely false and all is alienation,
with people totally incorporated into an inhuman social
order; or it is absolutely true, a state of total illumina-
tion which enables people completely to see through and
reject the social order. No 'in-between' states of
consciousness are allowed: consciousness cannot be
incomplete, partial, inconsistent, transitory, or in the
process of formation. There is no sense in which people
might quite consciously value sports as meaningful and
beneficial aspects of their lives, while at the same being
aware that ruling groups attempt to use sport as an
instrument of control. In this approach sport has to be
the exclusive possession of one class rather than another,
and so there is no room for conceiving that it might be
an arena of uneasy accommodation and conflict between
them.

What is lacking here also is a systematic interrogation
of a range of evidence from the different types and levels
of sport. Instead there is an exclusive pre-occupation
with the topmost levels and an assumption that the pattern
at the top determines everything else. Consequently, the
precise way is which most people are involved in sport is
ignored, and the conservative ideology of sports controllers
is taken at its face value as evidence of the effects of
sport on everyone. There are good grounds for thinking
that sport is not a homogeneous entity and that there are
crucial differences between levels and types - between
professional and amateur, local and national, and so on.
The approach is also peculiarly static or ahistorical for
one which purports to owe an intellectual debt to Marx.
One example is the way the bourgeois notion of the
universal virtues of competition is simply reversed by
these authors and held to be universally evil. Whereas
the meaning and significance of competition surely has
to be understood in its socio-historical context.
Competition in ancient Olympia was actually very different
in many respects from the kind of competition seen in
Wembley Stadium today. (42) Another example is the way
bourgeois ideology is equated with extreme conservatism
bordering on Fascism, a gross oversimplification which
allows the ideological effects of the more subtle liberal
and progressive face of capitalism to go completely
unobserved.

Lastly, the argument that sport is essentially the same
in state socialist societies and capitalist societies
obscures very important differences between the way it is
organised in each, and this point will be returned to in
a moment.

Such faults are not all to be attributed to critical
theory as such: they stem rather from a relatively
unsophisticated attempt to apply it to a particular realm.

V

Something has to be said also about the influence of
structuralist Marxism, because of its general impact on
cultural analysis in the last few years here (on the work
of the Centre for Contemporary Cultural Studies at
Birmingham, for example) and for its potential influence,
rather than for the relatively small amount of work on
sport it has stimulated so far. Structuralist figures
like Barthes and Bourdieu, who hover around Marxism,
have interested themselves in a marginal way: the former
in a semiological analysis of wrestling and the latter in
an analysis of the role sport plays in cultural reproduction. (43) But for the obvious reason that his has been
easily the most seminal influence, I shall focus on the
leading figure, the French philosopher, Louis Althusser.
(44)
    In Althusserian Marxism sport is characterised, together
with a whole range of other institutions - education, the
arts and literature, the churches, the media, the family,
trade unions and political parties - as an 'ideological
state apparatus'. The latter is distinguished from the
'repressive state apparatus', in that while the function
of both is to reproduce the relations of economic
production, i.e. the exploitation of labour by capital,
ideological state apparatuses perform this function
through ideological work, whereas the repressive state
apparatus does so through coercive practices exercised
through the legal system, and by the police and the army,
etc. So, the role of cultural institutions is seen as
crucially instrumental in the reproduction of class
relations, each ideological state apparatus doing so
through its own particular kind of ideological work.
The fact that education, which is closely associated
with sport, is said to be the dominant ideological state
apparatus, and that sport seems to be accorded the status
of an ideological state apparatus in its own right,
suggests that Althusser regards sport as very important
in reproduction.
    In Althusserian theory the object of analysis is
structure: people are not the subject of history or of
social processes; they are the bearers or agents of
structural relations determined in the last instance by
the mode of production. The function of the ideological

state apparatuses, therefore, is to place agents with the
requisite skills and dispositions where they are required
in the social formation, i.e. those destined for subordinate positions are invested with certain skills to make
them productive and inculcated with appropriate dispositions to make them submissive, while those destined for
dominant positions are trained to lead and manage and
manipulate. Althusser heavily emphasises the structural
determination of social relations: whether agents are
aware of it or not, ideological state apparatuses
invariably reproduce the dominant social relations.
The teacher or coach may be progressive and non-authori-
tarian, but he or she is still an agent of the system
destined to carry out an ideological function.

It is difficult to see how this framework can be
helpful. It is couched at so high a level of generality
that there is effectively no guidance as to how precisely
the sports ideological state apparatus, or indeed any
specific ideological state apparatus, works. We are
simply given a list of 'bourgeois virtues' it is supposed
to inculcate. Secondly, in effect the categories of
ideology and culture are assimilated, so that the latter
disappears and all culture becomes ideological. What
remains - ideology - is then rigidly distinguished from
what is defined as its antithesis, namely science, so
that science seems not to be part of culture at all, but
to exist in a separate realm together. This has the
unfortunate result of establishing a polarity between
on the one hand the minority with access to, or capable
of understanding, culture 'scientifically', like himself
and his followers, and on the other hand the masses, who
are ideologically crammed, so that they are unable to
appreciate that their culture is a structurally determined
ideological state apparatus.

There is similarly little room here for an analysis
in terms of consciousness as an active element in the
process whereby people experience social relations like
sport and are able to respond to that experience in any
real sense autonomously. There is little conception
either that control from the point of view of dominant
groups can be highly problematic. In education, for
example, almost everybody knows how wide the fit is
between what employers require in the way of trained,
docile labour power and what the education system is
actually able to provide, and that a substantial proportion of students in schools are negatively influenced
by the way sports are put over in that context. In other
words, as in the previous approach discussed, there is
no real explanation of why conflict should ever arise,

let alone an explanation of conflict that is actually present; so while conflict is acknowledged, it has to be dealt with in ad hoc terms and in a rhetorical fashion - references to the class struggle are copious - rather than as a constituent element of the theory. In this respect, paradoxically, Althusser's Marxism would seem to exhibit much the same defects as functionalism, even though it is formulated in Marxist categories.

Lastly, Althusser assimilates society to the state, in that he rejects the distinction on the grounds that it is merely a bourgeois legal category and that its effects are therefore merely ideological. The result is that every superstructural element then becomes an apparatus of the state. This reasoning is quite fallacious and has very serious analytical consequences (let alone consequences for political judgments and commitments which will be left aside). For, while the distinction between state and society - or more accurately between state and civil society, a distinction Marx himself insisted on - may indeed be bourgeois in origin, it cannot be ignored because in practice it is strongly institutionalised. How else could one explain the powerful resistance to further encroachment by the state on the private sector in Britain, and the fact that elements within the state itself are a crucial element in that resistance? Without the distinction between state and civil society it becomes impossible to analyse and establish the way structures of hegemony work in different types of system. The fact is that the state plays a very different role in general, and in relation to culture and sport specifically, in liberal-democratic, capitalist societies, in Fascist dictatorships, and in state socialist societies. (45)

It may be for these reasons that, although a debt is acknowledged to Althusser in some of the Birmingham Centre's work, a critical distance is maintained from him. (46) In the work that the Centre has accomplished so far on sport his influence is hardly in evidence: no general theory of the role of sport has been attempted and instead, the focus of the Centre's work has been very much on discrete topics and issues, concerned mainly with working-class youth and football. Unlike Althusser, there has also been a welcome stress on the problematicity of control, and on the rationality of subordinate groups' reactions, which stems from the evident interest at the Centre in interactionism as it has been used in more radical versions of deviancy theory. (47)

VI

I want to pull these remarks together now, and draw out
what has been implicit, in the form of some suggestions
which might begin to extricate us from some of the
difficulties we have been discussing. What in fact I am
proposing is an approach which leaves open the possibility
of relating sport as an element in culture to the structure
of hegemony.

Let us look once more at the concept of culture, which
certainly cannot be hived off into a separate sphere of
leisure activity. It seems to me that a concept is needed
which concedes the principle that cultural processes are
no less material or real, i.e. no less important a feature
of social life than economic and political processes: all
are integral to social existence, and indeed, the cultural
is a vital condition for the existence of the economic and
the political. (48) In fact, all three are equally
important in their own ways in the construction of hegemony.
Culture therefore is not just a mental product: it is a
lived practice formed by conscious human beings from their
lived experience, and constituting for them a whole way
of life. There are two internally linked dimensions to
this process of cultural formation: culture is both
constituted by people consciously making choices and
evaluations of their experience AND simultaneously,
because culture is also inherited from the choices and
evaluations people have made in the past as tradition, it
is also constitutive of choice and action, and therefore
culture can also, though it never does entirely, act as
a powerful constraint on understanding social life in
appropriate terms and on taking appropriate forms of
action. As Williams puts it so cogently, in commenting
on Gramsci's conception of hegemony and its relation to
culture:

It [hegemony] is a lived system of meanings and values -
constitutive and constituting - which as they are
experienced as practices appear as reciprocally
confirming. It thus constitutes a sense of reality
for most people in society, a sense of absolute
because experienced reality.... It is, that is to
say, in the strongest sense a 'culture' which has
also to be seen as the lived dominance and subordination
of particular classes. (49)

Some, as opposed to others within the Marxist tradition
of social analysis, are not too happy with this conception
of culture. As it has been articulated in the work of
Raymond Williams and Edward Thompson it has come under
fire for what one critic has termed 'culturalism', i.e.

for allegedly underplaying the importance of structural determinations and of especially the role of the economic base. (50)   There is a certain amount of truth in this criticism when it is applied to particular representatives of cultural analysis, or to individual pieces of work: it is largely true of Hoggart's work, for example; (51) it is more true of Williams's earlier than his later work, as he himself has recently admitted; (52)   but it is scarcely true of Thompson's work. (53)   So, recognising the centrality of culture does not necessarily deny the effectivity of the mode of production, which can and must be granted the status of exerting crucial pressures and limitations on people's ways of life.   Quite obviously, for example, the restricted access to higher education of most working-class people, which has been reinforced by the cuts recently, cuts off a whole section of the population from certain kinds of cultural experience.

But once economic constraints, i.e. the class power which is based on ownership and control of the means of production, is given its due weight, there remains a lot to be explained, and talk about economic determination often turns out to be trivially true with respect to the solution of specific problems.   It is doubtful, for example, whether it is very helpful beyond a certain point in explaining the importance of football to working-class people in this country, as opposed to cricket or rugby, or in explaining the significance of the great plebian underground of disorderly, rowdy and 'rough' sports which have passed into working-class cultural tradition, and which is especially manifested in the strong association of sports with gambling.

Nevertheless, there may still be some doubt or uneasiness about the utility of seeing culture as a whole way of life, not only because it can so easily become a rather vague catchall for all that is not economics or politics (in the current state of conceptualisation this seems to be a perennial problem), or because in some usages of the concept we have noted already, social life is depicted in such a way that economic and political reality fade away into the background; but also because of the danger that 'culture' becomes virtually synonymous with the category of society.   Thus there is nothing that is not culture and the distinction between political and economic relations, as opposed to other forms of social relations, is lost.

However, in attempting to resolve this difficulty there would seem to be little analytical utility in defining where culture ends and politics and economics begins strictly in institutional terms, because we are dealing

here with processes, that is, with forms of social life
which are historical, and which are tightly interwoven.
Of course, given institutions do tend to be more associated
with one or other major social process - political parties
and interest groups with politics, firms, trade unions and
professions with the economy, sports and the theatre with
culture (in the conventional sense of habits, customs,
style of life, and achieved state of 'civilisation').
But the relationships are not necessary or fixed, for
clearly a given institution from a processual point of
view may partake of a variety of functions, depending on
the historical and social context. Kinship systems and
institutions, for example, especially in non-industrial
societies, may perform to varying degrees important
economic, political and cultural functions.

In broad terms, if we understand that economic processes
refer to the production, distribution and control of
relatively scarce resources; that political processes are
concerned with the mobilisation and organisation of
perceived opposed interests; and that cultural processes
refer to the habits, customs, pastimes, rituals, style
of life, and the achieved state of knowledge and learning;
then it does make sense to speak, as we often do, of the
culture of work and of politics, of the economics of
political and cultural instituions, and of the politics of
economic and cultural relations. Thus sports partake of
the economy, in so far as they require resources, which
in capitalist societies are mostly allocated on a
commercial basis; they partake of politics, in so far as
they serve as an agency of political mobilisation on
occasions; and they partake of culture, in so far as they
are a popular form of leisure activity.

Provided we bear the above distinctions in mind, the
utility of the second and broader sense of culture, that
is, as a whole way of life, can be appreciated. For it
possesses the capacity of enabling us to capture the
connected, processual, dynamic nature of political,
economic, and other relationships and experiences - in
fact the varied, complex nature of social life as such.
We can, and indeed we must maintain at the same time the
analytic distinction between political, economic and
cultural processes, and this is possible if, firstly, we
retain the concept of 'society' to refer to the totality
of social relationships and, secondly, if we conceive of
people's experiences of a range of institutions and
processes within a given society as constituting definite
sets or complexes of common experiences - in other words
as constituting cultures or different ways of life within
the social totality.

Now let us take the concept of ideology. A notion of ideology is needed which does not collapse the distinction between culture and ideology, so that all culture becomes ideological, or simply the common sense world view of particular groups or classes. Of course, ideology has to be seen as a pervasive and crucially important phenomenon, but it has to be seen also as a specific type of representation of social relations: one which is embedded in key social processes, and which conceals the interests of specific groups and classes. In this way it therefore conceals the contradictions between the present social order and the potential it contains for change. (54) For example, the pervasive notion that egoistic, competitive individualism is universal and that one's social position and the good of society are dependent solely on individual merit and achievement, is widely encouraged in our type of society, and it may be that sport is one of the major ways such ideas and practices are encouraged.

But if we are to avoid a Zhadanovist and philistine condemnation of all bourgeois culture - which Marx's own example clearly does not warrant - it is vitally important to keep in mind that by no means all the culture characteristic of a capitalist society is ideological in this sense, and further, that not all incorrect or mistaken beliefs are necessarily ideological. So where sport is concerned we need to distinguish the ideological from the non-ideological elements, unless we wish to write off sport in toto as an illusion and thus deny the experience of a large section of the population.

In any case it is simplistic to think of ideology as mere illusion. Beliefs and practices which are based on them are only accepted and adopted by people if there is some 'rational' kernel to them, i.e. if there is some aspect that makes sense to people in their particular situation. People do not believe things unless they are some way socially prepared and therefore predisposed to believe them, and if ideology were merely illusion it would be far easier to expose and shake off. This suggests that the attraction of a popular cultural item like sport is very deep-seated, and if it is possible for ruling groups to cash in on it, as it were, for their own purposes, as they demonstrably try to do at times, it is because people are already organically involved with it as part of their culture. In other words, ideology has a material base in social practice and is not merely the antithesis of science.

The third point is that it is absolutely necessary to recognise the centrality of popular culture and of sport within it. The latter aspect is very much under-recognised -

even by so perceptive a cultural analyst as Williams.
Nationally, it is an influence, to one or other extent,
on the lives of people in all classes, and thus it may be
one of the most important factors cutting across class
divisions and helping to create a sense of local and
national identity. Furthermore, it is a central feature
of working-class culture, much under-rated in studies of
working-class life.

There is a need to identify the specific appeal of
sport as a cultural form, compared with others such as
cinema, theatre and dancing, which enables it to convey
meanings so powerfully, and which perhaps at times
uniquely lends itself to ideological usage. I have
suggested elsewhere, for example, that ritual practices
surrounding sport and its dramatic qualities are important
in this connection. (55) The simplistic understanding
of popular cultural forms like sport in terms of a
totalitarian, valueless, fraudulent imposition on people
blocks understanding of their importance, both of their
autonomy and of the way they function within an overall
hegemony. As such it is a debilitating elitist mistake
that a socially aware artist like Brecht, who used
popular songs, music and stories in his work, or
commentators like Benjamin and Enzenberger, never make.
(56) To exert such an enormous appeal sport must be
significantly different from work and everyday existence.

Fourthly, the analysis of sport must be carried on in
historical terms, if the present patterns are to be in
any way adequately understood. A start has been made,
but much more work is required. Above all in this
respect the development of sport has to be systematically
related to the major phases in the development of
industrial capitalism and to phases in the structure of
hegemony associated with it. For example, in my own
work I have tried to trace this development and
characterise its different phases in the case of Britain:
the repressive phase concurrent with the transition to
industrial capitalism; the successive phase when folk
sports are reconstructed in a process of accommodation
between dominant groups; the diffusion of reconstructed
sport as an aspect of the process of 'remaking' the
English working class; and the massification of sport
as it increasingly merges in many respects with the
entertainment industry in the twentieth century. (57)

Fifthly, the process of development and the present
patterns need to be understood in dialectical terms - a
much-abused word admittedly. By that I mean a process of
reciprocal interaction between groups and classes which
is full of tension, rather than a process of one-way

determination of and imposition by one group or class on another. Without some notion of the autonomy of popular cultural tradition and of the power of subordinate groups to resist manipulation and control from above, manifestations of conflict and resistance involving people who are also sports enthusiasts cannot be explained. The development of football in Britain illustrates the point. The initial transformation of the game under the control and patronage of the earlier Victorian bourgeoisie (who established the amateur tradition in fact) and its later transformation under the auspices of the bourgeoisie, who made football into a business, did not prevent working-class people colonising football and in a restricted sense making it their own. As a rider to that, this colonisation did not prevent, and in fact, co-existed with, administrative control over the game by dominant groups in society at large. We need to understand this aspect of hegemony as full of tensions, contradiction and limitations on the influence and on the actions that any class or group can take.

Or let us consider the repercussions of the increasing rationalisation of sport, not only from the perspective of how it makes control of people easier, but also as in some ways itself an inner limit on the use of sport for these purposes: rationalisation tends to increase the predictability of outcomes and the level of standardisation in sports, and therefore tends also to reduce the level of excitement, etc., i.e. it tends to erode the very kind of appeal which is a precondition for dominant groups being able to trade off it. Or again, there seem to be limits to the exploitation of sports workers in the interests of increased productivity and profits and on the exploitation of sport for promoting respectability, or national prestige, or whatever; for the more intensive the competition, the more there is a tendency, it seems, for those involved, from administrators down to participants, to try to win by breaking the rules (drug-taking, undercover payments, violent tactics, etc.). This has obvious repercussions for the credibility of sport as a convincing symbol of dominant values and norms, and therefore for its utility in the construction of hegemony.

Lastly, in terms of the general requirements for an analysis of sport, a theory is needed which attempts to encompass sport as a whole, i.e. a theory which integrates the many scattered studies on football, boxing, wrestling, racing, and so on.

VII

I would like to conclude by very briefly pinpointing some of the major institutional areas on which more empirical research is required if advance is to be made.

The role of capital has so far only received piecemeal, somewhat sensationalised and fascinating illustration, rather than systematic investigation. At the moment there is little to match, for example, the historian Charles Korr's careful analysis of the role capital played in the foundation and early development of West Ham FC. (58) We need to know far more about the specific role of capital - of big versus small and medium capital, of old versus new capital, in relation to the type of power and influence it confers on the owners and controllers of sports organisations, on advertisers and sponsors. And we need to know more about the significance of commercialised sports in general in promoting particular ways of life, especially that of the 'consumer'.

Though the means of mass communication are now probably the main promoters of sport and one of the prime ways in which a framework for interpreting its meaning and significance is established, there is as yet no major or substantial study of the media in this respect. In marked contrast we do have studies of the way the media handle other important issue areas and their relation to hegemony, such as law and order, political demonstrations, industrial relations and race relations. (59)

The modern state is everywhere increasing its intervention and therefore its potential control and influence over sport, yet there is almost no sustained work on the phenomenon as a whole, let alone on discrete aspects, such as the role of the Sports Council in Britain. Even in that area which constitutes the longest standing influence of the state on sport, namely state education, there is little work available of the kind that is needed, most of what has been done coming in the category of descriptive history. (60) A study of the role of the physical education profession, for example, and its precise relationship to the state in helping shape what is an important aspect of the school curriculum, would seem to be well worthwhile. Also, the fact that physical education, or movement education in general, is virtually the only subject on the curriculum at the secondary level in which the sexes are still largely segregated, suggests that an analysis of this aspect in relation to sexual divisions in our kind of society might prove most rewarding. (61)

Finally, a study of the role of youth organisations of different kinds which promote sport - religious, secular, political and para-military - would be likely to pay dividends, in that the experience of youth seems to be very important in class formation and in creating a sense of class identity. Most youth organisations have traditionally de-emphasised class differences and promoted social mobility by attempting to inculcate certain norms of respectability. Also sport, it seems, has traditionally provided an avenue of social mobility for ethnic minorities and it would therefore be interesting to examine the significance of sport in this respect, given the current highly pressurised position of the black and brown communities.

It is time now for the analysis of sport to shift somewhat from the terrain it has so far largely occupied to a more critical and advanced level of understanding. It may be that on the way something concrete can also be accomplished with respect to the way that sport itself is practised.

NOTES

1   C.H. Page, The mounting interest in sport, in J.T. Talamini and C.H. Page (eds), 'Sport and Society: An Anthology', Boston, Little Brown, 1973.
2   Page, a past editor of the 'American Sociological Review' has complained that during his tenure not a single article dealing with sport as a sociological problem was submitted.
3   Some notable exceptions are: R. Frankenberg, 'Village on the Border', Harmondsworth, Penguin, 1957; M. Stacey, 'Tradition and Change: A Study of Banbury', Oxford University Press, 1960; B. Jackson, 'Working Class Community', London, Routledge & Kegan Paul, 1968; N. Dennis et al., 'Coal is Our Life', London, Tavistock, 1956.
4   J.H. Goldthorpe, et al., 'The Affluent Worker', 3 monographs, Cambridge University Press, 1968, 1969.
5   R. Hoggart, 'The Uses of Literacy', Harmondsworth, Penguin, 1958; R. Williams, 'Culture and Society', Harmondsworth, Penguin, 1958 and 'The Long Revolution', Harmondsworth, Penguin, 1961.
6   M.A. Smith et al. (eds), 'Leisure and Society in Britain', London, Allen Lane, 1973 (the collection contains one paper on football); M. Young and P. Willmott, 'The Symmetrical Family', Harmondsworth, Penguin, 1973.

7 See for example J.W. Loy and G.S.Kenyon (eds), 'Sport, Culture and Society', London, Macmillan, 1969; E. Dunning (ed.), 'The Sociology of Sport', London, Cass, 1971; Talamini and Page, op.cit.; G.H. Sage, 'Sport and American Society', London, Addison-Wesley, 1973; R. Albonico and K. Pfister-Binz (eds), 'Sociology of Sport', Switzerland, Maggligen, 1971; J.A. Mangan (ed.), 'Physical Education and Sport: Sociological and Cultural Perspectives', Oxford, Blackwell, 1973. Other examples are given below.

8 H. Edwards, 'The Sociology of Sport', Illinois, Dorsey Press, 1973.

9 Social historians frequently ignore the subject altogether. See for example, H. Perkin, 'The Origins of Modern English Society 1780-1880', London, Routledge & Kegan Paul, 1968; F.M.L. Thompson, 'English Landed Society in the 19th Century', London, Routledge & Kegan Paul, 1969 (with the exception of hunting); G. Steadman Jones, 'Outcast London', Oxford, Clarendon Press, 1971. Others give sport a mention in passing: E. Hobsbawm, 'The Age of Capital', London, Weidenfeld & Nicolson, 1975; R. Samuel, 'Village Life and Labour', London, Routledge & Kegan Paul, 1975. The following give it more attention: H. Cunningham, 'Leisure in the Industrial Revolution', London, Croom Helm, 1980; J. Walvin, 'Leisure and Society 1830-1950', Harlow, Longman, 1978; J. Lowerson and J. Myerscough, 'Time to Spare in Victorian England', Hassocks, Sussex, Harvester, 1977; R.K. Ensor, 'England 1870-1914', Oxford University Press; G. Best, 'Mid-Victorian Britain 1851-75', London, Fontana, 1971; See N. Polsky, On pool playing and pool rooms, in G. Stone (ed.), 'Games, Sport and Power', New Jersey, Transaction Books, 1972, for some apposite critical comments on the neglect of sport by American professional historians.

10 D. Brailsford, 'Sport and Society: Elizabeth to Anne', London, Routledge & Kegan Paul, 1969.

11 See Stone's remarks in Introduction to 'Games, Sport and Power', op.cit.

12 See especially the contributions by Sage in Sage (ed.), op.cit.; A. Guttman, 'From Ritual to Record', New York, Columbia Press, 1978; C. Lasch, 'The Culture of Narcissism', New York, Norton, 1980.

13 Take the following from a Director-General of UNESCO: Whether we consider the ascetism of training, the ideal of balanced personality, the sense of justice implicit in obedience to rules, or the brotherhood of classes, races and peoples evinced on the field

and in spectator sport, these major ethical virtues
are satisfied in our modern civilization by sport
more than anything else. I know of no social,
ideological or intellectual movement able to bring
home the gamut of these basic values so directly
to the young, to every class and, overcoming
political barriers and differences of race and
language, to all peoples of the world. (R. Maheu,
Sport and Culture, in Mangan, op.cit.)

In a somewhat similar vein see also: P. Weiss, 'Sport:
A Philosophic Inquiry', South Illinois University Press,
1969; H. Slusher, 'Man, Sport and Existence',
Philadelphia, Lea & Febiger, 1967; F. Inglis, 'The
Name of the Game', London, Heinemann, 1978; E. Gerber,
'Sport and the Body', Philadelphia, Lea & Febiger,
1972, who quotes K. Schmitz, 'Sport and Play'.

14   The familiar difficulties of categorising sociological
work are encountered in the sociology of sport. Some,
being eclectic or agnostic where theory is concerned,
resist ready categorisation, while a relatively large
proportion ostensibly does without any theoretical
framework at all, i.e. the field abounds in examples
of abstracted empiricism (see especially the collection
edited by Sage for examples of the genre, but most of
the other collections are also fairly liberally
sprinkled with examples). Most of this work in essence
is functionalist in the sense that the established
pattern of society is taken for granted or equated
with 'normality', and is not therefore taken to be
problematic. I leave aside discussion of the
'positivist' nature of work conducted within the
predominant approach as an epistemological question
beyond the scope of this paper.

15   J.W. Loy and G.S. Kenyon, Towards a sociology of
sport, in Loy and Kenyon (eds), op.cit.; G. Luschen,
The sociology of sport, 'Current Sociology', 1967;
G. Luschen, The interdependence of sport and culture,
in G. Sage (ed.), op.cit.; H. Edwards, op.cit.;
A. Guttman, op.cit.; J. Dumazadier, The point of
view of the social scientist, in E. Jokl and E. Simon
(eds), 'International Research in Sport and Physical
Education', Springfield, Mass., Thomas, 1964.

16   C.H. Page, Pervasive themes in the sociology of
sport, in Talamini and Page, op.cit.; Sage, op.cit.;
Mangan, op.cit.; Lasch, op.cit.; Introduction to
Dunning, op.cit. and E. Dunning, Some conceptual
dilemmas in the sociology of sport, in Albonico and
Pfister-Binz, op.cit.; E.E. Snyder and E. Spreitzer,
'Social Aspects of Sport', New Jersey, Prentice-Hall,

1978, and their Sociology of sport: an overview, in
A. Yiannakis et al. (eds), 'Sport Sociology', Dubuque,
Iowa, Kendall Hunt, 1976; H.L. Nixon, 'Sport and
Social Organisation', Indianapolis, Bobbs-Merrill,
1977; J.M. Roberts and Sutton Smith, Game involvement
in adults, in Loy and Kenyon, op.cit. and Child
training and game involvement, in the same volume;
A. Beisser, 'The Madness in Sports', Bowie, Maryland,
Charles Press, 1967; A.G. Ingham and J.W. Loy, The
social system of sport: a humanistic perspective,
'Quest', vol.19, 1973 (an attempt to combine a form
of interactionism derived from Peter Berger's
Schutzian phenomenology with structural-functionalism
which merely gives the latter the appearance of a
human face while retaining all its defects);
Frankenberg, op.cit.

17   K. Roberts, 'Leisure', London, Longmans, 1970;
S.R. Parker, 'The Sociology of Leisure', London,
Allen & Unwin, 1976.

18   N. Smelser, 'The Theory of Collective Behaviour',
London, Routledge & Kegan Paul, 1965; C.Geertz,
paper in D. Apter, 'Ideology and Discontent', New
York, Free Press, 1964.

19   J. Huizinga, 'Homo Ludens', London, Paladin, 1970;
for the critique of Huizinga see: R. Caillois,
'Man, Play and Games', New York, Free Press, 1961;
Dunning, Sociology of, op.cit.; Loy and Kenyon,
op.cit., Edwards, op.cit., Guttman, op.cit. For
recent works which, like Huizinga's, place the
category of play at the centre of historical, social
and cultural development see R. Sennet, 'The Fall
of Public Man', Cambridge University Press, 1977;
F. Hearn, 'Domination, Legitimation, and Resistance',
London, Greenwood Press, 1978.

20   Dunning, 'The Sociology of Sport', op.cit.; Page,
op.cit.

21   SSRC/Sports Council, 'Public Disorder and Sporting
Events', London, HMSO, 1978.

22   H. Edwards, 'The Revolt of the Black Athlete',
New York, Free Press, Macmillan, 1969; E. Dunning
and K. Sheard, 'Gentlemen and Players', Oxford,
Martin Robertson, 1979.

23   A. Gramsci, 'The Prison Notebooks', (ed.), Q. Hoare
and G. Nowell Smith, London, Lawrence & Wishart,
1971.

24   E.P. Thompson, 'The Making of the English Working
Class', Harmondsworth, Penguin, 1963, and Time,
Work discipline and industrial capitalism, 'Past
and Present', vol.38, 1967; S. Pollard, Factory

discipline in the industrial revolution, 'Economic history review', 2nd Series, vol.16, 1963-4.

25   R.W. Malcolmson, 'Popular Recreations in English Society', Cambridge University Press, 1973; R.D. Storch, The plague of blue locusts: police reform and popular resistance in Northern England, 1840-57, 'International Review of Social History', vol.20, 1975, and The policeman as domestic missionary: urban discipline and popular culture in Northern England 1850-1880, 'Journal of Social History', vol.9, 1976; P. Bailey, 'Leisure and Class in Victorian England', London, Hutchinson, 1978.

26   Malcolmson, op.cit.; Bailey, op.cit.

27   Ibid.

28   See for example on horse racing W. Vamplew, 'The Turf', London, Allen Lane, 1976; on cricket C.C.P. Brookes, Cricket as a vocation, unpublished PhD thesis, University of Leicester, 1974; and 'English Cricket', London, Weidenfeld & Nicolson, 1978; on association football, Tony Mason, 'Association Football and English Society 1863-1915', Hassocks, Sussex, Harvester, 1980; and rugby union, Dunning and Sheard, op.cit.

29   Bailey, op.cit. On the working men's club movement in this connection see R. Price, 'Imperialism and the Working Class', University of Toronto Press, 1973. Another well-documented example is the Volunteer Force, for which see H. Cunningham, 'The Volunteer Force: Leisure, Class and Social Control', Hamden, Shoe String Press, 1976.

30   R. Roberts, 'The Classic Slum', Harmondsworth, Penguin, 1971; J.R. Gillis, The evolution of juvenile delinquency in England 1890-1914, 'Past and Present', vol.67, 1975.

31   W.D. Smith, 'Stretching Their Bodies', Newton Abbot, David & Charles, 1976.

32   Jennifer A.Hargreaves, 'Playing like gentlemen while behaving like ladies': The social significance of physical activity for females in late 19th and early 20th century Britain, unpublished M.A. Thesis, University of London, Institute of Education, 1979.

33   P. Cohen and D. Robins, 'Knuckle Sandwich', Harmondsworth, Penguin, 1978; R. Ingham, Towards some recommendations, in R. Ingham, et al., 'Football Hooliganism', London, Interaction in Print, 1978.

34   H. Meller, 'Leisure and the Changing City', London, Routledge & Kegan Paul, 1976; S. Yeo, 'Religion and Voluntary Organisations in Crisis', London, Croom Helm, 1976.

35 For example, the British and American governments'
    positions on the Moscow Olympics and the Afghanistan
    issue. See also J. Riordan, 'Sport in Soviet
    Society', London, Blackwell, 1977.

36 Bailey, op.cit. Having thus characterised the
    predominant paradigm, it should be noted that in
    North American sociology of sport and especially its
    Canadian branch, an interesting, if inconclusive
    attempt at a critical distancing from the predominant
    paradigm is developing. See for example R.S. Gruneau
    and J.G. Albinson, 'Canadian Sport: Sociological
    Perspectives', London, Addison Wesley, 1976.

37 E. Goffman, Fun and games, 'Encounters', Indianapolis,
    Bobbs-Merrill, 1961, and Where the action is,
    'Interaction Ritual', New York, Doubleday, 1972;
    G. Stone (ed.), op.cit.; M.B. Scott, 'The Racing
    Game', Chicago, Aldine, 1968; C.E. Ashworth, Sport
    as symbolic dialogue, in Dunning (ed.), op.cit.;
    P. Marsh, et al., 'The Rules of Disorder', London,
    Routledge & Kegan Paul, 1978; D. Whitson, Method in
    sport sociology: the potential of a phenomenological
    contribution, 'International Review of Sports
    Sociology', vol.4, no.2, 1976.

38 E.P. Thompson, The moral economy of the English crowd
    in the 18th century, 'Past and Present', vol.50,
    1971; E. Hobsbawm and G. Rudé, 'Captain Swing',
    Harmondsworth, Penguin, 1969.

39 Cohen and Robins, op.cit.; I. Taylor, Soccer violence
    and soccer hooliganism, in S. Cohen (ed.), 'Images
    of Deviance', Harmondsworth, Penguin, 1971.

40 See A. Gouldner, 'The Coming Crisis in Western
    Sociology', London, Heinemann, 1972, for some
    pertinent comments on Goffman and interactionism in
    general.

41 Jean Marie Brohm, 'Sport: a Prison of Measured
    Time', London, Ink Links, 1978; P. Hoch, 'Rip Off
    the Big Game', New York, Doubleday, 1972; G. Vinnai,
    'Football Mania', London, Ocean Books, 1973;
    B. Rigauer, 'Sport and Work', New York, Columbia
    University Press, 1981.

42 M.I. Finley and A. Pleket, 'The Olympic Games: The
    First Thousand Years', London, Chatto & Windus,
    1976.

43 R. Barthes, 'Mythologies', London, Paladin, 1973;
    M.A. Bouet, The significance of the Olympic
    phenomenon: a preliminary attempt at systematic and
    semiotic analysis, 'International Review of Sport
    Sociology', vol.3, no.12, 1977; P. Bourdieu, Sport
    and social class, 'Social Science Information',

vol.17, no.6, 1978; P. Bourdieu and J.-C. Passeron, 'Reproduction in Education, Society and Culture', London, Sage Publications, 1977.

44   L. Althusser, Ideology and ideological state apparatuses, 'Lenin and Philosophy', London, New Left Books, 1971.   It may be objected that since Althusser never intended this essay to be more than programmatic, and his views have changed somewhat since it was first written, that it should not be taken as representative of his position.   While the first claim is certainly correct, there has been ample time for Althusser to have developed the ideas therein, but curiously, he has not done so. The second claim is extremely contentious.   Although he has produced an auto-critique of some aspects of his previous work in 'For Marx' and 'Reading Capital' (see his 'Essays in Self-Criticism', 1976) he has never explicitly repudiated the ISA essay, and whether his self-criticism actually amounts to a change of substance as opposed to cosmetics, i.e. a restatement of his previous position, is debatable. See especially E.P. Thompson's assessment in The poverty of theory, 'The Poverty of Theory and Other Essays', London, Merlin, 1978.   Lastly, an examination of his ISA essay is certainly justified, simply in terms of the great influence it has exerted in such fields as the sociology of education.

45   R. Miliband, Reply to Nicos Poulantzas, in R. Blackburn (ed.), 'Ideology in Social Science', 1974; Riordan, op.cit.; R. Mandell, 'The Nazi Olympics', London, Souvenir Press, 1974.

46   See for example S. Hall et al., 'Working Papers in Cultural Studies', vol.10, 1977; R. Johnson, Three problematics: elements of a theory of working class culture, in J. Clarke, et al. (eds), 'Working Class Culture', London, Hutchinson, 1979.

47   C. Critcher, Football since the war, in Clarke, ibid.;   J. Clarke, Football and working class fans: tradition and change, in R. Ingham, op.cit.

48   The argument is based on R. Williams, 'Marxism and Literature', Oxford University Press, 1977.

49   Ibid., p.110.

50   R. Johnson, op.cit.

51   Hoggart, op.cit.

52   Williams, 'Culture and Society', op.cit., is the most obvious example.   For Williams's own assessment in the light of this type of criticism see his 'Politics and Letters', London, New Left Books, 1979, especially pp.137-51.

53   See especially the interweaving of the economic and
     political with the cultural in his Patrician society
     plebian culture, 'Journal of Social History', vol.7,
     part 4, 1974.
54   J. Larrain, 'The Concept of Ideology', London,
     Hutchinson, 1979.
55   John Hargreaves, 'Sport and Hegemony in Britain',
     London, Macmillan, forthcoming. See also S. Lukes,
     Political ritual and social integration, 'Sociology',
     vol.9, no.2, 1975; O. Patterson, The cricket ritual
     in the West Indies, 'New Society', no.352, 26 June
     1969.
56   P. Slater, 'Origins and Significance of the Frankfurt
     School', London, Routledge & Kegan Paul, 1974;
     H.Y. Enzenberger, 'Raids and Reconstructions',
     London, Pluto, 1977; W. Benjamin, The work of art
     in the age of mechanical reproduction, 'Illuminations',
     London, Fontana, 1973.
57   John Hargreaves, op.cit.
58   C. Korr, West Ham United FC and the beginnings of
     professional football in East London 1895-1914,
     'Journal of Contemporary History', vol.13, 1978.
     See also T. Mason, 'Association Football and English
     Society 1863-1915', Hassocks, Sussex, Harvester, 1980.
59   S. Hall, et al., 'Policing the Crisis', London,
     Macmillan, 1978; Glasgow Media Group, 'Bad News',
     vol.I, London, Routledge & Kegan Paul, 1977;
     S. Cohen and J. Young, 'The Manufacture of News',
     London, Constable, 1974; J. Halloran, 'Demonstration
     and Communication: a case study', Harmondsworth,
     Penguin, 1970; J. Curran et al., (eds), 'Mass
     Communication and Society', London, E. Arnold, 1977
     reprints some of the more useful papers in this
     connection.
60   P. McIntosh, 'Physical Education in England Since
     1800', London, Bell & Hyman, rep. 1979.
61   J.A. Hargreaves, op.cit.

Chapter 3

'Highlights and action replays' - ideology, sport and the media

Alan Clarke and *John Clarke*

I IDEOLOGY AND SPORT (1)

Recently, the proposition that politics should be kept
out of sport has been endlessly debated. It is a proposition which assumes that politics and sport are two clearly
separated fields of life. Anyone, it assumes, can tell
the difference between the world of politics - with its
political parties, parliaments, international conferences
and so on - and the world of sport - games, contests and
physical activities. But to describe politics in this
way is to leave out a different level of political
relations. These relations lie outside the formal arena
of party politics, and operate in the maintenance of
social patterns of power, domination and subordination
throughout the whole of society. It is this aspect of
politics that is involved in 'managing' a society composed
of divided and conflicting classes and groups. It is,
as we shall show, a level of political activity that
stresses the importance of ideology, particularly, in the
role of presenting a divided society as if it was an
harmonious unity.

It is this link between politics and ideology that
directs this approach to sport and the mass media. From
this view of politics, it becomes impossible to treat
sport as if it stands outside of all the other social
relations within which we spend our life. Sport is not
a 'privileged space' into which we can retreat from real
life - rather it is systematically and intimately
connected with society. Sport as an activity, or an
object of interest, is socially constructed; it is defined
and given meaning. It is these meanings which give us
the value of being involved in sport - they provide us
with identities and identifications. It is the meaning
attached to the game - rather than the bare physical

fact of '22 men chasing a little ball around' - that gives
football its popularity. (2) It is this theme that is
explored in the first section of this paper, for unless
this social positioning and valuation of sport is understood, we cannot properly make sense of the media treatment
of sport. The manner in which the media portray and
present sport is, as we shall see, dependent on this already
existing 'social construction of sport'.

There is one more general point to be made by way of
introduction. Sport does not merely passively replicate
these wider ideological definitions. It contributes
something of major significance to the production of these
images. Because it appears as a sphere of activity outside society, and particularly as it appears to involve
natural, physical skills and capacities, sport presents
these ideological images *as if they are natural*. They
appear to rest on natural, or extra-social truths, rather
than being the products of human social and political
construction. This may be easier to grasp if we turn to
some of the specific ideological images which we can
identify as associated with sport in English society. (3)

Let us begin by taking what appears as the most
natural characteristic of sport - that it involves
individuals locked in competition. Playing sports demands
the application of individual skills and powers;
successes and failure are individual accomplishments.
Sport provides the opportunity for individuals to pit
themselves against others, and be judged by their competitive performance. It appears as the most primitive and
natural form of interaction between humans. This may
seem 'self-evident', but it is connected to propositions
about this as the natural state of society - that social
life is 'competitive individualism'. From this standpoint, it is possible to see the cross-connections that
are constructed between sport and social images. Thus,
competitive individualism as a political ideology is
presented as the natural human condition. This draws on
images from and analogies with sport to construct this
'naturalness'. Thus, socially, individuals are
presented as engaged in a race or contest, in which
success goes to the 'fittest'. Success or failure lies
in the hands of each particular individual - it rests
on natural talents, and the capacity to apply them, to
be a 'good competitor'. And, as in sport, we recognise
that such talents are unequally distributed, and that
there will always be winners and losers.

This conception passes us backwards and forwards
between sport and political ideology. On the one hand,
it is 'naturalised' by its reference to sport. On the

other, through our socialisation to a political identity
as individuals, we can recognise ourselves in sport - for
it validates and reinforces our identities as 'competitive
individuals'.

But, it will be said, not all sports are individualised:
there are team games. Here, too, though, there are cross-
references to ideological themes and practices from
other areas of social life. Team games, especially in
their professional forms, have increasingly come to
stress managerial direction and co-ordination, the
importance of an organised and systematic division of
labour, and even such themes as 'work rate' and productivity. These are practices and images drawn from an
industrialised economy. (4) Outside sport, divisions and
conflicts between managers and managed, dominant and
subordinate social groups are masked through the use of
sporting metaphors and imagery. From the factory to the
nation, we are presented with images of ourselves as
members of a team, having to make sacrifices and dedicate
ourselves to the good of the team. We are exhorted to
compete against other factories and other national teams
in the olympics of profitability.

There are other forms of social identification
constructed through sport in our society, which are
produced through the social organisation and distribution
of sport. Sport draws on and gives a symbolic value to
particular local identities, constructing 'communities'
of interest and support. This is probably most visible
in professional football, where historically football
was provided for its mass working-class audience by
local businessmen and traders as one of the means through
which local cross-class loyalties could be established.
It is 'our' town, 'our' team - no matter what the real
patterns of ownership and power are. Even today, local
businessmen on the boards of directors of successful
football clubs speak glowingly of the ways in which the
teams' successes contributed to industrial harmony,
lower absenteeism and increased output. (5) But it is
not just local identities and rivalries that are
mobilised through sport: regional ones are also represented. One of the most visible in England has been the
north-south division, which has proved a constant source
of resentment and hostility for northern sports
followers. This resentment has been directed at the
perceived aristocratic and/or public school domination
of sports administration and team selection in the south.
Though this division is expressed through particular
sporting issues and controversies (usually the exclusion
of a Yorkshireman from an England cricket team), it

mobilises other deeply rooted social divisions. Myths of the hard, serious and honest northerner pitted against the soft, but all-pervading old boy network of the south, may not be truthful, but they provide popular representations which draw on real economic unevenesses in the development of the north as against the south east since the 1920s. They register the concentration of social, economic and political power in the south. What is significant is that such resentments are expressed as powerfully, if not more, through discussions of the MCC than they are about the banks and finance houses. Sport provides a cultural arena through which such identities and conflicts are expressed. But it is also an arena through which they are displaced from their real social basis.

Beyond these local and regional identities, however, stand the most socially visible identification constructed and maintained through sport as a cultural symbol. This is the connection between sport and nationalism. There are a number of points that we wish to make about this here, but some of the more substantial issues about sport and English nationalism we shall return to later in this article. First, and most obviously, there is the articulation between sport and political nationalism. In the era of sporting boycotts of various kinds, sport has become a significant international currency. It can possess this status only because of a major ideological construction of the activities of particular athletes and teams as the representatives or bearers of national prestige. They are 'our boys/girls', and represent us in the international sphere. This level of nationalism and sport has two aspects. The first is the existence of a popular identification with the sporting representative of the nation - the acceptance that the equation between athlete X or team Y with the nation is a real and significant one. It is only with the existence of this first level, that the second, a more self-consciously political appropriation of sporting achievement, is able to work. Without this popular commitment, the equation of Harold Wilson with England's 1966 World Cup victory, the reception by the military junta of the victorious Argentinian team in 1978, and the significance that the South African government attaches to sporting links, would be meaningless. It is solely the ability to draw on popular sporting nationalism, that makes this linking of political nationalism and sport possible. Sport is a forum that allows the construction of the nation as 'us' - rising above and displacing whatever 'minor' internal divisions there may be.

There is another connection between nationalism and sport in which international competition is interpreted through the imagery of national (and racial) divisions. In this, athletes (and sometimes spectators) are the living, breathing representatives of national or racial characteristics which explain their behaviour. The catalogue (much beloved of sports commentators) is endless: the 'suspect' latin temperament (sly, but unstable); the 'natural sense of rhythm' of blacks; the 'fiery' determination of the Welsh; the 'inscrutable' faces of the Chinese table tennis players; the devil-may-care-casualness of Brazilian footballers (not to mention the samba rhythms of their passing); and so on. Here sporting competition is invested with, and helps to keep in circulation, a whole repertoire of national and racial mythologies - myths of 'their' strangeness, difference, peculiarity, which help to reinforce the ethnocentrism of our own culture.

But we should not forget, from the standpoint of our ethnocentrism, that there are other nationalisms at stake in international competition. These may have something to prove, and may draw on past or present resentments, hostilities and conflicts of their own experience - experiences which lie outside sport. Scottish and Welsh competition against the English provide occasions for the display of the existence of separate nations that are, for much of the time, submerged in an England dominated Britain. The seemingly eternal dominance of West Indian cricket teams provides a spectacle for black spectators of an occasion where white superiority cannot be effortlessly assumed. Nor does it seem likely that the intensity of Czechoslovak-Russian ice-hockey contests can be solely explained through friendly rivalry.

Finally, we should remember that this elevation of nationalism through sport does not always comfortably override or elide the divisions and tensions within nations. The Olympic black power salutes stand as a persistent reminder that the ideological construction of national unity through sport is not always success-fully accomplished.

There is one final arena of ideological connection between sport and other social practices that we need to mention and that is its relation to sexual divisions. (6) Let us begin with the most obvious. Sport provides apparently incontrovertible evidence, decisive testimony, for the inevitable superiority of the male over the female. Men beating women at tennis, women playing

football, men running faster, throwing things further
than women, are all added to this natural catalogue of
male dominance. No matter that all kinds of doubts may
be raised about the status of such judgments of 'natural'
superiority; it is there before our eyes, in the most
'natural' forms of activity. It is as if all arguments
about sexual divisions of labour, the effects of different
economic, social, political, legal processes and statuses,
different processes of socialisation, can all be resolved
by referring to Bobby Riggs beating Billy Jean King.

But the reproduction of sexist ideologies through
sport extends further than this. Sport itself often
appears as intrinsically and naturally male. It is a
forum which reproduces the myths of masculinity - reaffirm-
ing that men are active, aggressive, competitive, strong,
challenging, forceful, courageous and so on. And it is
in sport that men can find validation of their masculine
identities - by competing, striving and succeeding. The
arena of sport is one which is defined in masculine
terms of reference, and where women are consequently
only allowed entry into subordinate positions. For
example, the involvement of women playing traditionally
male-dominated sports is usually greeted in one of two
ways. One is by almost total neglect (women's cricket,
for instance). The other is by transforming into an
object of fun and patronising humour - women's football
becomes something for the men to laugh at. For instance,
the use of women's football as a half-time entertainment
at football matches both asserts the superiority of the
'real (male) thing' and reaffirms sexual valorisation
of women. They are there as women, not as footballers.

In other areas of sport less clearly male-dominated
sportswomen are persistently referenced to criteria
other than sporting ones. Apart from the recent sexual
valorisation of a few male sporting 'pins ups', the idea
of sexuality within sport has always pointed in one
direction. Women athletes are always framed by their
status both as athletes and as women (i.e. the assumption
is that athletes are male). This referencing of their
femininity can appear in a variety of forms. It may
appear through registering their sexuality - 'lithe,
lissom, graceful, glamorous, attractive', etc. Or it
may be referenced through their performance of other
female roles - 'housewife/mother of two/newly married,
etc.' - carrying the implication that these women manage
to remain feminine *in spite* of being athletes. We can
see the reversal of this in the third form of referencing
of femininity - that which casts aspersions on the
femininity of women athletes by virtue of their involve-

ment in athletics.   That is, by virtue of training,
dedication (or drugs), these women have sacrificed their
'essential' femaleness to an unnatural goal - that of
sporting competition and achievement.   A goal, which, on
the other hand, is perfectly natural for men.

We have tried to show how sport as a socially
constructed and meaningful activity is enmeshed in the
reproduction and transmission of ideological themes and
values which are dominant in our society.   We have also
tried to show that it not only reproduces them, but adds
weight and significance to them by appearing as a realm
which is pre-eminently natural, non-social, outside
politics.   But at this point, we need to make some
qualifications about this argument.   The reproduction of
dominant ideologies through sport is not uncontested or
uncontradictory.   It does not form one single seamless
sheet of ideology.   There are tensions within these
images and themes, they do pull in different and
sometimes antagonistic directions.   At points, subordinate
and competing definitions make their presence felt
through sport.   We can see this if we consider some of
the examples above.   Thus, the importance of sport in
developing cross-class local identifications achieves
this to some extent, but also forms the basis for
'illegitimate' extensions of such identifications and
rivalries by groups of football fans.   The playing out of
local rivalries on the terraces rather than the pitch is
condemned as irrational, stupid and 'meaningless'. (7)

But it also never completely obscures real local
divisions - football fans do not see themselves as the
same as boards of directors.   They have, and recognise
that they have, a different relation to 'their team'
from those who own and control it.   And, quite often,
this provides a source of antagonism, with blame for
failure being laid at the door of those who do own the
club but 'know nothing about football'.

In different ways, these local and regional identifications can militate against the construction of the
national unity through sport.   Accusations of regional
bias, behind-the-scenes manoeuvring, and so on, provide
the basis for often uneasy mixtures of support for, and
hostility to, the national representatives.   The 'nation'
persists in remaining more difficult, more complex and
more intractable than the image of the nation proclaims.

This first section has tried to demonstrate the
connections between the culture of sport (how it is
defined and experienced) and wider social and political
ideologies.   If this seems a long detour, it is a detour
made necessary by the power of the idea that sport stands

outside society.   If this definition is allowed to stand,
then we reduce the relationship between ideology, sport
and the media to one in which the media 'corrupt' the
world of sport by importing undesirable elements from
outside.   There are many examples of this corruption
argument around - advertising, commercialism, the
dictates of media coverage changing the character of
sports.   We are not suggesting that the media have no
effects on sport, but that these effects cannot be
adequately understood as 'external corruption'.   The
intersection between sport and the media rests on the
fact that sport is an already socially constructed
activity, and it is here that the 'effects' of the media
have to be sought.   It is this connection between the
culture of sport and the processes of media presentation
that concerns us here - the question of how the media
portray not just 'sport', but sport as a socially defined
object.

2   THE MEDIA AND SPORT

We have suggested that sport is not a neutral arena which
is 'corrupted' by the entry of the media, but there is an
inversion of this argument that we need to be wary of.
This suggests that the media offer a reproduction of the
real world - a mirror in which we can see the reflections
of reality. (8)   This assumption of the 'transparency' of
media reporting is a seductively misleading one.   A
moment's thought about the media's reporting of sport
gives us the first reason for not accepting this
proposition: for that reporting is *selective*.   It
selects *between* sports for those which make 'good
television', and it selects *within* a particular event,
it highlights particular aspects for the viewers.   This
selective highlighting is not 'natural' or inevitable --
it is based on certain criteria, certain media assumptions
about what is 'good television'. (9)   But the media do
not only select, they also provide us with definitions
of what has been selected.   They interpret events for
us, provide us with frameworks of meaning in which to
make sense of the event.   To put it simply, television
does not merely consist of pictures, but also involves
commentary on the pictures - a commentary which explains
to us what we are seeing.   In this section, we want to
examine these processes - the process of selection and
the process of interpretation.   In both of these, the
media are also involved in highlighting and reinforcing
some of the ideological values about sport which we have
just discussed.

First, though, it is worth drawing attention to the
obvious fact that the media presentation of sport takes
place within clearly demarcated 'slots': 'World of Sport',
'Grandstand', and the back pages of newspapers. This
physically, visually, marks sport off from the rest of
media content - it isolates it as separate and distinct.
It reproduces the belief that sport forms a special
arena, removed from the rest of society - literally a
separate 'world of sport'. This demarcation is *routine* -
it is part of the regular, predictable ordering of the
world in the media, and provides us with conventional
expectations about location and content. We know what
will happen at 12.30 on Saturday afternoons. The
importance of this sense of routine, in giving us a sense
of continuity and predictability of the world, is demonstrated in the fact that during the Second World War the
press attempted to maintain its coverage of the domestic
sporting calendar, helping to promote a contrived sense
of 'normality'.

The exceptions to this routine demarcation - when the
media coverage of sport breaks out of its normal 'slots' -
indicate some of the selective processes at work in the
media. They occur for the major events - the 'cream',
and especially when British success is involved. Thus,
Robin Cousins's gold medal at the 1980 Winter Olympics
was able to push other *news* stories out of the news
headlines. (10) The criterion is national pride through
sport playing on the investment which we discussed
earlier.

But these occasions involve merely the accentuation
of the normal values which govern the media treatment
of sport. For, in the routine treatment of sport, these
selections also go on. The mid-week football slots are
not filled by the third and fourth division mid-week
games, but by the drama of the cup competitions. In
summer, the cricket coverage is not of the three-day
county championship matches, tennis does not feature
the round-Britain Pernod trophy. In all these instances
the attention is given to the dramatic - the 'knock-outs',
the big name championships. Even here, we are not shown
the whole game, but what the media define for us as the
dramatic, the highlights: the goal mouth scrambles,
the winning runs off the last ball, the match-winning
rallies and so on.

These selections are socially constructed - they
involve decisions about what to reveal to the viewers.
The presentation of sport through the media involves an
active process of *re*-presentation: what we see is not the
event, but the event transformed into something else - a

media event. This transformation is not arbitrary, but governed by criteria of selection, which concentrate and focus the audience's attention, and, secondly, those values which are involved in the conventions of television presentation: concentration and *conventionalism*. We can identify four main values which inform the concentration of the presentation of sport: 'spectacle'; 'drama'; 'personalisation' and 'immediacy'. (11)

'Spectacle' refers to both the status of the event and the location of the event. The status of the event involves the significance or importance attached to the event itself - the 'big time' events, no matter where they are held. In addition, some events are spectacular because of *where* they are held - thus, the impact of the winter sports is intensified by the naturally spectacular quality of their settings in snow-covered mountains. In other instances the significance of the event is underlined because they take place in particular valued locations - the single finals at Wimbledon, the F.A. Cup Final at Wembley. In these cases, event and location combine in the spectacle.

'Drama' is related more closely to the content of the event itself, it is the 'highlights' of the action. At its most dramatic, it is the goal of the season, the record-breaking sprint and so on. It is the drama of success - or failure - that is sought for 'good' television. It is the moment of crisis into which the emotions are concentrated. It cannot be completely divorced from spectacle, since the spectacular occasion invests the event with special drama - it heightens the tension necessary for drama. But even in routine coverage, it is the 'dramatic' that is sought out. Thus, for the horse trials, the focus of attention is the water jump because it provides the potential for dramatic failure. Similarly, in the coverage of darts or limited-overs cricket, it is the finish of the event that is the focus, for there the dramatic tension is at its highest. The example of limited-overs cricket provides an instance of adaptation within the sport to the demands of the media for concentration of the drama. (12)

Even where the drama does not intrinsically exist in the event, it can be constructed through the media presentation and definition of the event. Thus in the build-up to knock out competitions, we will always be reminded of the 'uncertainty' of the game, the promise of potential 'giant killers' is held out to us. Similarly, 'Match of the Day' always manages to produce drama, the 'best action of the day', no matter what the quality of the games being shown. No matter how routine the coverage, there is always the promise constructed for us that it may contain something that is 'a bit special'.

'Personalisation' directs us to the tendency in the media to focus attention through concentrating on particular individuals – either famous sporting personalities or the more fleeting 'today's hero'. We are led to identify with particular individuals and the hopes, fears, achievements and failures. Through both the interview and the close-up of the action we are invited to witness the personal involvement of sport – through these individualised moments the media offer us a privileged 'insight' into the world of sport. (13) It 'reminds' us that sport is essentially an individual matter, resting on individual skills, capacities, temperament, etc. It might be thought that individual rather than team sports would produce this sort of reporting, but team sports are also subject to this process. We are introduced to the 'stars' and 'characters' of the teams – indeed, at times, the teams can be reduced to the contest between their star players (e.g. Keegan vs. ......). One example may serve to demonstrate this point. In the run up to the 1966 World Cup final, one of the most recurrent media comments on the English team was a lament about its *lack* of characters, stars, personalities. That lack affected not the performance of the team, but that of the media. Fortunately, we were eventually able to discover (ad infinitum) Nobby Stiles's 'gap-toothed smile'....

This personalisation also stands at the intersection between sport and the media in the more extensive use made of the superstars, not just in the commercial advertising, but as media personalities in their own right. For example, Brian Moore has presented a series of one-hour in-depth interviews with sports stars – Borg, Keegan and Lauda. A more established variant of this is the 'star column' in the sporting press written by a leading sports figure, giving an 'insider's' view of the game. The columnist needs to be well known nationally, preferably not only for his sporting ability, but also for his frank, controversial or outspoken view. Finally, some sporting figures also provide 'good copy' by their non-sporting activities – the status granted them by the media for their sporting activities also renders their private life media property. At this level, they become transformed from sporting personalities into media celebrities. George Best's drinking, Stan Bowles's gambling, Tommy Docherty's marriage – all are grist to the mill of the personalisation of sport. It culminates the process by which the media transform sport from the game itself into (another) example of the greater drama of human emotion, triumph, misery and despair.

The construction of sport through individual personalities - the creation of individuals with whom we, the
audience, can identify - is also one of the means by
which the value of 'immediacy' is realised. We are
taken closer to the action and to the participants than
we could ever be as mere spectators at the event.
Without inconvenience, television allows us to follow
the action, see it 'as it happens' - but also with the
added bonus of informative commentary, expert comment.
In television coverage, we can also have our attention
drawn to points that we might have missed, have the
chance of seeing 'highlights' again through action
replays, and even be 'talked through it' by the participants. Golf tournaments offer a very clear illustration
of media coverage, where we can follow several players
at the same time, see the best shots and the players'
reactions to them. Spectators on the course can only
follow one set of players on the course, or watch one
particular hole, relying on the scoreboard for the
knowledge which the television audience receives
immediately.

Sports coverage is also literally immediate, in the
sense that much of it is broadcast live from sports
stadia and race courses. Much of the appeal lies in
this rapidity - 'recorded highlights' being seen as a
poor substitute for live coverage, and requiring
condensing and dramatising to restore their attractiveness. The immediacy is also reinforced in the Saturday
magazine programmes, with their constant updating of
information, results, the latest news 'as it happens' -
particularly where the media cater for, in horse racing
or football, sporting gambling.

Yet this sense of immediacy - the transparency of
media presentation - is an illusory one. The immediacy
is, in fact, *mediated* - between us and the event stand
the cameras, camera angles, producers' choices of shots,
the commentators' interpretations - the whole invisible
apparatus of media presentation. We can never see the
whole event, we see those parts which are filtered
through this process of presentation to us. It locates
us as watchers in a very different position from the
spectator at the event itself - we cannot participate,
we cannot see what goes on out of sight of the cameras.
Rather than immediacy, our real relation to sports on
television is one of distance -- we are observers,
recipients of a media event. (14)

These elements of concentration operate within the
broader frameworks of sports programmes and they can be

illustrated by looking at the conventions, the formats of
such presentation. These conventions range from the
clichéd language of sports journalism, to the professional
conceptions of what is 'exciting', and to the actual
conventions of presentation. It is presentation that we
shall consider first, by looking at the formats of
'Grandstand' and 'World of Sport'. The programmes are
constructed around a single presenter, seated behind a
desk, who links different sporting presentations and
provides updating information on the afternoon's events.

The roles of the different types of presenters and
commentators are worth looking at in more detail here.
The 'anchorman' presenter, like Dickie Davies or Frank
Bough, has to be a competent professional performer in
front of the camera, but also needs to be able to
convince the audience that he has a genuine interest in
all sports from horse racing to clay pigeon shooting.
The anchorman's task is to set the tone of programme,
and to link us to the specialist sports commentators –
he is our gateway to the world of sport. The specialist
commentators are, like the anchorman, media professionals –
their primary characteristic is their skill as commentators, the ability to describe and interpret. They are
not required to have sporting competence, but must mix
their technical competence with a knowledge of the game
or sport, and demonstrate an enthusiasm for it. They
are, so to speak, our 'representatives' at the event –
the knowledgeable and enthusiastic spectator.

It is now common for the commentator to be supplemented
by an 'adjudicator', an expert – whose role is based
upon demonstrated expertise in the game: a player,
ex-player or manager. (15) Their summaries are intended
to highlight points of expertise, skill, technique or
strategy which may not be obvious to those who do not
play the game. They should also, preferably, be a
'character' to provide some colour of their own. In
football coverage, this on-the-spot expertise has its
parallel in the 'expert panel' who provide previews,
reviews and conclusions about the action. Their observations and analysis are supervised and linked to the
commentator by a studio presenter. In televised football,
Jimmy Hill and Brian Moore have in different ways combined
several of these roles – Hill being anchorman, adjudicator
and expert, Moore being anchorman and commentator. (16)

This cast can provide the whole array of devices
involved in the construction of the event for the
audience: the pre-match warm-up, with predictions and
guidance on what to look for; half-time analysis of the
progress of the game so far, with the panel highlighting

what they define as the key incidents through the use of action replays; and finally the post mortem on the game, when they define for us what we have just seen.

But these modes of presentation themselves become routinised, predictable and unexciting - like the clichés of the commentators themselves. (17) To counter this risk of repetitiveness, the media treatment of sport is always in search of something new, something different to supplement the established favourites. One way of doing this is to present a new 'angle' on an established sport - for example, the introduction to television of 'floodlit Rugby League'. In the case of Sunday league cricket, the game itself was adapted and proved highly suitable for televised coverage. Indeed, the decision to make the change was partly influenced by the successful televising of its forerunner, the 'Cavaliers' matches.

Technological advances can also provide new and dramatic additions. Our familiarity with the technique could lead us to forget that television has not always possessed the action replay. Even now, its use can still be a source of controversy between the media and the sporting authorities. The Football League has made complaints about the trial by television of referees, meaning, more precisely, trial by action replay. But not all innovations have established themselves as success- fully as the replay, as the 'image trace' proved. For the World Cup in Argentina, the BBC introduced a frame- stopping device, which, according to Jimmy Hill, would allow viewers to follow how the ball was being swerved. The principle was that the film was slowed to produce an after-image or trace of the ball, which would permit visible tracking of its flight. However, the trace showed not only the movement of the ball, but *anything* which moved on the screen - producing a blurred and confusing picture.

In addition, new sports are regularly introduced to television - again, with varied results. Some can be adapted to produce 'good television', while others fail. For example, darts was elevated from pubs and clubs to world championship status, and made successful television through the use of close-ups of the board and players. Audiences grew, both for television and in the halls, and the claims for greater time on television became stronger. But popular sport is not, by itself, a sufficient criterion for the televising of a sport - for which angling is the most striking instance. It is the most popular participation sport in the country, enjoys a significant place in sports coverage in the popular press, and even has its own papers. By contrast, television's attention to angling has been limited to the occasional local interview with a successful angler, a series of items within other programmes on technique and fishing spots, and only one series - 'Fishing Race'. This programme relied heavily for its effect on spectacular scenery and the imposed drama of the 'race' - one of the clearest examples of the media's reconstruction of sport into a media event.

'World of Sport' has a regular feature devoted to novelty items: sports which are either popular in other countries but rarely seen here (American or Gaelic football) or which are simply unusual or bizarre (the world lumberjack championships or the world car leaping championship). Such items pose presentational problems, because the rare, unusual or strange sports need to be 'translated' for the viewers, their rules, skills and principles explained in terms that we can understand. This is one of the most revealing moments of how the media simplify the sports they present. For example, in 'Sport's Special One', the slot devoted to these novelty items, Dickie Davies managed to describe baseball as a more complicated form of rounders. The effect of this sort of re-presentation is to trivialise - the sport becomes *merely* a novelty.

We have tried to describe the values and conventions involved in the media presentation of sport. Now we want to give an example of how these conventions combine, and how they highlight some of the ideological themes mentioned earlier. The programme we are using for this demonstration may not even be regarded by some people as a sports programme, but we hope to show that 'It's a Knockout' involves the culmination, the logical working out, of these principles of the media presentation of sport.

3   SPORT AND ENTERTAINMENT: THE CASE OF 'IT'S A KNOCKOUT'

The programme was developed from the mid-1950s series 'Top Town', which took the form of a weekly talent contest in which teams of amateur and semi-professional variety acts represented their local towns in what Willis Hall ('Radio Times', 5 May 1980, p.7) has described as 'a sort of mini-Olympiad of the Music Hall'. The creator of the series, Barney Colehan, developed this element of competitive rivalry between towns, but through games rather than entertainers. The games are races, adapting traditional sports, in which contestants have to use basic fitness, skills and dexterity to

overcome outsize obstacles or prevent the opposition from
succeeding. All the games are short, intensely competitive 'sudden death' affairs - maintaining the 'drama' of
competition throughout the programme. Points are
awarded for those who complete the course quickest, burst
the most balloons or carry the most buckets of water.
Part of the music-hall origins of the game remain, in
the extensive use that is made of 'slapstick comedy'
in that whenever possible games should involve water,
foam, or slippery surfaces, preferably simultaneously.
(18) These are coupled with making competitors wear
ridiculous, outside costumes - generically known to the
programme team as 'Tweedles'. These elements add to the
excitement of the contest by providing as many opportunities
as possible for falls, spills and duckings. The series
stands at the most obvious intersection between sport
and media values of presentation. (19) It features media-
invented games, but ones which draw on real sporting
skills and aptitudes, while its presentation involves a
mixture of sporting commentary and elements of presentational style drawn from other television 'contest' series.

Both of the presenters of the programme have sporting
connections, and are familiar television 'characters'.
Stuart Hall is both a football reporter and presenter of
'Look North'; Eddie Waring is the Rugby League commentator
and presenter. In 'It's a Knockout', they link the series
of pseudo-sporting events, collecting decisions on the
game from umpire Arthur Ellis (one-time football referee)
and passing on the points scored by the teams to the
eternally smiling and attractive scoreboard girls. The
presenters are the personalities of the programme, it is
their style and their enthusiasm which sets the tone for
the series. And, remembering the 'music-hall' traces in
the origins of the series, their role resembles more the
master of ceremonies than the sporting commentator.
Stuart Hall is the key figure here - explaining the nature
of the games, providing a stream of banal banter and
hysterical laughter which passes for commentary, urging
the supporters in the crowd to express their enthusiasm
and commitment as vocally as possible, and conducting
interviews with the contestants. The style set by the
presenters is one of homeliness, of familiarity. It
draws on our familiarity with the presenters as 'characters', on the 'ordinariness' of the people taking part,
and is registered through the way the presenters define
everyone involved in the contest as 'lads' and 'lasses',
even the Lord and Lady Mayors of the towns taking part.
And, from Stuart, Arthur and Eddie downwards, we are all
on first-name terms.

There is another sort of familiarity involved in the
programme - another form of recognition - for the
programme reproduces 'commonsense' assumptions about the
sexes.   It plays upon particular definitions of the
femininity of the 'lasses'.   This ranges from the
decorative scoreboard girls, (20) to the structure of
some of the games which require the men to rescue or
support the 'weaker' lasses, and to the paternal
familiarity which characterises Stuart's interviews with
the lasses - preferably just pulled, breathless and
dripping, from another encounter with the water tank.
     The games in the programme are simple (though often
wrapped up in complicated rituals), short, exciting and
dramatic.   The pace of the programme produces a sequence
of moments of triumph and moments of disaster.   (Some
of the 'best' 'Knockout' moments are disasters - 'and
they've fallen in the water *again*, hah hah hah hah....')
As at 'real' sporting occasions, the drama is heightened
by the atmosphere created by the spectators, endlessly
urged on by the presenters.   The whole of the programme
produces a unity.   It starts from the individuals - their
achievements, failures, excitement and (painless) suffering.
They are ordinary folks, just like you and me, not distant
'professional' athletes.   But they are not only individuals - they are members of the team, playing their part
for the greater good.   The team itself is representative.
Together with its supporters, it embodies 'community
spirit' - the ideal of collective action, loyalty and
harmony.   But there is also a larger community - the
community of sport - for the games take place in a spirit
of fun and harmony, without any of the professional
cynicism, hostility, aggression or tantrums which may
sometimes mar real sporting events.   The participants in
'It's a Knockout' reproduce the ideal sporting community -
enthusiastic amateurs enjoying the game for the game's
sake.   And, to complete the organic harmony, the programme
is a 'family' programme, providing good fun and entertainment for everyone.   The individual, the family, the town,
the sporting community - there are no tensions, no
conflicts, no divisions visible within this unity.   This
everyday harmony is summed up in Willis Hall's description
of one of the teams taking part:
     It contains policemen and policewomen, welders, a
     farmer, a mining engineer, electricians, a schoolboy,
     a student of agricultural merchanting, and a goodly
     sprinkling of P.E. teachers, naturally.   Each and
     every member of the squad is ready to give his or her
     all, to burst balloons, dress up as Tweedles, even, if
     duty calls, to take multiple duckings in tanks of ice-

cold water and still come up gasping for more.   'It's
a Knockout' brings out the battling best in all sports
persons. (21)
'It's a Knockout', with its Tweedles and custard pies,
comes perilously close to embodying the old adage that
'it's only a game', but it can never quite say that.
Because it's more than a game, it encapsulates a 'whole
way of life', an ideological image of what life ought to
be like.   When Willis Hall says that 'It's a Knockout'
brings out the battling best in all sports persons – he
could reasonably have said in all English sports persons,
for there is something essentially English about the
character of the programme.   Its settings, format,
presenters, games – the overall impression of homely,
quirky amateurishness all embody this image – by
comparison with which 'Jeux sans Frontières' appears
more spectacular, more sophisticated and more professional
in style.   In the final section we want to explore the
connections involved in this image of sport and the
English more closely.

4   THE SPORTING ENGLISH

Our decision to focus on the English here is not solely a
matter of convenience or ethnocentrism.   It also stems
from the 'peculiarities' of English national culture, in
which sport and sporting images play a significant role
in the definition of 'our way of life'.   Where else
could a society's character be summed up in the phrase
'it's not cricket'?   By national culture or nationalism,
we mean an ideology which constructs 'the nation' as a
distinctive and unique set of characteristics, traits
and habits which make up both a national character and
a national way of life.   It identifies those things
which we, as English, are supposed to have in common.
But the construction of nationalism also involves
suppressing internal differences and conflicts in order
to be able to present 'us' as a unity.   This discussion
of an apparently trivial example of how this 'unification'
works provides an excellent example of the caricaturing
of the national character:
    For the middle classes, she [Ann Dummett] argues,
    'tea' in the afternoon 'means ... a leisured and
    unnecessary refreshment between lunch and dinner.
    You take it around four o'clock;   the bread and
    butter will be cut thin, and you will not, except at
    a children's tea party, eat it in the dining room or
    kitchen'.   But tea 'to the majority of the population

is the meal of the evening, eaten about five-thirty
when father gets back from work and has had time to
wash and change his clothes'. Here, 'something
accepted both here and abroad as ... characteristically
English means, in fact, quite different things to
different groups of people in England. Nevertheless,
it is the first (minority) not the second (majority)
meaning of 'tea' which is thought 'characteristically
English'; the first not the second which has a
privileged place in English popular mythology. (22)

As this example illustrates, two things go on in the
construction of this image of a 'way of life'. The first
is producing a false unity out of differences. But the
second is that this unity is structured in a particular
direction. It draws its conceptions of Englishness from
a specific set of social images and practices - those of
dominant social groups. To put it crudely, 'we' appear
in their image. Nationalism as an ideology works in two
directions. One is to mark us off from the 'others' -
foreigners, strangers, aliens - it identifies and values
what is unique to us. The other is to draw us together,
to unite us in the celebration, maintenance and furtherance
of 'our' way of life. (23)

In encountering conceptions of the English way of life,
we meet the imagery of sport in a variety of forms. But
one particular image overshadows all others - that is
the image of sport-as-English. The English appear as the
founders, organisers and teachers of sport to the rest
of the world. England appears as the natural 'home' of
sport - Twickenham, Lords, Wembley, Wimbledon - all have
a reverential status in their particular sporting worlds.
Sport is a part of our imperial legacy - a part of our
greatness when we led the world and spread our civilisation.

This imperial past when we taught others to 'play the
game' should remind us once again that sport does not
stand outside society. For what was at stake in the
missionary spreading of sport was not simply to provide
enjoyable pastimes, but to use sport as a way of teaching
good habits, respect for the rules, and authority. It
was to instil a sense of order and discipline, and to
substitute the 'constructive' and healthy use of free
time for 'uncivilised', 'irrational' or 'undisciplined'
forms of recreation. We should also remember that this
missionary zeal for the civilising effects of sport was
not confined to our colonial conquests. It was also a
key aspect of the late nineteenth-century attempts to
civilise, discipline and order the dangerous masses at
home. It was this public-school-based civilising venture
of the late nineteenth-century middle classes that now

enables us to colonise the very notion of 'sporting' as peculiarly English. (24)

The notion of 'sporting' condenses many of the virtues of the English way of life. Within it are such themes as the sense of 'fair play', a proper respect for authority and the rules, the importance of self-control and self-discipline. These virtues help us to distinguish ourselves from others who fail to play the game - those who bend the rules, employ gamesmanship, intimidate or manipulate referees and umpires, and those who take the game too seriously and have a 'win at all costs mentality'. This distinction is particularly visible around the valued status of 'the amateur', where the true amateur has to compete against state-sponsored competitors, highly financed, highly trained and thus bending the rules of equal competition.

These 'moral tales' are not only lessons for the playing fields - they are part of the morality by which 'the English' live. Trade unionists are reminded that they should 'play fair' - be reasonable men, and not misuse their strength to take unfair advantage. Against such unsporting behaviour, there stand the rules of the game, the governing bodies and the referees. Here the moral code is backed by and enshrined in the Rule Books of Law and the might of Parliament. They, like referees and umpires in sport, are the final impartial arbiters - their authority unchallengeable because they are neutral. Their presence is necessary, it is claimed, because people cannot be trusted to play the game. (25) There are shirkers and cheats here, too. On the one hand, there are those who will try to dodge or avoid the competition - the scroungers, shiftless, workshy idlers. On the other hand are those who would bend the rules to their own advantage (the 'industrial hooligans') - or even 'bring the game into disrepute' by questioning the neutrality of the rules and their administrators. These are the militants, subversives and extremists who share with unsporting foreign athletes the 'win-at-all-costs' mentality.

It is these characteristics - their unwillingness to be reasonable, to abide by the rules, rather than any specific issues being contested - that defines such groups as 'beyond the pale', as constituting a threat to 'our way of life'. Such groups are portrayed as 'dangerous', not simply because they want more money, or want to make changes, but because they call into question the code, the 'moral consensus' which is supposed to govern the way in which we live, work and play together.

But before succumbing to the obvious and reasonable truth of this consensus, we might think about what it excludes, what it silences. In social terms, it silences as 'illegitimate', as outside the consensus, not only those who argue that parliamentary democracy is a political sham, or that the law has a class bias. It also has no place for those who think politicians are con-artists, have no principles, pursue vested interests or have no conception of real life .... Nor can it bear those who suspect that judges may be doddering old fools, that the law is an anachronistic ass, that the police may be something less wonderful than 'our boys in blue'. (26)

In sporting terms, the assumptions of 'fair play' and the neutrality of control also silence divergent experiences and expressions. The ideal of impartiality of authority co-exists with deep mistrust, suspicion, cynicism and even hatred of its particular representatives. Referees are biased, umpires incompetent, judges in international competition suspected of national bias and so on. We should remember that respect for authority goes alongside the belief that inside every referee (or any other figure of authority) there is a 'little Hitler' waiting to get out. Authority, the Rule of Law, the sense of order are not experienced as the universal, natural and inevitable good that the mythology of Englishness proclaims them to be. The mythology attempts to override and make invisible these divergent experiences.

A different element of 'sporting Englishness' lies in the conception which it offers of 'manliness'. This draws on many of the general themes of 'masculinity' within our culture - toughness, physical strength and capability, achievement, as the demonstration of virility, the importance of aggressive competitiveness. These qualities mark out the 'natural' character of the male. In doing so, they also construct by implication, the character of femininity, and the suspicion of the 'non-sporting' male as a real or potential deviant from masculinity.

But 'manliness' is more than merely masculinity, it has other connotations, too. It draws on another nineteenth-century aspect of the sporting English - that of 'gentle-manly' behaviour. It presents a peculiarly 'English' version of being a man, which stresses the virtues of being upright, moral, honest and decent, in which these values are counterposed to more devious and suspect forms of masculinity to be found in other cultures. The most visible, and persistent, counterposing of these different 'masculinities' has been in the reporting of international football, where the solid, honest endeavour of the English has to compete against the more subtle and dubious practices of other nations.

This conception of 'manliness' also draws some of its strength from a different class tradition of masculinity - a proletarian one. Here, life and work are acknowledged to be hard, a man ('the breadwinner') has to compete, strive and survive. He has to accept the severity of life, strive to overcome it, without complaint and without giving up. He must produce a 'workmanlike' performance, take pride in his honest endeavour. These two different traditions, arising out of different material circumstances, meet and are merged in the notion of 'manliness'. This form of construction of sexual identities is one of the most powerful ways in which 'cross-class' unities are composed. But they are always composed 'structured in dominance' - they take on the character of dominant rather than subordinate conceptions. And, in the construction of that unity, they produce, or reproduce, another subordination - that of women.

We can see in this conception of 'manliness' an ambiguous relationship to competition. Competition, striving, struggling to succeed are virtues - but not unconditional ones. They have to be kept within 'reasonable' limits, they should not be taken too far, or pushed to 'immoderate' extremes. This requires another English virtue - that of being a 'good loser'. We should take pride, not just in success - because success at all costs, for its own sake, is no real source of satisfaction, but also in having competed, having tried our best. It is this virtue which demonstrates those English characteristics of maturity, self-discipline, moderation. There is, after all, 'more to life than winning'.

This ambiguous relationship to competition is also mobilised in other areas of social life. It has been given a particularly powerful articulation in the recent Conservative 'revival' of the values of the English way of life. We are reminded that competitiveness is a vital and natural virtue - both for individuals and nations. Without it (under the creeping shackles of socialism, for example), our natural well-springs of initiative and energy will dry up, we will lack purpose in life, we will be stifled. Competition (by a fortunate harmony) serves our own private interests and those of the nation. Individually, we can be fulfilled by putting our natural talents to the test, we can take pride in ourselves by knowing that we have tried. Nationally, our combined efforts as private individuals will ensure that the nation is healthy, vital and competitive.

Competition also manages to ensure the proper distribution of rewards - everyone has the chance to attain their 'natural' level through competition. And, because we know

that talents are unequally distributed naturally, no one
can really complain: the success of the fittest is
'natural justice'. More than that, no one should complain:
everyone has the chance to compete, and having tried their
best, can take satisfaction from that knowledge. Having
tried is more important than having succeeded.

But this competitiveness should not be taken too far -
like everything English, it should be practised with
moderation. To ensure this, there are the rules and an
impartial authority to apply them. Because, we are
warned, without the rules, how do we control the shirkers
and the cheats who would spoil the game for everyone
else? Those who avoid competing must pay the penalty,
and those who try to steal unfair advantages must be
dealt with. And, if, as now, it seems that there are
more and more who are trying to win by dubious means -
then we must strengthen our controls. To deal with these
people - the shirkers, the cheats, the workshy, the
subversives, all those who won't 'play the game' - the
rules have to be changed, and the referees have to be
given stronger powers.

And for those to whom the game resembles nothing so
much as a carefully rigged one-arm bandit - for the
blacks, women, the unemployed, trade unionists, the one-
time beneficiaries of the one-time welfare state - their
'reward' is to be defined as 'un-English'. They are the
extremists who want to bring 'politics' into the
greatest game on earth - the English way of life.

NOTES

1 We have tried here to reproduce the paper given to
   the conference rather than adapt it by drawing out
   the theoretical issues and models on which its
   argument is based. The sources for the argument,
   for those interested, are referenced in the footnotes
   to the text.
2 For expansions of this point, see C. Critcher,
   Football and cultural values, 'Working Papers in
   Cultural Studies' no.1, 1971; and J. Clarke, The
   fan and the game, in Ingham et al., 'Football
   Hooliganism', London, Interaction, 1978.
3 Most of our references here are to ideologies and
   valuations of sport in England, for although there
   may be cross-cultural similarities, the ideologies
   we are concerned with have a specifically national
   character. This point is developed in the final
   section of the paper.

4   For a more detailed discussion of this point in relation
    to football, see C. Critcher, Football since the war,
    in Clarke et al. (eds), 'Working Class Culture', London,
    Hutchinson, 1979.

5   An investigation of the effect of Sunderland's F.A.
    Cup win has been undertaken by E. Derrick and J.
    McRory, Cup in hand, 'Working Paper', no.8, July 1973,
    available from the Centre for Urban and Regional
    Studies, University of Birmingham.

6   The questions of sport and sexual divisions are dealt
    with more fully in the papers by P. Willis and
    C. Critcher, Women in sport, 'Working Papers in
    Cultural Studies', no.5, 1975.

7   See the contributions by S. Hall and J. Clarke in
    Ingham et al., op.cit.

8   For reasons of space and convenience, our examples
    here are drawn primarily from television, though many
    of the arguments have more general application.

9   The processes of selection and interpretation apply
    not merely to sport, but to all media reportage;
    see, for example, P. Schlesinger, 'Putting Reality
    Together', London, Constable, 1979.

10 Disasters at sporting events also break out of this
    rule, becoming 'real' rather than sporting news - for
    example, accidents in motor racing or football
    hooliganism. See P. Schlesinger, op.cit.

11 Steve Chibnall has developed a similar analysis in
    relation to the news values involved in newspaper
    crime reporting. See S. Chibnall, 'Law and Order
    News', London, Tavistock, 1978.

12 Kerry Packer's intervention into cricket shows the
    potential for adapting even the most 'traditional'
    sports to television presentation - and also the
    conflicts and problems that such adaptations may
    create. The introduction of different coloured
    tennis courts has not yet raised the same level of
    criticism as did the multi-coloured outfits for
    night-time cricket, but many commentators raised
    their voices against the pink court erected specially
    in London for the 'Love Match Doubles' in 1980.

13 The close-up is used more extensively in this country
    than elsewhere. In football coverage, for example,
    British television will follow the player with the
    ball, rather than movement 'off the ball', focusing
    attention away from broader tactics. In Germany,
    however, the coverage relies more heavily on the
    'mid-range' shot which shows the audience more of
    the tactics of the game but less detail of individual
    player's skills and reactions.

14   We do not mean to imply by this argument that the
     audience is 'passive', merely taking what the media
     gives for the television presentation is subject to
     being interpreted, argued over, debated or even
     ignored by viewers. This response is, however, not
     to the game itself but to the media presentation of
     it.
15   On the role of the 'expert' in the television
     presentation of football, see E. Buscombe, 'Football
     on Television', London, BFI Television Monographs,
     1974.
16   The role of Jimmy Hill as an evaluator is discussed
     in Fiske and Hartley, 'Reading Television', London,
     Methuen, 1978.
17   The language of commentators is worthy of extensive
     discussion in its own right. Not least because the
     use of cliché as a routinely familiar or conventional
     way of registering drama is itself the source of an
     extensive folklore about the media presentation of
     sport.
18   This format is reproduced in 'It's a Knockout's'
     international version - 'Jeux sans Frontières'.
     Everything here is bigger and better. From the
     scene-setting travelogue sequence, to the size and
     scale of the games and the number of teams taking
     part, everything is more spectacular. The teams
     still represent towns, but localism is supplemented
     here by nationalism - for the teams represent their
     countries, too. Far from being 'games *without*
     frontiers', a key part of the programme's appeal
     is constructed *because* of national frontiers. It
     makes a clear-cut appeal to national loyalties and
     support - our attention is *always* directed to the
     fortunes of the British team.
19   This element of 'slapstick' invites us to laugh at
     'ordinary people' being willing to make fools of
     themselves - a device familiar in other television
     'contest' programmes, 'The Generation Game', for
     example.
20   The use of the 'scoreboard girls' is reminiscent
     of the positioning of women in other TV games as
     'hostesses' - 'The Golden Shot', 'The Generation
     Game', and 'Sale of the Century', for example.
21   Willis Hall, Newark! Newark! in 'Radio Times',
     3-9 May 1980, p.9.
22   The example is taken from Ann Dummett, 'Portrait
     of English Racism', Harmondsworth, Penguin, 1973,
     and the discussion is taken from S. Hall et al.,
     'Policing the Crisis', London, Macmillan, 1978, p.156.

23 For a more extended discussion of English 'national-
    ism as an ideology see Hall et al., 'Policing the
    Crisis', London, Macmillan, 1978; and S. Hall, The
    great moving right show, 'Marxism Today', March,
    1979.
24 This struggle to 'rationalise' recreation in Britain
    is discussed in P. Bailey, 'Leisure and Class in
    Victorian England', London, Routledge & Kegan Paul,
    1978.
25 The accusing finger is occasionally pointed at the
    'other side', too, in cases of bribery, corruption
    and other demonstrations of what Edward Heath
    described as the 'unacceptable face of capitalism'.
    But we should not mistake this for even-handedness,
    or neutrality, for as Douglas Hay reminds us, the
    Law has historically made great publicity out of a
    few symbolic cases of upper class crime. D. Hay
    et al., 'Albion's Fatal Tree', London, Allen Lane,
    1974.
26 Currently, criticism of the police indicates the
    power of this model, where any criticism is
    immediately identified as 'trying to undermine our
    way of life'.

Chapter 4

Women and leisure

Christine Griffin, Dorothy Hobson,
Sue MacIntosh and *Trisha McCabe*

INTRODUCTION

It is important to begin this paper with some clarification
of our emphasis on leisure for women, and its relation to
women's participation (and non-participation) in sport.
We would argue that an analysis of 'leisure' for women
must form a basis from which to think the position of
women in sport, because, in terms of women's restricted
access to *any* leisure time and/or facilities, there are
initial problems to be negotiated. It is important to
avoid straightforward comparisons between women's and
men's involvement in sport, without first analysing the
very different social conditions within which such
involvements must develop.

In this paper we suggest that the question of women
and leisure throws a completely new light on the whole
question of leisure, and that this has considerable
importance for existing conventional analyses, for
Marxist analyses, and for the implementation of policy.
First we take a critical look at some conventional
analyses (S. Parker and the Rapoports), and at a Marxist
approach to the work/leisure relation (E.P. Thompson).
We also consider briefly the relevant analyses of
culture (Hoggart), and particularly more recent analyses
of youth culture, including Angela McRobbie's work.
We than give an account, based on our own fieldwork, of
some of the characteristics of 'leisure' for white,
working-class women, at school, moving into waged work,
and in the home. We hope to illustrate that women's
position in waged and unwaged work in relation to the
family means that the existence of 'leisure' as a pure
category for women is questionable. In conclusion, we
outline the conceptual changes that attention to the
specificity of women demands of the study of leisure in

general, and some more practical implications for policies
on leisure.
  A Marxist critique of the leisure field would want to
expose the middle-class bias inherent in much existing
work, and the politics of current concern about leisure:
the possibility of leisure facilities provision being
slid into planned control of the unemployed is a real one.
  The second critical perspective involves an analysis
of race and racism. As yet relatively new to the field
of theoretical studies of culture, the 'race' perspective
might want to put the question of leisure into an
international analysis, connecting within this levels
of economic development and the ways of life of different
classes and racial groups. (1) Black people as providers,
or objects of leisure for whites (as in jazz, cricket),
would also be relevant to this analysis, as would the
ways in which leisure and musical forms may be connected
with styles of resistance for blacks within white culture.
Such an analysis might want to consider the position of
black women in prostitution as a result of recent
expansion in international tourism, and as 'cheap
entertainment' for visiting businessmen. (2)
  The main critical perspective around which this paper
is centred is that of feminism. As such we are interested
particularly in the male orientation (3) of almost all
the literature we have studied, the empirical absence of
women in this area, and the poverty of conceptualisation
as a result of this absence.
  There are ways in which clearly the dimensions of
gender, race and class are insufficient, since other
dimensions, such as age, physical ability, and level of
education, are also relevant. We would stress the
importance of race, gender and class as fundamentally
structured in relations of power, in ways which are
constructed and expressed through dimensions of age,
physical ability, and so on. More important still are
the ways in which the relations of race, class and
gender interweave. There are some groups, such as
black women, whose position demands that we articulate
these three sets of relations. If this is true for
oppressed groups, then it must also be true for
powerful groups. Thus, the white, bourgeois male, for
example, should also be seen in terms of gender, race
and class.
  We have here attempted a critique and an analysis
of leisure from the specific point of view of women.
Whilst the best analysis would aim to articulate gender
with at least race and class, we cannot apologise for
not giving such a full and detailed analysis here.

that heterosexual intercourse is largely male-defined, and
that sexual activity of this sort does not always mean
'leisure' or the 'satisfaction of physiological need'
for women. It seems that there is a real danger of the
reproduction of men and their labour power being conflated
with 'leisure' in this definition.

The fourth category is that of 'non-work obligations';
Parker says they are 'roughly what Dumazedier calls semi-
leisure plus the domestic part of work obligations'.
Here again the category clearly refers to men. Discharging
duties is an activity seen as marginal to work, but·
constituting an obligation on otherwise 'free' time. For
women, the content of this category fills a large part of
their day: 'discharging domestic duties' is, after all,
the sum total of their work in the home. Is women's
work therefore to be equated with male 'semi-leisure'?
Or is it that this categorisation can only be used for
men?

Finally, we have 'leisure' - with a mental sigh of
relief. He's been to work, done the overtime, eaten and
eliminated, taken the wife and kids for a run, and now at
last he's free. To do what? Parker says 'leisure is freedom from obligations either to self or to others - time
in which to do as one chooses.' The problem for a woman
is that she has very little of this time. So little, in
fact, that it may become a threat when it exists, pointing
up in relief the *lack* of autonomy and time for herself
in the rest of her life. In addition, few facilities
do exist for women's leisure: the crêches, the proximity
to home, and the cheap entry fees.

Women may well (or may not) accompany men on some of
their leisure activities. The 'night-out' may well be
constructed for both the man and the woman. However,
the freedom truly to choose where to go, who to talk to,
and how to enjoy the evening may not be there for the
woman having time off with her husband. The culture of
the 'night-out' makes it difficult for the woman to see
herself as the *definer* of the entertainment. In the pub,
for example, she is distinctly 'with her man' - and owes
her presence in such a male culture to being with him.
(8)

In all five categories, therefore, Parker has in mind
not simply 'a person' as presented, but 'a man' quite
specifically. On p.29, at the end of the introduction
to the whole analysis, Parker says somewhat disingeneously:
'One important qualification must be made to the analysis
of life space. In considering the various categories we
have had in mind men in full-time employment. Certain
modifications to the scheme are necessary if it is to fit

the cases of other groups.' However, this male bias is not
made explicit in the analysis itself, and it is assumed
that it forms the *general* case, while women form *one
particular instance* containable within a modified version
of that scheme. It is precisely this assumption (that
women form a specific offshoot from the male category
which is synonymous with the neutral, general category)
that constitutes what has been described as masculine
hegemony.

Parker does spend one paragraph looking at women, at
the end of the chapter on definitions. (Other groups
meriting a paragraph are prisoners, the unemployed and
the idle rich ...) Here Parker acknowledges that women
at home often do more than one thing at the same time.
However, this is interpreted as follows: 'In this sense
at least', he says, 'the lives of housewives may be
fuller than those of other people.' This refusal to
consider seriously the *specific* and *oppressive* nature
of these women's lives is evidenced also in his overall
outline of their position. He begins well - 'The life
of the housewife, like that of the prisoner, tends to be
restricted at both ends of the constraint-freedom scale.'
However, he goes on - 'There is for her no real difference
between work and work-obligations, and the responsibilities
of the household, particularly if she is a mother, must
often restrict the range of her leisure activities, even
though' (and this is the crucial phrase), 'her "free
time" may be greater than that of her working sister.'
To equate being at home with having 'free time' is a
thoroughly male assumption. For all women, employed or
not, being at home is quite definitely not an experience
involving much leisure.

Patriarchy is the critical dimension totally missing
here. For it is not simply that women's work at home is
different from that of men - *it is constructed by it* and
subordinate to it. Women's work reproduces men at work;
women's work allows for men's 'existence time' or
reproduction, and women's work produces leisure for men.
We can say that all five of Parker's categories in the
work-leisure spectrum operate for men only, and constitute the demands on women by men - i.e. women's work.

In their book, 'Leisure and the Family Life Cycle',
Rhona and Robert Rapoport have attempted to study changes
in patterns of leisure activity. (9) This is seen in
terms of various stages in the 'family life cycle', and
this approach does begin to recognise women's specific
relation to work and leisure. For the Rapoports, the
family life-cycle is one possible framework through which
to think the relation between 'the institutions of leisure-

facility providers and the wishes, "needs" and requirements
of people seeking to develop meaningful whole life
experiences' (p.19).   They are chiefly concerned to
investigate the various influences which impinge on the
individual's 'life line' of development, which moves
along three lines: the family, work and leisure.   So,
rather than attempting to provide a structural analysis
of the relation between leisure, waged work and the
family, the Rapoports aim to identify the 'variables'
which influence individual's patterns of leisure activity
at different stages in the family life-cycle.

The Rapoports' use of a social-psychological approach
to the motivations and preoccupations which are seen to
underly particular leisure activities has specific
implications for their analysis of women's leisure.   They
are aware of the social constraints on women's leisure
time and activity; for instance, the ways in which women's
24-hour childcare responsibilities, and domestic work,
mean that women cannot experience leisure in the same
terms as men.   For the Rapoports, these social constraints
are barriers to be overcome, based on the conception of
sex as a variable (along with age, education, etc.), rather
than material conditions which are based on sets of power
relations inherent in patriarchal society.   Their analysis
is unable to consider the ways in which challenges or
resistances to these constraints can have real and
problematic effects on women's lives.

So, even if women can arrange babysitters, or if they
have no children, their men (whether husband, brother,
father, lover or co-habitee) may well say 'no', and forbid
women's involvement in leisure outside the home.   In a
similar manner, husbands frequently forbid or discourage
their wives from staying in, or moving back into, waged
work and a young woman's 'steady' will often tell her to
stop seeing so much of her girlfriends, once they are
courting.   These social constraints do not simply
constitute barriers to be overcome through determination
and individual resourcefulness.   The threat of male
violence in the home is very real for many women, and it
constitutes a considerable material constraint on women's
leisure, and on the whole of women's lives.   Women's
involvement in leisure outside the home is also constrained
by the threat of male violence on the streets, especially
at night, and by the fact that fewer women than men have
access to cars which they can drive. (10)

The Rapoports see 'individual resourcefulness' as
centrally important in overcoming such social constraints,
and they define this quality as 'knowing and being able
to make a meaningful whole life for oneself, with the

realities of one's existence, as well as how to change
these realities' (p.26). Resourcefulness is a capacity
that can be trained, so that eventually, state leisure
provision can be decreased to an absolute minimum, as and
when we are all able to create 'meaningful whole lives'
for ourselves, within the realities of our own existences.
Resourcefulness for the Rapoports means being able to
cope, and to adapt on an individual level to the material
conditions of existence.

The Rapoports see age, sex, type of residence and
education as 'important variables in explaining observable
behaviour' (p.23). They use the family life-cycle framework as means of losing class-specific patterns of leisure
activity, and race is simply not included, even as a
variable. This approach produces a universal, ahistoric
account, in which sex (not gender), is seen as an important
variable, but not in terms of a set of social relations
with its own specific determinations. So the Rapoports
can provide a limited descriptive account of women's
leisure, with no theoretical means of analysing the
material and cultural/ideological forms of patriarchal
relations.

However, the Rapoports' approach does have some
advantages for considering women's leisure. Their initial
account of the variety of meanings which have been related
to the notion of 'leisure' does partly overcome the chief
limitation of previous approaches to women's leisure.
That is, the tendency to see women's domestic work as
part of leisure time in an unproblematic manner, which
does not consider the relation of women's unpaid labour
to their position in waged work, and to men's leisure
(e.g. S.R. Parker). The Rapoports do point out that:
'the burdens of household work fall inequitably on
married women, even when they work equally to their
husbands. Weekends therefore become a matter of overtime
work for married women, and more a matter of recreation
for men' (p.13). As the final section of this paper
indicates, most women do see much of their domestic
work as work: hard work, unpaid work, and work which is
continual, rarely praised or acknowledged.

A CRITIQUE OF A MARXIST ANALYSIS OF LEISURE

We turn now to a consideration of a Marxist analysis in
the field of the work-leisure relation. The number of
contributions to this field from a Marxist perspective
is very small: perhaps with the greater attention being
given to leisure, this will now change. Rather than take

any of the very recent analyses available, (11) we have
chosen to look briefly at a much earlier intervention,
partly because of the undeniably Marxist credentials of
its author, partly because of its historical emphasis,
and partly because it specifically does not look at
leisure as a single category, but at the time dimension
of both work and leisure. The article in question is
E.P. Thompson's Time and industrial work discipline
(December 1967: 'Past and Present', no.38).

Thompson is here concerned to trace the changes in
the conception and experience of time for ordinary people
before, during and after the industrial revolution in
Britain. His main theme is the change from 'task-
oriented' time to rational time-structures. His main
focus is work, but leisure and its relation to work are
intimately connected with his analysis.

He begins by looking at pre-industrial conceptions of
time, drawing on anthropology and history. 'It is well
known', he says, 'that among primitive peoples the
measurement of time is commonly related to familiar
processes in the cycle of work or of domestic chores.'
He quotes time-measures such as 'a rice-cooking' (from
Madagascar), and from medieval England 'a paternoster
wyle' and 'a pissing while' - as he says, 'a somewhat
arbitrary measurement'.

He traces the shift *from* this type of time conception
with the growth of employment. The independent craftsman may himself have task-oriented time, but his family
may represent a division of labour, and the distinction
between employed time and one's own time becomes more
marked with the employment of non-family members. The
incentive to measure time with increasing precision
arose largely from the employers' interest in the use of
paid labour. The development of the factory system,
with its emphasis on the synchronisation of labour with
machinery, underlined this trend. Thus, 'rational time'
reaches its apotheosis in the time-discipline of the
factory and in the associated institution of the school
which Thompson describes in horrific detail: the penny-
pinching of the industrialists, the rules forbidding
workers to carry watches or clocks, the regimentation of
children in the schools.

Our interest here is of course in the implications
of this for the work-leisure relation. Where in
'primitive' society this distinction might be by no
means clear, Thompson describes lovingly the pattern of
the week worked by the independent craftsman. Work
would proceed in sharp concentrated bouts, followed by
three or more days of leisure. Thus Sunday would lead

into 'Saint Monday', Tuesday would be spent recovering,
Wednesday would show a slow return to work, and on
Thursday, Friday and Saturday excessively long hours would
be worked to complete the task. Leisure patterns were
slow, collective and relaxed. With the development of
the factory system, and rational time, Thompson traces
the parallel development of religion and morality, and
the Puritan emphasis on the husbanding of time and the
use of leisure for improvement. Leisure also became
rationalised. Thompson ends by looking at current and
future trends in leisure patterns and leisure studies,
suggesting that it is now the developing nations which
are stressing rational work and leisure, while the
'developed', more automated societies are seeking new
ways of using non-employed (unemployed?) time.

We will look first at the way Thompson sees women.
This will not take long, for women surface only occasionally and peripherally in the article. This is, of
course, because the subject in question is work-discipline,
and most 'workers' are male. However, private work in
the home *is* also work, and women have historically acted
also in the public work-sphere, as agricultural workers,
shop- and inn-keepers, craftsworkers (such as brewers
and spinsters), and sometimes as managers and traders.
However, of course what we mean here is that 'work' as
a domain has traditionally been defined as masculine -
and Thompson is no exception to this custom.

Women do merit *some* attention - and Thompson admits,
in his discussion of the craftsman's working week, that
heavy drinking (and over-observance of 'Saint Monday')
could produce conflict with wives. He quotes a Sheffield
song: 'The Jovial Cutlers'. The wife says:

Damn thee, Jack, I'll dust thy eyes up
Thou leads a plaguey drunken life;
Here thou sits instead of working
Wi' they pitcher on thy knee;
Curse thee, thou'd be always lurking
And I may slave myself for thee.

The implications of this for the whole analysis - that is,
that the work-leisure patterns referred to are male ones,
imposed on women, are left unspoken and the whole point
is trivialised by Thompson's coy remarks on 'domestic
tension' and (referring to her threat to deny him her bed),
her 'general strike'. But the point is an important one,
and it is clear that the long days of unwinding and
relaxing for men relied to some extent on the labour of
wives (and children) to make up the slack.

Later in the same section (like Parker, one paragraph
at the end), we have more serious consideration of domestic

labour. However, the short shrift given to this area once
again undermines the possibility of an analysis emerging.
It is, of course, hard to find evidence on the history of
women's lives, but it *has* been done; (12) indeed, Thompson
himself in the course of the article produces some quite
useful evidence as cited above, but tends not to follow it
up. However, the generalisations Thompson goes on to make
are disappointing. His main point is that women only put
up with the additional burden of domestic work because it
seemed 'necessary and inevitable'. This may well be true,
although we have no way of knowing. Thompson then moves
in an extraordinary way to extrapolate a contemporary
analysis from this. Women still think this way, he says -
indeed, the job is still much as it was. It is 'task-
oriented' and therefore feudal; the woman in the home,
he says, has not moved into capitalist time-sense (despite
'school times and television times'). I quote: 'The
mother of young children has an imperfect sense of time
and *attends to other human tides*' (our emphasis).

This is a very telling phrase, and one which indicates
Thompson's perspective here. For, in his dualism of
'natural' and 'rational' time-rhythms, feudalism and
capitalism are allocated their place, and women and men,
respectively. This is all very neat, but vastly over-
generalised and therefore misleading. Women thus belong
to the 'natural feudal' side of the equation. Thompson
commits two errors here. Firstly, the analysis is
ahistorical, since it is a question to be asked, rather
than a statement to be made, that women's situation today
is the same as that of two hundred years ago. Secondly,
Thompson insinuates that the feudal order had something
'natural' about it. And, in similar vein, he suggests
that women's work in the home is also 'natural' - she
'attends to other human tides'. This, of course, connects
with the ahistoricism. For what need is there for
historical specificity when a 'natural' role is in
question? This naturalisation of what is a *socially*
constructed, oppressive set of relations, is all the
stranger in the light of Thompson's statement, two
sentences earlier, that women themselves see their
situation as necessary and that this legitimises it. One
is tempted into a Spike Milligan-type logic: 'No wonder
they thought that way if their history was written by
someone like Thompson'.

Curiously, in the light of the claims we are making in
this article, women have often been seen as having nothing
but leisure, as basically doing nothing, at least in
comparison to men who do 'real' work, i.e. waged work.
This seems to be even more the case when girls are

considered. The main leisure pursuit of working-class
girls - talking - is easily dismissed, as with older
women, as gossip, doing nothing.

Within, loosely, sociological and cultural writing
about 'youth' it is precisely girls' active involvement
in 'leisure' that provokes panics about, principally,
the consequences of their visibility for their sexuality.
When girls *do* appear, which isn't often (youth as a
category means young men), their pursuit of enjoyment or
pleasure is interpreted as potential or actual insubordi-
nation. Fears about their relative independence, which
are provoked by their involvement in social life, quickly
become fears about their willingness to conform to
authority. References to girls in this literature
reflect patriarchal social relations; most writers are
concerned about girls' lack of seriousness and the
potential immorality this implies for them. An example:
Richard Hoggart in 'The Uses of Literacy' describes
teenage girls as having 'little interest as committed
individuals in anything, they take no interest in trade
union activities and little in the home. Surely they are
most of them flighty, careless and inane?' (13)   A major
worry for these writers centres around girls' use of
make-up and fears of permissiveness - the fear that they
will 'cheapen' themselves and sell their sexuality below
the market price, i.e. outside marriage. What is important
about this work is that it concentrates on the potential
misuse of the girls' sexuality - that *is* the threat their
volatility represents. The 'problem' is actually about
the consequences of girls' participation in leisure for
their future role in the family and their *sexual*
stability. Dancing, another major leisure pursuit of
adolescent girls, is often regarded by (male) teachers
or youth workers as immoral - meaning it makes them
uncomfortable - because it is perhaps the only legitimate
way for girls (and women) to use their bodies expressively
and sexually.

The more recently developed model of youth sub-
cultures ignores girls; they are not only absent but
invisible. (14) One of the reasons for this is that
this model is particularly concerned with boys' *resistance*
to exploitation. McRobbie and Garber (15) have shown that
the invisibility of girls is a structured absence, since
cultures of femininity are structured in relations of
subordination to the dominant male youth cultures. The
whole discussion of youth cultures is predicated on this
structural absence since it is impossible within this
model to recognise that boys oppress girls; the possibility
of the boys' resistance actually comes from their power

We shall be interrogating each stage of this schema
with reference to the situation of women working in the
home - not because we wish to deny the reality of work
both inside and outside the home for many women - but in
a heuristic sense, to provide the polar opposite case to
full-time employment. Our final section on the ethnographic work with women at home makes this critique all
the clearer, as we shall show.

Parker defines work as 'the activity involved in
earning a living, plus necessary subsidiary activities
such as travelling to work'. This is the first category
and is, in fact, the one by which the others are defined.
The assumption here is that work is what is done for
money, that it takes place outside the home, and that it
is a distinct area, capable of producing subsidiary
categories. For women at home, however, work is not
done for money, but for 'love' or maternal duty; it
takes place *in* the home; and, as the final section shows,
it is not a distinct area.

The second category is that of 'work obligations',
which for Parker, 'include voluntary overtime' (a strange
categorisation), 'doing things outside normal working
hours associated with the job or type of work, that are
not strictly necessary to a minimum acceptable level of
performance in the job, or having a second job'. Once
again we have here the use of full-time employment as
the yardstick - even to the point of relegating overtime,
or a second job, to the category of 'work obligations'.
The fact that 'women's work' in the home is not so
clearly defined, means that for them the boundary between
work and work obligations is very blurred. (6) In a
sense, *everything* that women do in the home is 'work
obligation'.

The third category of Parker's is the first of his
'leisure' categories. This is 'existence time', or 'the
satisfaction of physiological needs'. Of this, Parker
says, it 'follows the conventional definition of these
needs', and elaborating, he gives 'sleep, eating, washing,
eliminating' as examples. There is an immediate problem
here for a woman. That is, she is not simply doing these
things for herself, but facilitating them in other
people: whether feeding her husband, or changing the
baby's nappies. A further problem Parker *does* see:
the possible overlap with leisure. Eating may be for
pleasure, sexual activity may be 'beyond the call of
purely physiological need' (p.26). Bypassing the somewhat
quantitative mentality of this latter distinction. it is
worth noting that the ambiguity may be considerable for
women. Recent, and not so recent, research (7) indicates

position within patriarchy and a model developed to understand the oppression of 'youth' cannot come to terms with their actual dominance.

The impression we are left with from the 'youth cultures' literature is that girls either do not participate in social life, or that their leisure consists of doing nothing - which is precisely why it is seen as a problem. 'Doing nothing', and apparent passivity, mean that girls are taking risks by putting themselves in situations where things may be *done to* them.

McRobbie and Garber (16) have provided the most detailed analysis of women's 'leisure' to come out of the 'youth cultures' work. They have concentrated on the position of white, working-class girls in the context of a critique of the male bias of literature on youth culture and sub-cultures. They point to the existence of the specifically feminine culture of the teenybopper, which is centred on fandom, and situated within the home. McRobbie's work has begun to develop from critiques of existing approaches, to a more positive consideration of the contradictory representation and involvement of white, working-class girls in the leisure sphere, and of the complex relation between class and gender. (17)

We have considered the work of several contributors to the 'leisure' field. The crucial point is that it is possible, not simply for conventional analyses, but also for Marxist analyses, to fall into essentially the same traps in the consideration of women. These are: absence, token reference, a naturalisation or denial of women's oppression, and, crucially, the failure to see the radical implications which analyses of women's position present for the *rethinking*, not the minor adjustment, of categories. As long as this last move is not made, women will continue to appear as marginal within existing categories. To quote Judy Keiner: 'Just tacking on "the problem of women" to existing theories of social reproduction, which are not gender specific, all too readily confirms the marginality of women, or finds that they are just like men, only less so.' (18) This problem does not apply only to theories of social reproduction, but to all areas of life.

ETHNOGRAPHIC ANALYSES OF LEISURE FOR WOMEN

This section is based on three ethnographic analyses of the position of white, working-class women, and their experience of 'work' and 'leisure', both in and outside

the home. The first part centres on school-age girls,
the second on the transition from school to waged work,
and the third on young married women who are full-time
housewives and mothers. This work is based on qualitative
ethnographic methods of cultural analysis, as developed
partly through the work of the Birmingham Centre. (19)
Although this approach involves working with relatively
small groups, the stress on the importance of subjective
experience, and on the 'personal', gives it particular
relevance to feminist analysis. Consideration of women's
position and experience is so often absent or marginalised
in most academic work, that the ethnographic method has
specific political importance in making women visible. (20)

The work presented in this section is intended to
extend the critiques discussed in the first part of the
paper, and to act as a starting point for the development
of a fuller analysis of leisure which begins from women's
position. In deconstructing the notion of 'leisure' as
a pure category, we hope to show that what these girls
and women actually *do* in their 'leisure' time cannot be
seen as leisure in a straightforward sense, nor in
relation to a simplistic comparison with men's leisure
activities. We would situate these differences in terms
of women's specific relation to, and position in, the
family, and hope to illustrate and develop our analysis
from the following ethnographic accounts.

SCHOOL-AGE GIRLS AND LEISURE

The 'commonsense' view of schools is that girls are
frivolous, unable to concentrate and are not motivated
to keep their attention on anything serious. Girls are
perceived as being only interested in 'leisure', in
'impractical' things like boyfriends, gossip and the
disco; any discussion of girls and work is often
transformed into moans about girls and 'leisure'. Girls'
interests, as the following quote shows well, are
transferred from the world of work into her future world
of (in common sense) leisure:

Take a girl whose list of interests showed she spent
most of her time out with boyfriends and going to
dances. Suppose she chose to go and work in the
local factory operating a machine ... if her job was
easy to learn and could be done after a short spell
of training there is no reason why she shouldn't do
it well. And if all she asks is to work with her
friends and not have a job with a lot of responsibility then she could be quite happy, couldn't she?

Of course, if it were a job which did take some time
to learn and needed a lot of skill with your hands then
it might be different. You would expect a boy who wanted
an apprenticeship in joinery ... to have been quite good
at woodwork in school and (be interested in practical
things). (21)

What is missing from this is any recognition that in fact
the girl's 'interests', so easily dismissed as leisure,
are in fact central to her future economic and social
survival. They bear a direct relation to her future work -
getting and keeping a man, permanently - but without some
grasp of women's oppression, this fundamental activity is
seen as 'leisure', as doing nothing (or at least nothing
serious, practical, responsible...).

In fact girls in schools do typically use tactics of
silence, obvious boredom or deliberate immersion in their
private concerns to undermine teachers and the masculine
and middle-class ideologies of the school; (22)   this
response makes sense. 'Real work' is not their central
preoccupation, and crucially is not open to them
culturally (even if some of the official barriers to sex
discrimination are removed). Their futures, culturally
and economically, depend upon their relation to the
family and to men, and the necessity of waged work, which
is most likely to be low paid and low status, and is not
something to relish or look forward to.

Girls' responses to school and work, transforming
both into social life, a particular form of leisure,
through using their own definition of, and culture of,
femininity, make sense in minimising the oppressive
features of their situation. At school, girls invest
their uniform or dress with their own definitions of
adult femininity, wearing the school colours but not the
uniform clothes, battling over hem lines, competing with
female teachers over style, wearing subtle, difficult-
to-detect make-up, struggling for the right to wear
engagement rings if jewellery is forbidden.

Angela McRobbie has pointed out that this refusal to
abandon adult femininity and its claims to be taken
seriously indicates how girls 'gently undermine [the
school's] principles and [indicate] that they do not
recognise the distinction between school and leisure.
Symbolically at least the school is transferred into an
extension of their social life.' (23) Going to school
is less boring than staying off, you can have a laugh
and piss off the teachers. You can make your own space,
and small but essential spaces in the school are transformed by girls into their own areas: the corridors,
toilets, cloakrooms and, partly, the classroom. Hiding

behind typewriters, reading 'Jackie' or 'My Guy' under the desk, talking to each other in lessons or painting nails, *and* developing techniques to get away with it.

It is precisely this construction of leisure in the classroom - passing time, doing nothing - that results in some girls being branded as trouble-makers by teachers, and in some cases by boys. As one teacher put it to me,

Bouncy girls are seen as a nuisance, rough, they're put down for it. Boys get more attention, they're seen as a real lad, a good laugh. But teachers really don't like girls who behave like that.

The point seems to be that boys are entitled to have a laugh, that their resistance to the teacher through disruption or whatever is acceptable, is understandable. Boys are perceived as entitled to leisure in a way that girls are not. To try and transform the classroom into social life, space for them, through any obviously disruptive means, rather than the typical tactics of boredom and inattention, is unfeminine and is often frowned upon. Girls and women don't *earn* leisure, and in taking it cannot be seen as proving they're real women in the sense that in doing that boys prove themselves to be real lads. Typically, West Indian girls are often perceived as trouble-makers by white teachers because they may not conform to the white middle-class model of femininity, which has no real relation to their lives, and consequently they are not defined by the school as real women but as trouble-makers. If boys make trouble, on the other hand, it can result in more attention being paid to them, more effort being made to get them interested, often at the cost of the girls. Careers lessons are a good example both of this in practice, and of the dominant male definitions of what is real work, and of work as central to life.

The most important space in the school for girls is the toilets. Characteristically, bathrooms are the only women-only spaces in our society. Male bars or clubs, football matches and the night out with the lads which cannot be interrupted - even the streets to hang around at night - have no female equivalents. In schools toilets are used as somewhere to escape from the class-room and teachers, for trying out make-up, smoking and, most important of all, for talking. Talking for girls and women is not simply relaxation, but is centrally about managing contradictions and gaining support, and its centrality to girls' leisure is no surprise. They (rightly) see talking as positive, sorting out problems with friends, establishing their own space and time; nevertheless it is usually over-determined by boys and men.

The amount of male 'humorous' folklore about women
spending hours in the bathroom is an indication of how
jealously women guard their own space. Bedrooms where
girls can talk, listen to records, read magazines and
fantasise about stars they'll never meet (they're much
nicer than the real thing) eventually give way to
'sharing'. The bedroom, like the kitchen, becomes another
place where women must work to satisfy men - and home
economics and sex education have remarkable similarities
in the way they are taught (as do 'teach-ins' on romance
in girls' magazines and recipes in women's). Sex, like
cooking, is something to be *learnt* and for girls this
means learning how to negotiate the thin line between
being sexually loose and sexually 'frigid', attractive
but not available, petting but not intercourse, or at
least not just yet. Sex as a popular leisure pursuit
for men cannot be simply applied to women too; it changes
its significance when overlaid by worries about how far
you can go and still keep him, whether he'll tell his
mates, whether you'll get pregnant, whether he'll notice
you're faking, whether he'll drop you if you say no,
drop you if you say yes....
    Finally, the leisure of girls is restricted materially
and physically in a way quite unlike that of boys. While
middle-class girls may have more money to spend on
recreation, or mothers who can pick them up from clubs or
concerts (two-car families often 'free' the wife to
spend her time running her kids around), most working-
class girls don't even have access to these types of
leisure pursuits. Their lack of money, often only from
babysitting or pocket money in exchange for housework,
(24) fundamentally restricts them to their own bedrooms,
or friend's of their own locality. Going to gigs and so
on are overlaid by worries about 'trouble', a part of the
real fears both girls and their parents have for their
safety. The threat of violence, and particularly of
rape, is something against which girls have no protection.
They are restricted geographically - cannot go out without
the means of getting home safely - and parents will impose
restrictions on the time they can come home because the
threat of violence induces a fear which is just as
powerful in forcing girls and women 'voluntarily' to
limit their own freedom. Needless to say, there is no
equivalent threat or limitation for boys because boys
and men *are* the threat to girls.

THE TRANSITION FROM SCHOOL TO WAGED WORK

This section of the paper will consider the move into
full-time waged work for young white, working-class
women, specifically in relation to their leisure
activities. This is based on recent ethnographic work
on the contemporary position of young women at work and
in the family. (25) For young women, it is not the move
from school to work which primarily structures their
leisure, but the shift from a 'best' girlfriend, or
group of girlfriends, to going out with boys, and then
'going steady'. As 'Cosmopolitan' of January 1980 stated
in an advert for their 'Careers Guide': 'Choosing the
right career is as important as choosing the right mate.'
For young, working-class, white women, 'choosing the
right mate' is a vital part of waged work and leisure,
and it can be seen as their primary 'job'. Women's
central position will be in the home, married and with a
family, and finding a bloke with a skilled apprenticeship,
or a secure, clean office job is of primary importance
to their lives.

The move from school into full-time waged work - if
you can get it - means moving into one of three sectors
of employment for young women in the Birmingham area:
  (i)   Factory work, mainly in the 'light' industrial
        sector, food, distribution, etc.
  (ii) Shopwork, in supermarkets, boutiques, hair-
        dressers, department stores.
  (iii) Secretarial and clerical work, telephonist/
        reception work.
In all cases the sexual division of labour pervades,
and girls move into areas of 'women's work'.

Factory work is seen as the least attractive, as
dirty work which is less secure and 'not a nice job for
a girl'. Even if a girl's parents have no positive
desire for her to move into any particular work, her mum
especially would tend to see factory work in a similar
light, although it offers much the best wages. Secretarial work is seen as the most attractive, and of the
highest status, despite being far less remunerative
than factory work, and frequently just as monotonous.
However, it is clean, and provides one of the most
appropriate means for working-class girls to meet men
in secure middle-class jobs: 'steady blokes'.

One of the central criteria according to which waged
work is seen as more or less attractive, is the relative
possibility it offers for meeting eligible men. The
young women themselves recognise this, and once in full-
time work, they begin to assess the men as possible

partners at once. As one 16-year-old girl, who had been
working in an office for only two months, has put it: 'The
work's pretty boring, but no one bothers me, and there's
a few dishy blokes here - you know what I mean?'

This fundamentally structures women's experience of,
and position in waged work and 'leisure'. Women's
primary job is finding a man, and this is not specific to
working-class women. Talking to young middle-class women
in the sixth form of a prestigious local girls' school,
I found that university or college, where most will go
when they leave school, is recognised as a marriage market
for women. The spate of engagement rings which begin to
appear during the first year of college bear this out.

And it is *work*. For working-class women, the first
wages go on clothes: £30 boots, £60 for a coat, make-up,
etc. Constructing your own femininity to attract men is
hard work, and it does take time and money, as Janice
Winship has pointed out. (26) The construction of
femininity takes a considerable amount of women's
'leisure' time, both inside and outside work. It is of
crucial importance in attracting 'a steady bloke who
won't bash you around', and who has a secure job. It
must be seen as work for women, since - quite literally -
their lives will depend on it. The time, effort and
money spent on the construction of femininity is an
integral part of women's final appearance at the disco
or club.

So, it is impossible to see women's position in waged
work and leisure without reference to gender, and this
must be reflected in any analysis of women's leisure.
Considering specific changes that the move into waged
work brings, the most obvious is the wage itself. From
earning perhaps a few pounds a week babysitting, or in a
Saturday job, girls can earn between £20 and £30 a week.
However, the patterns of girls' consumption, and their
use of 'leisure' time does not change radically at this
point. Some of the wage goes to their mothers for keep
(about £5 or £6 a week), (27) a varying amount might be
saved for the 'bottom drawer', and the rest goes on the
construction of femininity, clothes, make-up, etc. By
far the most radical shift in girls' patterns of consumption and leisure activities comes when they begin to go
out with boys. This shift must be seen in terms of an
analysis of changing cultural forms, as the chiefly
feminine culture of best girlfriends centred in the
home, shifts to the heterosexual couple, and the pre-
liminaries to married life.

With the move from school to waged work - or unemployment - girls' 'leisure' still centres around the domestic

sphere, with perhaps more frequent visits to the pubs and clubs to meet older blokes - money permitting. Consider-able ideological pressure is focused on young women at this point, in which femininity is constructed in terms of heterosexual attractiveness to men. Although in an important sense these activities can be - and are seen by the girls - as 'fun', they cannot be viewed unproblema-tically as enjoyment.

Once a girl has started going out with a 'steady' boy, whether before or after leaving school, contacts with girlfriends will begin to drop off, and sometimes cease completely at the boy's insistence. Whilst a boy will keep up his leisure activities once he has started going out with girls, such as football, or going to the pub with the lads, his girlfriend's leisure time will be trans-formed. Her boyfriend begins to monopolise her time - even when he is not there. Leisure activities centre around the couple, staying at her or his parents' house watching TV, with the girl servicing her boyfriend, making him cups of tea and snacks, in a sort of anticipa-tion of married life. For girls, consumption patterns shift from clothes and make-up to saving more intensively, and the discos and pubs are now rejected, particuarly by the boy, as 'cattle markets'. If the courting, or 'serious' couple do go out in the evening, it is to the cinema, or to the pubs frequented by other young couples and older people.

YOUNG MARRIED WOMEN AT HOME

This section draws on research that involved interviewing young working-class women at home with small children or babies. (28) We do not propose to make any broad or generalised assertions about the lives and leisure of working-class girls and women, but simply to give an account of the lives of the women interviewed, to try to show how their class and sex limited their choices of work and leisure opportunities both before their marriage and now in their married lives.

The concept of 'leisure' is difficult to consider in relation to women who are not engaged in paid work because leisure itself is a corollary to work and the one is unthinkable without the other. Thus working-class women who did not develop strong leisure activities before their marriage have difficulty in feeling that they have the 'right' to leisure, which is something that they associate with the 'right' to work which is afforded their husbands but not possible for themselves.

Leisure before marriage

> DH   Before you, when you left school ... what did
>   you used to do in your spare time?
> Lorna   Oh, I used to go out a lot then.
> DH   How often was 'a lot'?
> Lorna   Well, I used to go out Fridays, Saturdays,
>   Sunday and Monday and probably just round to
>   friends the other nights. I was never in.
>   (laughs)
> DH   When you did go out, where did you used to
>   go?
> Lorna   Oh, dancing, or pictures, you know, up town.
>   (...)
> DH   Who would you have gone there with?
> Lorna   I've got three friends, girls ((mm))
>   one's getting married soon, but the other two
>   they're still single, they still go out a lot,
>   and I miss all that. (laughs)

This extract could have been spoken by any of the women
in the study, for without variation the period between
leaving school and meeting their husband has been the
time when they have enjoyed most freedom in terms of
their leisure. The period between leaving school and
'settling down' to married life has been traditionally
considered as one of freedom and enjoyment for the young
working class both male and female. The 'reality' of
marriage for the working class is posed as the end of
freedom for working-class women. Certainly, they may
not make open challenges to their new situation but
nevertheless they do feel real regret and resentment that
they have lost that freedom. In contrast to their
present situation their past with respect to their
leisure time is a phase of their lives which is remembered
with excitement and pleasure.

In contrast with the freedom which they experienced
were the restrictions which were imposed on them and
which they *accepted*, when they met their future husbands.
When they began 'courting' they abandoned both their
spare-time activities and their girlfriends. There is
an acceptance that women 'give up' their freedom; there
was no sight of assertion of their *right* to continue
their own leisure activities.

The women interviewed would have liked to continue
going to dances and discos now that they were married,
but not only did their husbands stop them from going to
discos now; once they had started a serious relationship
they often found that their boyfriends would no longer
to go dances or discos nor allow them to go. If they

shared leisure pursuits once they were 'going steady' it
was the male leisure pursuits that they both shared.

In order to consider the 'problem' of leisure for
women at home it is also necessary to look at their work
within the family. The location of women's domestic
labour and their responsibility for the welfare of their
husband and children, within the privatised sphere of the
home, has meant that for women there is neither a physical
nor an emotional separation of the spheres of work and
leisure. The privatised nature of housework which
necessitates the isolation of the individual woman in the
home is one of the most recognisable sites of her
oppression. The male worker returns to the private
sphere of his home to be 'reproduced' in a fit state for
work the next day. This period away from work can be
seen as the time when the man has leisure time. However,
there is no space for leisure for women at the same time.
The woman works in the home during the day when the man
is at work but when he returns from work, she still has
to work.

DH   So you think there's more of a separation
         between men's work and their spare time than
         there is for a woman?

Betty   Yes, I think men have got more spare time
         'cause their work they have to go to and so
         when they come out of it they're away from
         their work so what they do then really it's
         up to them. I mean, if they don't want to
         help the wife, I mean, nobody can force them
         and they can just sit down all night if they
         want to and do what they like. ((yes))
         Whereas, with a woman they've got to keep on
         working and they don't clock out at 5 o'clock,
         They've still got to cook the tea and do
         anything else that needs doing. Like, if one
         of the children make a horrible mess of the
         room or something, or throw a bottle of milk
         on the floor or tip something on the floor,
         then they can't say, 'Oh, it's gone 5 o'clock,
         I'll stop, it'll stop there now till 9 o'clock
         tomorrow morning.' They've got to clean it up.

This extract poses the distinction between the working
life of men and that of women. As Betty says, men have
to go to their work and they leave work behind when they
leave the site of production. Men have a choice of what
they do because there is a distinct non-working period
in their working day. There is no official working time
for women. Recent figures reported the length of the
working week for housewives as being an average of 77

hours. (29)   However, although women are not forced to
work such long hours, their own self-compulsion drives
them on even when they feel that they should be at
leisure.   This compulsion to work must come in part from
the absence of boundaries and from the structurelessness
of housework;   there are no boundaries between work and
leisure and no notion of how much housework is 'enough'.
The repetitiousness of housework intensifies the compulsion
which women experience in managing it.   Nothing is really
achieved even when the task is finished because it still
remains to be repeated the next day.   Yet for women there
is no escape from housework.   It is ever present, cyclic
and infinite.

DH	That's what I wanted to ask you, do you miss going out?
Lorna	Yes, Yes, I don't go out much now. I used to go out with me husband, you know, when I was expecting the baby but since we've had the baby I haven't been out.
DH	Does he go out?
Lorna	Yes, he goes out Monday and Tuesday and Saturday. On the Monday and Tuesday he plays dominoes for the pub and then on the Saturday he goes with one of his mates down to the 'Blues' match. You know, then he goes to his Mom's on the afternoon and then he'll go for a drink on the night with his mates.
DH	And would you like to go out?
Lorna	Yes, I'd love a night to go out.

One of the most obvious changes which has occurred in
the lives of the women since their marriage is the lack of
any 'leisure' or time which they consider to be 'spare'
when they could do what they wanted.   The lack of
opportunity to go out is also in sharp contrast with
their husbands who still go out with their friends or
mates to football matches or to the pub.   In terms of
what they actually do in their spare time, the concept
of a 'hobby' as actively 'doing something', is obviously
considered as something different from simply 'going out'.
At one point when one of the women was asked about her
interests before she was married, she said,

'I went out nearly every night, I was hardly ever in.
I don't suppose there was time for a hobby then'.
She clearly differentiates between 'going out', and 'doing
something'.   It is the former which the women in this study
miss, they would like the opportunity to go out particularly
with their old girlfriends.

The length of time which has occurred since they went
out on their own is quite horrifying and, coupled with

their isolation in the home during the day, it is not surprising that they indicated signs of depression and dissatisfaction with their lives. The following extract reveals how one woman's isolation during the day is reinforced through her lack of opportunities to 'go out' in the evenings. She tells how she has not been out on her own since before she was married eight years ago, and she and her husband have not been out together since before her eldest child was born, five years ago. What is particularly depressing about her account is that she said that she would not know what to do if she did have the opportunity to go out.

DH   Did you ever, have you ever been out on your own since you've been married?

Betty Oh gosh, I don't think I have. Oh, I used to go a couple of times to bingo with me husband's mom, ((yes)). I think about a year I used to go on a Saturday, most Saturdays ((mm)) but I'm not really all that fussy about bingo. It was just sort of to go out, you know, somewhere to go out to, but otherwise I don't go anywhere.

DH   Do you go out very much together?

Betty No, we never go out together 'cos we've got no babysitters. ((no)) So we never go. I don't think we've been to the pictures, I don't think since before Shane was born. Last time I went was when I was expecting Shane, that's the first one, and we sometimes, we used to go out for a drink when I was expecting Shane, usually on a Friday night. ((mm)) But since I've had him, you know, I didn't go out really anywhere. ((yes)) (...)

DH   Do you mind that and would you like to go out more?

Betty I would do but I've got that used to not going out that I'm just not bothered really. I don't think I'd know what to do if I did go out, (laughs), you know; you just get used to not going after a bit.

The women in this study did not have any real notion of time which was their own in which they could do what they wanted. They were always conscious that they could be called on at any time to get food for their husbands or look after the children, even during the evenings. They did, however, feel that they should have spare time during the evening and they said that they would watch television or do knitting. In fact, television was the main 'leisure' pursuit of the women in this study, but this could always be interrupted if their domestic role demanded their attention. They did not have any notion of a 'right' to any time which was entirely their own.

Although they did not go out on their own or with their friends, these women did enjoy any time which they spent with their women friends. What they experienced as a pleasurable activity was the opportunity to be with other women and spend time together talking or 'gossiping'. Lorna articulates her idea of spare time and what she does for a 'hobby'.

DH   Have you got any hobbies, anything you do in your spare time?

Lorna   No, really most of me time is spent with these and cleaning and washing. The only hobby is sitting and talking and drinking coffee, and just going down the road, that's as far as we get, you know.

Similarly, Ann tells of how she spends time with her girl-friend when she visits her.

DH   And do you see her very much?

Ann   She's working part time, she came down yesterday, she used to come down every Wednesday but her mother's been ill so she's been going down there. ((mm)) But it's generally every week.

DH   And what would you do when she came?

Ann   Just have a good old natter. (laughs)

DH   What would you natter about?

Ann   Her husband, my husband, (laughs) all their faults ... what we're going to do next to the flat.

Clearly, women see the time which they spend with other women talking over their 'problems' as a form, if not of relaxation, certainly as a means of 'managing the contradictions' or tensions in their lives. However, women have to contend with the whole negative attitude to female interests. Because the notion of women 'gossiping together' has been denigrated and treated with humorous contempt, women do not see their own pleasures in positive terms. They feel that they do not pursue hobbies as men do, yet they do not feel able to claim a 'space' for going out with their girlfriends, as their husband has the same right to go out for a drink with his mates.

CONCLUSION

Because leisure for women and men is constructed in different ways through femininity and masculinity, their

leisure is experienced through a power relation. Men's
leisure in relation to their work depends on women's
position in the family and employment. The family is
relaxation for men, but only because of the work women do
to create that area of relaxation. Men's leisure is work
for women, women are leisure for men. This leads to a
fundamental critique of the meaning of leisure - traditionally seen as non-work - and we have tried to show that
girls experience their so-called leisure precisely through
their femininity. That experience of femininity is
structured by class and by race in different ways.
Despite the volumes written on economic class, the concept
has been inadequately theorised *within* the overall
structure of patriarchy. Thinking through economic class
within a theory of patriarchy is a relatively new project.
Race and racism has been virtually ignored on both counts -
both from the point of view of class and patriarchy - and
we can only suggest that the experience of being a black
girl in a racist society is different in relation to the
dominant white society than within black cultures. At
this stage, seeing both these structures as operating
within the overall structure of patriarchy, we think it is
clear that the central determination of women's and girls'
experience of leisure is the fact of being a woman in a
society where women are oppressed.

NOTES AND REFERENCES

1 For an analysis which places 'leisure' in the context
   of imperialism and new technology, see A. Sivanandan,
   Imperialism and disorganic development in the silicon
   age, in 'Race and Class', vol.XXI, no.2, 1979.
2 See, for example, K. Thitsa, Tourist Thailand - women
   for sale, in 'Spare Rib', vol.103, 1981.
3 We define maleness as the social construction of
   masculinity as it is superimposed on biological
   differences between women and men.
4 Parker's earlier work has been chosen because, as his
   PhD thesis, it concentrates on spelling out the
   definitions of leisure in more detail. He sees work
   as the prime determinant of leisure patterns, and his
   whole study concentrates on that connection, whereas
   his later work looks at other institutions in more
   detail.
5 J. Dumazedier, quoted by Parker, 1971, p.22.
6 See final Ethnographic section on women's work in the
   home.
7 Research exploring women's sexual potential, and its

frequent limitation in heterosexual intercourse includes: W. Masters and V. Johnson, 'Human Sexual Response', Edinburgh, Churchill, 1966; A. Kinsey et al., 'Sexual Behaviour in the Human Female', Philadelphia, Saunders, 1953; and more recently, S. Hite, 'The Hite Report', New York, Summit, 1977.

8   Recent events such as the 'Knit-In' staged in a London pub (February 1980), illustrate the need for women to assert our right to sit alone in male-dominated public spaces.

9   R. Rapoport and R. Rapoport, 'Leisure and the Family Life Cycle', London, Routledge & Kegan Paul, 1975.

10 See M. Talbot, Women and Leisure, review for the joint SSRC/Sports Council Committee, 1979.

11 J-M. Brohm, 'Sport: A Prison of Measured Time', London, Ink Links, 1976.

12 See, for example, J. McCrindle and S. Rowbotham, 'Dutiful Daughters', Harmondsworth, Penguin, 1977; S. Rowbotham, 'Hidden from History', Penguin, Harmondsworth, 1973; I. Pinchbeck, 'Women Workers in the Industrial Revolution', London, Cass & Co., 1966; and J. Mitchell and A. Oakley, 'The Rights and Wrongs of Women', Harmondsworth, Penguin, 1976.

13 R. Hoggart, 'The Uses of Literacy', London, Chatto & Windus, 1957, pp.51-2; for a fuller account of this literature, see A. McRobbie, Working class girls and the culture of femininity, MA thesis, CCCS, University of Birmingham, 1977.

14 The literature in this field is considerable, but see S. Hall and T. Jefferson (eds), 'Resistance Through Rituals', CCCS, 1975, and M. Brake, 'The Sociology of Youth Cultures and Youth Subcultures', London, Routledge & Kegan Paul, 1980, for reviews of this area.

15 A. McRobbie and J. Garber, Girls and subcultures: an exploration, in S. Hall and T. Jefferson (eds), op.cit.

16 Ibid.

17 A. McRobbie, op.cit., and A. McRobbie, Working class girls and the culture of femininity, in Women's Studies Group, CCCS, 'Women Take Issue', London, Hutchinson, 1978.

18 J. Keiner, Introduction to 'Mind you do as you're told' by A. Davin, in 'Feminist Review', vol.31, 1979, p.86.

19 See ethnography section in S. Hall et al. (eds), 'Culture, Media, Language', London, Hutchinson, 1980, for a fuller discussion of these methodological questions.

20   See D. Hobson, ethnography chapter in A study of
      working class women at home: femininity, domesticity
      and maternity, MA thesis, CCCS, University of
      Birmingham, 1978, for a discussion of the political
      importance of ethnographic work with women.
21   T. Crawley, 'Choosing a Career', London, CRAC, 1972.
22   Key to transcripts in the Ethnography section:
          ...   pause
          ( )   non-verbal communicate, e.g. laughs
          ..   speaker interrupted
          (( ))   phatic communication, e.g. ((mm))
          (...)   passage edited out
      This section is based on Trisha McCabe's work with
      groups of girls in a local school, which was carried
      out as part of the research for a PhD thesis. Some
      of this work has been developed in 'Feminism for
      Girls', edited by T. McCabe and A. McRobbie, London,
      Routledge & Kegan Paul, 1981.
23   A. McRobbie, 1977, op.cit.
24   The amount of housework which girls are expected to
      do varies enormously, though the differences are
      nothing like those between girls and boys, whose
      leisure opportunities are rarely restricted by
      domestic responsibilities.
25   This section is based on Chris Griffin's fieldwork
      as part of a project on 'Young Women and Work',
      which is concerned with the transition from school
      to work for white, working-class girls.
26   J. Winship, Sexuality for sale, in S. Hall et al.
      (eds), op.cit.
27   This refers to June 1979 - some young women to whom
      I have spoken since (November 1980) have given as
      much at £10-£12 to their mums for keep, out of a
      net weekly wage of between £30 and £40.
28   This section is based on Dorothy Hobson's work with
      young working-class housewives at home with young
      children. For a fuller account of the research see
      D. Hobson, Housewives: isolation as oppression, in
      Women's Studies Group, op.cit., and D. Hobson, MA
      thesis, 1978, op.cit.
29   See A. Oakley, 'The Sociology of Housework', Oxford,
      M. Robertson, 1974, pp.92-5.

Chapter 5

Women in sport in ideology

Paul Willis

What follows is an essay in ideas. It is only a fragment
towards the final critical mapping of sport within the
social totality. It provides no proper empirical basis
for analysis, provides no history of women in sport and
does not develop an inclusive theory of ideology. In a
way it may be seen as a long footnote to John Hargreaves's
general survey of the area. My limited aim is to explore
one of the crucial questions within the larger operation
of ideological processes in the specific area of women
in sport: how a set of ideas which bear a particular
'guilty' relation of support and formation to dominant
groups and dominant ideas nevertheless appear 'freely'
on the market place of ideas: unbiased, neutral and the
property of any independent mind prepared to use 'common
sense' and 'work things out for itself'. This is the
now classic area defined for us in John Hargreaves's
opening article of where 'cultural hegemony' meets the
realm of 'common sense', or where more precisely the
potential 'good sense' of 'common sense' is displaced
and makes room for what are 'dominant' views – but
'freely' taken on. (1) Approaching our chosen area with
such an open and apparently simple question may throw
some light on women in sport as well as perhaps illumina-
ting some of the ways in which ideology colours 'the
natural'.

Sport and biological beliefs about gender difference
combine into one of the few privileged areas where we
seem to be dealing with unmediated 'reality', where we
know 'what's what' without having to listen to the
involved self-serving analyses of theorists, analysts,
political groups, etc. Running faster, jumping higher,
throwing further can be *seen* – not interpreted. 'The
natural' is one of the grounds of ideology because of
its apparent autonomy from 'biased' interpretation.

Obvious domination or even insidious infiltration of such areas would, it seems, be spotted very easily: after all Jesse Owen did win X number of gold medals in the 1936 Olympics and Fascism could not dominate sport to show its 'superiority'. Nor should we rush to our socio-cultural cynicism here. John Hargreaves is surely right to insist that sport isn't simply 'the front' for other kinds of social domination. It is wrong to ransack the variety of experience and practice in the area to come up with simple social fits and reflections: sport helps the rulers rule. There is an enjoyment in activity, there are pleasures in competition that cannot be reduced to capitalist competition. Much sport is undoubtedly organised in commercial ways for profit and it is timed and measured like activity in the factory, (2) but people of both sexes do enjoy watching and/or participating in activity, dexterity, co-operation and movement. Most importantly, there are different meanings at play, contested meanings over the same event, the same happening. It is precisely here, I shall be arguing, in the real separation of sport from other areas of society, its differences, its autonomy, wherein lies its power for legitimation – it would not be believed if it did not show this independence and apparent capacity to carry social meaning separately from what the powerful say. This is exactly the freedom, rest and release, that non-political joy in sport, which participants experience as its particular quality and defend precisely against 'political interference'. It is how this complexity is actually nevertheless taken up into ideology that is the focus of this paper – in the concrete example of comparative sports performance of women in sport.

Women in sport and the ideological effect I want to outline are also important in providing us with one of the few examples of the 'circuit of the media' and especially with how the experience of a phenomenon and its communicated meaning relate or differ. Too many media accounts deal with the communications of the powerful or with the adaption of received views, or add on the 'amplification effect' (3) as an internal media process. It is important always in my view to place the *situated generation* of meaning as well as to outline the process whereby it is disseminated, and also to suggest some notion of the structured articulation between them. The area of women in sport and its relation to ideology provide a very revealing case study also of the media's operation in our society.

At any rate sport has attracted more and more attention over recent years as perhaps the central constituency of the burgeoning area of 'leisure'. It is central to *active* notions of 'leisure' and to passive reception. It raises questions both about the event and its media meanings. Though in no way directly related, during the same period there has also been a greatly revived interest in, and opposition to, the oppression of women in society. The intersection of these two important themes, therefore, in the area of women in sport may offer us an unlikely and revealing, concrete manifestation of crucially modern concerns and feelings. We may find that the particular *conjunction* of the two lines helps us to understand better each line even as they lead away from women in sport to more central and abstract concerns.

It may be noted, perhaps unexpectedly, that there is also methodological importance here to a student of social thought, because so many of the approaches to women in sport exhibit the clearest aspects of positivism in contemporary social research. They share an assumed deterministic model, isolated from the general culture, composed of dependent and independent variables. The usual project is to identify and measure the variables in the system, so that causal relations may be uncovered. The system invoked is often the female body, and the aim is to isolate the crucial variables involved in its ability to achieve in sport. Where the system invoked is the body *plus* its social and cultural location, the uneasy aim is simply to add another few variables on to the chain, and identify, with scientific rigour, that such and such cultural factors are ultimately responsible for particular levels of sports performance.

However, this linear determinism will not do if we are interested in the social meaning of a phenomenon. I mean, for instance, that to know, more exactly, why it is that women can muster only 90 per cent of a man's strength cannot help us to comprehend, explain, or change the massive feeling in our society that a woman has no business flexing her muscles anyway.

Even if one could identify all the 'variables' at play in a national culture one would end up with such a vast number that it would be quite impossible to plot co-variation and determination. Secondly, in dealing with cultural meaning we are crucially concerned with the *nature* of symbolic systems, social attitudes and cultural values, and there is no way to qualify this. Thirdly, and perhaps most importantly, it is impossible to think of cultural processes in a linear way. It is not the case that there is a culture over here that affects sport over there, in a simple one-way relationship. The understanding of interrelationship and interconnection is

of the essence if we are even to set the right questions.
Sport is influenced by the state of the general society,
and reflects that society. Sport, in its turn, influences,
and for the most part reinforces, that society. Furthermore, we cannot conceptualise society as a great monolithic
entity, with a protuberance - sport - stuck on the outside.
The society, itself, is nothing but a layered complex of
elements all intricately and dialectically interrelated
with each other.

I should like to propose a very different approach to
women in sport: that of analytic cultural criticism.
This approach is different because it is concerned with
meaning, and values, and social explanation, without
attempting positivistic rigour. It accepts differences
in sports performance between men and women, accepts that
cultural factors may well enlarge this gap, but is *most*
interested in the manner in which this gap is understood
and taken up into the popular consciousness of our society.
In this perspective the fact of biological difference is
incontrovertible, (4)but it is an 'inert' fact, socially
speaking, until we have explained the colossal social
interest in it. After all there are many factual
differences facing us in the social world, some people
are short, others tall, some fat, some thin, some have
blue eyes, others brown, some have black skins, some
white, some people speak with deep voices, others with
high. The analytic socio-cultural task is not to
measure these differences precisely and explain them
physically, but to ask *why* some differences, and not
others, are taken as so important, become so exaggerated,
are used to buttress social attitudes or prejudice.
What activates these 'inert' facts, then, is the business
of critical qualitative analysis - why do people *think*
a particular difference is important, how do they *use*
the difference, is this use related at all to a general
system of attitudes and beliefs: to ideology?

The course of this article is briefly to identify
some of the basic characteristics of how sport is seen
in our society, and then to take a preliminary and
necessarily perhaps impressionistic view of how the area
is inflected through 'patriarchal' ideology in our popular
views of the specific area of women in sport. After a
'theoretical detour ' - a general abstract view of how
ideology 'invades' commonsense understanding - some of
the specific mechanisms will be analysed of how this
general ideological view of the physical inferiority and
'femaleness' of gender is implanted in 'commonsense' views
of women in sport, thereby reinforcing particular notions
of women in sport as well as more general notions concerning female genderedness.

THE SOCIAL AND PATRIARCHAL CHARACTER OF SPORT

Sport in general seems to be freer and more voluntary than other activities. It is away from the productive process and away from the family. Though participation and interest is, of course, deeply structured by age, class, gender and race, the fact that its site of operation is structurally separate from the main domains of 'necessity' (waged work for men, domestic *and* waged work for women) seem to confer upon it (and in some ways really does) a freedom not enjoyed in those areas.

And in one very simple straightforward way sport's basis in physical activity and movement does provide a real materialism of expression and freedom because the body and its movement are prescribed by quite freely humanly made rules and methods – not by the 'dull compulsion' of the workplace or the cloying blackmail of the home (which bears, though unequally, on both sexes). It seems to be, one might paraphrase, activity for activity's sake. It is also a field of relative simplicity, where right and wrong, good and bad, are taken to be easily identified. One expects greater strength, or skill, to bring commensurate rewards in sport. It is the area where the apparently unpredictable chance of normal living intervenes least between ability and achievement. The regulation enquiries between sportscasters turn on 'Was it a fair result?' The very fact that so much sports commentary is concerned with who 'deserved' to win, goes to demonstrate the overwhelming expectation of simple physical justice. In some ways sport provides the morality drama of our electronic age: the ideal expression of unfettered social relations – not worker against manager but player against player.

But this apparent freedom and separate internal life of sport evaporate when we come to women in sport. We realise at once that our ideal description above is a *male* description concerning males. Where women become at all visible, then the terms of reference change. There is a very important thread in popular consciousness which sees the very presence of women in sport as bizarre. Frequently, reporting of women's sport takes its fundamental bearings, not on sport, but on humour, or the unusual. The tone is easy to recognise, it's a version of the irony, the humour, the superiority, of the sophisticated towards the cranks – the UFO believers, the end-of-the-world disciples on the mountain top. Dr Johnson's hackneyed old phrase cries out to be released in new ways again and again, 'It's like a dog standing on its

hind legs. It is not well done - rather one is surprised
to see it attempted at all.'

The fundamental anxiety seems to be that men and women
have to be continuously differentiated; male preserves
continuously guaranteed. One way of emphasising this is
to promote laughter or cynicism when females take to the
field, another way is (cf. Bobby Riggs) to set out to
prove incontrovertibly that women are inferior through
direct challenge. Another way is to draw attention to
unarguable physical differences out of context. In a
'Daily Mirror' article (5) there is an excellent example
of this. In the photograph accompanying the text the
female athlete is actually shown with her baby in the
background. Even in the case of a successful athlete
you see at a glance that she is different from men,
defined essentially by sex rather than athletics, and
perhaps even a freak for being able to have a baby and
be successful in sport.

Games and sports played by women could be judged
purely for themselves, without reference, all the time,
to what are taken as the absolute values, the only
yardstick, of achievement - *male* achievement. And
furthermore, the wide spread of characteristics through
both sexes, the considerable overlap of the spectrum of
physical characteristics between men and women, and the
greater salience of fitness rather than gender (6) to
performance means that a team of high-ability women will
be better, even in so-called masculine qualities, than
a low-ability men's team. And yet, the meanest local
5th division, male works' team gets more respect, in
popular consciousness, than a women's national team.

Another powerful way in which the sexual identity is
given precedence over the sport's identity of female
athletes is the vein of sexual innuendo running through
much sports commentary. The male may comfortably suppose
that even if the sports woman affronts him on the field
of play, at least she likes 'a bit of the other' in another
field of play. Sometimes the women themselves are
guilty parties to this, and collude with being 'sexy'
and 'attractive' at the same time as being sportswomen.
In such ways the female athlete is rendered a sex
object - a body which may excel in sport, but which is
primarily an object of pleasure for man. A useful
technique, for if a woman seems to be encroaching too
far, and too threateningly, into male sanctuaries, she
can be symbolically vapourised and reconstituted as an
object, a butt for smutty jokes and complacent elbow
nudging.

It is also clear that sport is strongly associated with

the male identity, with being popular and having friends. Rugby and football are archetypal here. We imagine men to be at their most gregarious, expansive and relaxed in the pub after the match. It's not hard to see that the stereotype, 'I'd like-to-be-with-them' males of the beer adverts, 'if you can't beat them join them', are really rugby or football players. Achievement particularly strengthens male identity; it is assumed that sports success *is* success at being masculine. Physical achievement, and masculine activity, are taken to be the same.

When we think of women in sport, the situation is entirely contrary. One thinks of female athletes as alone - there is no popular image of back-slapping in the pub afterwards. Indeed there is an important element in the popular response to the female athlete, of uncertainty before the deviant, distrust of the strange, dislike of the marginal. As the athlete becomes even more outstanding, she marks herself out as even more deviant. Instead of confirming her identity, success can threaten her with a foreign male identity. In so far as she is affected by popular consciousness - and she can hardly ignore it - the female athlete lives through a severe contradiction. To succeed as an athlete can be to fail as a woman, because she has, in certain profound symbolic ways, become a man. Indeed, in certain areas it is not only a symbolic power she faces. The demand for sex tests on female athletes shows us the power of the suspicion - 'if she's successful, she's a man'. A moment's reflection that no male athlete lives this painful contradiction of success-being-failure-really, to say nothing of this failure being physically tested, throws up for us once again the severe interest which sport manifests in differentiating the sexes.

Ironically, even in those sports like ice skating and gymnastics, in which girls and young women excel and are publicly acclaimed, sex-role differences are further clarified. Success is to do with fitting the youthful, lithe, nubile, stereotypically 'perfect' popular image of femininity.

I want to suggest that what we have been considering is an ideological inflection of our basic social characterisation of sport. How does ideology gain an entrance here? (7)

IDEOLOGY AND COMMON SENSE

Ideology for our purposes here can be understood as the

process of legitimation, in its different forms, within
all existing societies, whereby a certain social
organisation - most pertinent for us the patriarchal
relations of the family and society - system of order
and power, and access to reward is constituted as the
only possible, or the only fair, pattern of human
relations. Crucially it can only achieve this by
dissembling its own nature. If it does not succeed in
this it may be transparently seen as a dominating interest
and may be obeyed only through physical coercion. Unless
ideology, in its deepest character, can induce assent to
itself, it is only the manifesto of a group that has
power over others.

We can only understand this 'dissembling' nature of
ideology if we realise that the general notion of
ideology is an abstraction, and that ideology proper
exists only through its manifestations at the level of
apparently concrete circumstance within the zone of
common sense, within what is taken to be reality. In
order to find a starting point, it is necessary to posit
the abstraction of ideology and to indicate its essential
parameters, but unless we can show how this abstraction
is taken up as the real in the social world, we shall
have done nothing more than point to a manifesto.

I should like to represent the operation of ideology
in three stages. Though I can only describe them
sequentially and separately, they should be thought of
as simultaneous, mutually dependent and reinforcing
elements of continuing process. These three stages are:
(a) the ideological force of definition, (b) the re-
interpretation of discrepancies in social sub-regions,
(c) the located rebirth of ideology.

In the first instance I posit an ideological content,
a general account of what the ideology 'says', as if
indeed it were a manifesto. In our own society this
would be something like the importance of work, the
justice of meritocratic advancement as well as, of course,
the natural superiority and aggressiveness of men coupled
with the weakness and caring/emotional nature of women.
Essentially these 'contents' are beliefs about the nature
of reality, and can only be upheld if reality seems to
comply with them. We must of course be extremely
sceptical of 'reality's' ability to speak for itself, to
confirm beliefs held about it. Rather we must recognise
that belief seeks to define reality, to find in reality
what will satisfy itself, and to neutralise or change
what seems to contradict itself. The content of our
general notion (abstraction) of ideology, then, is
basically a powerful force of definition seeking its own
reflection from reality in order to confirm itself.

Now there are competing forces of definition in all the sub-regions that make up society, and the individuals and groups inhabiting every area of the culture have their own at least partially independent forms of understanding and living their own immediate environments that won't immediately yield to an outside version of what is happening to them.

To follow up some of our previous examples: factory workers do not always believe in the 'work ethic' and may seek ways to control and limit production; (8) working class students often realise that success does not seem to depend on merit but more on class, accent and wealth; (9) women know that in many situations they can be more dominant, able and hard-headed than men. But I have argued that ideology can only exist precisely if it can embody itself in the concrete common sense of the actors in such sub-regions. This embodiment, I suggest, is likely to take place in areas of discrepancy within these sub-regions, that is in areas which the immediate forms of understanding have not already been taken up into their own definitional field of force. One way of conceiving this was mentioned at the beginning - the 'inert' fact, an aspect of reality which is visible but not yet taken up into a system of belief. Another way is to regard it as a mismatch felt within particular experiential sub-systems, felt *discrepancies* which the actors involved are puzzled by and cannot adequately account for. In such areas the countervailing local forces of definition are not strong enough to resist ideological forces, and the 'unknown quantity' can be interpreted globally by ideology for its own purposes - can be used to embody general beliefs in a located social example.

To resume our examples: factory workers may not like work but they know that some form of production is necessary to support human life, resistance to work does not account for this and so the capitalist logic and organisation of production can be 'naturalised' as the only possible one so that capital can proclaim on its own behalf 'if you don't work, you don't eat'. Working-class students might know the importance of class, wealth and accent to success, but they also confusingly recognise that the 'successful' seem also to have those 'qualifications' which they find it so hard to obtain. This is difficult for them to explain, but meritocracy can proclaim 'advance through merit for all in our education system'. Women may know their own real competence and power in some situations but they are also the ones who must leave work to bear children. They can also be physically beaten up or raped by men. Patriarchy strides in to this physical territory to claim superiority in general in all social and cultural fields.

There has been another simplification of course in suggesting that 'inert' facts or social discrepancies are just lying idly by waiting for a more powerful mistress than their local ones. In fact they have always been in a state of having been interpreted, since to have remained uninterpreted is to have remained invisible to social meanings. However, to separate them artificially for a moment from the manner of their cultural investment at least shows the theoretical potential for the incursion of ideological meaning into located social sub-regions.

An important consequence of this incursion is that apparently concrete instances can be used for general legitimations that are quite distinct from the inherent logic of the particular social sub-regions from which they came. Examples can be quoted out of context to support more global versions of reality which may even contradict the organising perspective of the system from which the example is taken. In the modern era of tele-communications, and a central societal consensus based on information provided by the mass media, such out-of-context citations are commonplace and the most important mechanism for allowing the illusion of a central and agreed normative value system. The media could never succeed in presenting their unifying consensual vision of social reality unless it can be continually embodied in a wealth of concrete news items. Television, as the purveyor of the ultimate concrete image, has greatly augmented this process. The contextual disengagement practised by the media certainly gives news reporting a reassuring continuity and feeling of straightforward reasonableness, but for those involved in the real events which are being reported there is a characteristic, if muted, sense of colossal misinterpretation. The continuity of real events has been sacrificed in the media to the continuity of much larger myths about the real. The profound needs of society to embed its ideology in empirical reality totally overrides the participants of particular scenarios, even renders their own reality unintelligible to them, in the interests of a larger coherency, a larger version of social reality.

The distribution of this ideological penetration is most uneven, and a further cause for the rage of the participant actors. There are a number of factors accounting for the degree of penetration of a certain area. The relative powers of definition are always changing within a particular sub-region, and a particular

definition of an element of social reality is never won
outright.   There is always uncertainty and the sway of
real events may transform the ability of the various
actors to reclaim areas of meanings. Furthermore the
various social sub-regions vary greatly in their capacity
to be usefully invaded by ideology. An area that seems
to exhibit great apparent autonomy is a prime candidate:
for instance the areas of the 'natural' or the biological
are enormously important to ideology, they seem quite
free from human manipulation, and apparently self-
determined, the most basic form of external reality.
If an example can be won here it offers the ideal
opportunity for the embodiment of ideology in the real.
The plea to common sense is 'why, even in that separate
area the same things are true!'

Even though a particular social sub-region may not
offer the advantage of being apparently autonomous it
may still be a frequent ideological target if its values
and norms in some way impinge on an important principle
of ideology. If the particular area throws up values or
definitions which challenge ideological beliefs, the
field clearly has to be contested. Even if ideology
cannot totally submerge itself as common sense, it can
at least forward plausible suggestions for the reinter-
pretation of events. Ideology can never afford to let
contradictory interpretations of reality go free from
at least a crippling ambiguity. At the other extreme,
sub-systems that produce definitions of the real which
run parallel to ideological definitions are clear
candidates for insurgency. Again, though the meanings
derived from such areas may not always have the
unquestioned hallmark of the real, or the undetermined,
they may all add to a gathering weight of a certain
version of reality. It's all cash in the bank of a
growing deposit of the 'obvious'.

This investment with ideological meaning of disputed
elements in local social systems does not however, fully
account for the ideological process. The real dynamic
is supplied to the system in our third stage, where the
concrete social elements invested with ideology take on
an ideological life of their own, and give a genuine
rebirth to those beliefs with which they have been
invested. This rebirth comes about because the local
social actors surrounding an element that has been
'ideologised' do not remain neutral to it - social life
is of course continuous and always monitoring and
adapting its meanings and actions to its social and
cultural environment. Within this reaction lies the
basis for the rebirth of ideology (in fact the only real

manifestation) in concrete reality. It does not matter
whether this reaction is positive or negative so long as
the underlying definition of the situation is accepted.
Within this response any reaction short of a wholesale
counter-redefinition accepts the incursive ideological
meaning and inducts elements of that meaning into the
system as a whole. Frequently the immediate response of
the actors involved will be one of opposition, but the
opposition, unless it is extremely self-aware, can only
take up the issue in the terms within which it has been
offered, the terms which render the phenomenon apparently
concrete and real. The reaction of the local actors,
then, though hostile to the surface forms of the penetration, in fact gives completely new life to the underlying
definitional power of the ideology. To take certain
questions up is already to have given up the right to
challenge the epistemological foundations of those
questions. The 'battle' so to speak, is conceded as
soon as it is started, *by* starting it. If the local
cultural participants do not attempt to challenge the
immediate apparent issue, and have no other account of
reality, then they have no choice but to collude in the
ideological definition of what confronts them. They may
well be puzzled and uncertain as to quite why they are
behaving in such and such a way but they have in fact
given a mute rebirth to the ideology. They are living
the ideology in that social area because they have no
other voice to speak with, they act in the only mode that
is open. They have conceded the battle without even
realising that there was a 'battle'. These points may
become clearer by example, one of a 'battle' apparently
fought, and another of no 'battle' at all. In both cases
I will point to what would have been successful grounds
for repelling ideological 'invasion'.

Trade union opposition to employers which is couched
in the form of a demand for more money accepts the
legitimacy, and gives new life to the legitimacy, of
wage labour in general. Even the most vociferous and
militant demands for more money, which seem on the
surface to challenge the functioning of the capitalist
economy, at a deeper level underwrite more forcefully
the legitimacy of the market economy and its exchange
values. Union activity could only directly challenge
the capitalist system if it challenged the terms on which
workers are rewarded at all, and offered an alternative
account of how the workers could be related to their
product. (10)

To take the very different area of crime and deviance,
so long as the miscreant herself makes excuses for her

misdeeds, she is powerfully supporting the normative
structure of the main society. For to make excuses for
her conduct (perhaps for no other reason than to attract
a more lenient sentence) accepts the whole definition,
recreates the definition, which first defined her behaviour
as antisocial. The criminals or deviants who are truly
a threat to the 'fabric of society' are the ones who place
their own definitions across their acts and find them
just. It is no accident that such defendants frequently
claim the status of political prisoners; the belief
system which is strong enough to counter the ideological
definition of their actions must be well supported by a
complex political analysis of society and its internecine
unequal struggle to define reality.

It is not the case, then, that located actors are
doomed carriers of ideology. A sufficiently strong
repossession of the definition of the situation can
reverse the process. But by and large we can see that
particular actors in local social areas who are not armed
with an analysis, will always struggle in the obvious
way. If they are told they are asking for too much
money they will reply that they deserve what they get,
if they are told that they are evil, they will reply,
'please forgive me'. By not challenging the basic terms
of the exchange, they will have given rebirth to the
legitimacy of defining the whole situation in terms of
money or evil.

The argument at this third stage is that the ideologically imbued concrete elements of particular social sub-
regions take on a life of their own, and produce
spontaneously the essential elements of ideology. This
is the manner of the continuing life of ideology in the
commonsense realm of the concrete. If we can accept
the continuous complex functioning of this process in
all the diverse areas of our social life, we can see that
what we take to be the general force of ideology is only
ever a set of continually reconstituted beliefs and
definitions occurring in empirical circumstances.

PATRIARCHAL IDEOLOGY AND SPORT

If we trace our three processes of ideology through women
in sport we shall see just what a fertile and unsuspecting
field there is here for the legitimation of a certain
dominant version of social reality. Taking as our
starting point the general belief that the sexes are
innately different, and males superior, we can posit a
powerful force of definition seeking confirmation in

social sub-regions. The area of sport generally offers
itself as an important target because of its apparent
autonomy. Sport is just itself and part of the ideologically important area of the 'natural'. If evidence can
be found here for ideological belief, then it will have
the cache of the real, it will be admirably suited to
citation out of context. But within this already
privileged zone there is the further sub-region of women
in sport which can offer the bonus of biological, and
apparently incontrovertible differences between the sexes
once the question of sexual comparison arises. Now
within the local terms of reference - those women involved
in sports performance - this biological difference is
noted as discrepancy, but is not necessarily mobilised
as the main definition of their social reality in that
region. Their main social reality is presumably connected
with sport for its own sake, and the frustrations and
hopes of that world: for its own enjoyment and meaning.
But ideology can claim biological discrepancy fully for
its own: to present cultural legitimations as biological
factors. There is the tailormade opportunity for
transforming ideological belief into an aspect of
concrete reality at the plane of common sense. The fact
that no one can deny female difference becomes the fact
of female sports inferiority, becomes the fact that
females are innately different from men, becomes the fact
that women who stray across the defining boundary are in
a parlous state. An ideological view comes to be
deposited in our culture as a commonsense assumption -
'of course women are different and inferior'.

Looking at the third stage of the ideological process,
the situation of women in sport offers even more to
ideological development. For local cultural participants,
the sportswomen, unarmed with a counter-definitional
force of their own, either immediately collude with the
ideological definitions (the female athlete conspiring
to be sexy with the news reporter) or take up the
challenge totally within the terms of the preferred
ideological definition (the angered sportswoman setting
out to prove male equivalence in her sport's performance).
In many cases the latter is even preferable to collusion,
since it makes the case so much more visible, and so
eminently suited to citation out of context. One can
think of many examples: Billie Jean King's response to
Bobby Riggs is an archetypical example here - not least
because she won.

The popular press abounds with examples of how
ideological definitions can seek to take over and highlight
apparent biological differences to thus render the meaning

of women in sport in a specific way - as a commentary on, and therefore reinforcement and reproduction of, gender differences in our society. The clearest move here is when 'sports stories' leave their home at the back of the tabloids and find their way into the centre spread and the general 'human interest', titillating or unusual category. A story concerning female weight-lifting in the 'Sun' (11) is headed 'Building up a Body Beautiful' and 'Muscle Misses' and most of the copy concerns not their sports identity but their gender identity. The male trainer is reported as saying that most women take up weight-lifting to improve their figures and to achieve 'that Raquel Welch look - wide shoulders, slim waist and hips and firm, high breasts'. The story concludes with the vignette of how one woman's weight-lifting career had repaired her marriage - now she could train alongside her re-united weight-lifting husband. No male weight-lifter could face this confusion of his sport and his personal sexual life. The only alternative reading given is that in so far as the sport is taken seriously for itself, then the women become masculinised 'swinging weights which most men could scarcely lift', and give up much that is normal in a female life. Furthermore, the motivation for this apparently, again, concerns the archetypal negation of supposed female qualities and the inflation of supposed male qualities - 'I took up body-building because I didn't want to be a passive, weak, dependent female'. Clearly, it's the unspoken 'good' to be aggressive and strong. Guess of which sex that is the general social specification! These are the basic news value of the story: (a) the unusualness, the dog on its hind-legs-ness, of women lifting weights and becoming 'muscly' (hence the liberal use of photo-graphs), (b) through this strangeness, either the lengths to which women will go to *attract* men, or the lengths to which they will go to *emulate* men. Either way, men, and what they stand for, reign supreme. An original ideological definition has framed 'the experience' of female weight-lifting in a certain fashion and the (at least reported) responses of the women - given no doubt the immediate framing of the interview to which they're subjected - either collude in the sexualisation of the topic or reinforce the standards of male comparison used in the original definition.

Researchers and positivist enquiry also bear some responsibility here, since they so often take it as their task to *explain* differences in performance - thereby dignifying that difference. Sometimes they offer a base for closing the gap between male and female sports

performance. To accept that it is a worthwhile endeavour
to push female performance closer to that of a male, even
surpass it, admits at a stroke the stigma of femininity
and the legitimacy of that male eminence which coined the
standards. So no matter how the actual physical gap is
closed, there is an equal and opposite reaction which
expands the cultural and ideological resonance of that
gap. It creates anew the frame of reference in which,
and by which, the gap was measured in the first place.
By accepting the terms of the ideological definition,
the attempt to approach male performance levels, in fact
strengthens popular prejudice about femininity. It
creates an expanding bank of the obvious examples of
female 'inferiority', which in their turn aid the ideological imbuement of other areas of society, as well
as the discrediting of values associated with femininity.
Meanwhile male values are firmly established at the
natural 'centre-stage' of life and judgment.

The response of the participants in the area of women
in sport and of the researchers of positivist academics
may, therefore, produce profound and unintended
consequences, and actually exacerbate the processes which
in the first place brought unwelcome attention.

Some recent work seems to be at odds, somewhat, with
the drift of this analysis. (12) The 'biological gap'
or the 'inert fact' of female inferiority in sports
performance may be much less than is popularly suggested.
The 'fitness' factor far outweighs the sex factor and
it is now suggested that in some sports, namely swimming
and long-distance running, women could actually outperform
men - even in the traditional 'hard' male qualities of
performance and time. The addition of such success to an
accepted female capacity for greater skilfulness and
artistry, say in things like dancing and gymnastics,
could offer the prospect of a direct physical challenge
to ideologies of male ascendancy.

It should be noted still, however, that the biological
arguments continue to indicate greater male powers in
direct strength and high-oxygen-needing 'explosive'
activity.

Such suggestions perhaps make it necessary to specify
and differentiate this analysis more. It may well be
that a strong sporting or feminist frame of definitions
could focus on certain kinds of female sports performance
and argue for success or superiority here as a *general*
claim to defeat simplistic, across-the-board notions
about male superiority. This is, in a way, precisely
strengthening the countervailing local force of definition
of 'inert items' to struggle against the trivialisation

and ideological incorporation of more general views about
gender. There does seem scope for serious and dignified
mobilisation here.

On the other hand we should not forget the massive and
important area of popular culture and consciousness and
its relation to sports reporting and activity. On the one
hand we may expect the relative downgrading of sports in
which women do excel with a further inflation of speed
and strength in sport. On the other hand we should not
underestimate the sense in which even success in some
areas of sport may be *popularly* presented as the success
of male standards in which, now, some women 'happen' to
be represented. This would reinforce those notions of
competition, effort and measurement which, for instance,
are still likely massively to turn young women off sport
(13) in general, and to make the 'ideological choices'
of successful but non-radicalised athletes and performers
still more wretched: either they conspire to be 'feminine'
under the even bigger contradictions of their now superior
performance, or they accept an even stronger cultural
definition of their inbuilt masculinity.

So much depends again on definition, and the relation
between a cultural and biological definition of gender.
If for sports women and feminists, physical performance
can be properly posed not simply as a challenge to
biological definitions but to a wholesale cultural
definition, specifically to invalidate the basis of a
cultural definition, then excellence in sport may be an
important antidote to popular culture. But it must be
remembered that this culture/biology relationship is anyway
a variable and constructed one - a relationship of
relative autonomy. Definitions are not tied to individuals
- only to stereotypes. The cultural definition can give
up, even thrive on, many individual exceptions: the
'exceptions that prove the rule'. These general specifi-
cations of 'maleness' might be strengthened by a few
well-publicised examples of a few women *meeting* them.
A concession, or a little more commonality between the
physical attributes of the sexes, can easily be met anyway
by the power of other aspects of the cultural definition -
that to behave in that 'masculine' way denies what is most
valuable about the other intrinsic aspects of being female.
Heroic sports success amongst a few women - without a
massive, corresponding ideological battle to change the
field of force of meaning - will not lead to greater
participation regularly in schools and sports centres by
girls and women, nor to a liberation in their sense of
gender. A particular notion of masculine standards may,
paradoxically, be reproduced and further 'negative' examples
of femininity made regularly available.

CONCLUSION

In the general terms of my analysis I would like tentatively to suggest that the culturally effective way for sports women (and others) to counter their role as the unwilling victims in a larger legitimation of belief about the nature of sexes is to offer much more strongly their own version of sports reality which undercuts altogether the issues of male supremacy and the standards which measure it. In some ways such a view would be rooted in part, not in the *negation* of popular images about women, but in a selective reinforcement of some of their strengths. I mean that sport could be presented as a form of activity which emphasises human similarity and not dissimilarity, a form of activity which isn't competitive and measured, a form of activity which expresses values which are indeed unmeasurable, a form of activity which is concerned with individual well-being and satisfaction rather than with comparison. In such a view of sport, differences between the sexes would be unimportant, unnoticed. We wouldn't have the measures to realise that there was difference, or to be able to base conferences, or research projects, on measured differences - there would not be the fuel to supply popular consciousness with its prejudices about femininity.

If such a counter-definition of sport could be mounted, and it's here that research might play a more helpful role, then there would be the possibility of influencing society in the positive direction of challenging received ideas about the nature of men and women. As it is we must pessimistically conclude that, for the most part and for the moment, the responses of women involved in sport, sports reporting and most of the research done on sport, have been a force for reaction. They have been trapped in ideology.

NOTES

1 For the classic reference on hegemony and common sense, see A. Gramsci, 'Prison Notebooks', Lawrence & Wishart, London, 1973.
2 See J. Brohm, 'Sport: A Prison of Measured Time', Ink Links, London, 1978.
3 See S. Cohen and J. Young (eds), 'The Manufacture of News: Deviance, Social Problems and the Mass Media', Constable, London, 1973; and J. Ditton, 'Controlology: Beyond the New Criminology', Macmillan, London, 1979.

4 It is clear that one cannot propose an absolute 'gap'
   here. It is changeable subject to effort/training,
   and can in some sports operate to the advantage of
   women. I deal with the 'cultural' implications of
   this at the end of the article. See A. White, Sportswomen and society, in 'Report of the Langham Life 1st
   International Conference on Women in Sport', published
   by the Central Council of Physical Recreation, 1978.
5 'Daily Mirror', 20 July 1973.
6 See A. White, op.cit.
7 The focus here is necessarily limited to the operation
   of ideology as lived experience in particular concrete
   areas, and does not attempt to outline a general
   theory of ideology and its connections with social
   and material relations.
8 See P. Willis, Shop floor culture, masculinity and
   the wage form, in C. Critcher et al. (eds), 'Working
   Class Culture', London, Hutchinson, 1979.
9 See P. Willis, 'Learning to Labour', Farnborough,
   Gower Press, 1977.
10 This is, of course, a very limited and foreshortened
   view of trade union activity which misses very
   important elements of opposition and struggle in the
   whole, complex relation of trade unions to the working
   class. The purpose here is one of exemplification.
   This central case is used not to show the total
   incorporation of trade unions, but to show generally
   the deep, 'obvious' and organic structure of ideology.
11 'Sun' 'centre spread', 18 March 1980.
12 See note 4.
13 For a lively indication of just how far adolescent
   girls turn off from organised competitive sport,
   see M. Talbot, Girls' games - are they really
   worthwhile?, 'ILEA P.E. Journal', Summer 1974.

Chapter 6

Sport and youth culture

David Robins

Mass spectator sport in Britain increasingly resembles a
branch of capitalist showbusiness. Soccer and motor-
cycle racing, to take the two most popular examples, are
heavily marketed as 'entertainment', and are watched by
an adoring and overwhelmingly youthful population.   On
the terrace, at the track - the sports stadium is the
place for people to be diverted from the 'real' problems
into a spectacular dream world of glamour and excitement.
(1)   But there is another side to the picture ...
   Fortunately the lessons people learn from sport are
not always the ones that promoters, coaches, or the media
seek to impart. The following is an everyday scene
from a working-class housing estate:

   Despite the sign NO BALL GAMES, every evening
   improvised games of football would be played out
   on the courtyards and bare patches of grass around
   the Monmouth and Denby estates. Kids of all ages,
   shapes and sizes would take part in these, often
   in platform heels, smart jackets or tight trousers.
   Rules, playing area, goals, team numbers were all
   negotiable. What was harder to negotiate was the
   co-operation of the tenants. The broken windows,
   noise and disturbance caused by these games were
   amongst the biggest source of complaints that the
   Tenants Association Committee was called upon to
   deal with. Invariably such matches would end in
   heated confrontations with angry tenants and the
   police being called.

      Such casual disruptive exertions of physical
   energy tended to be seen by school coaches and youth
   club men as little more than self-generating rituals
   practised by the kids as they are supposed to have
   done since time immemorial. Part of the local
   scenery. Quite different from the mini-professional

training, coaching and adult-controlled sporting
discipline as practised in club and school soccer.
As one coach put it: 'There's very little
competitiveness, very little possessiveness, on or
off the ball, when they play in the street. They
just get pleasure from making the ball move from one
to another in a certain way, or just mucking about
or showing off. But without any real energy put
into it. In the youth club there's a lot more real
fire goes into it ... mind you, if I left them in
the gym by themselves, if I wasn't there to watch
them, they'd play like that ...' Indeed, exactly
the same kids would play these two styles out. (2)
The above example shows how young people resist
regimentation or manipulation more effectively in sport
than in many other activities. Games learned and
appreciated in youth exert their own demands and inspire
loyalty to the game itself, rather than to the programmes
that the bureaucracy that controls sport, not to mention
media and business interests, seek to impose on them. (3)

The notion that capitalism has created sport in its
own image (4) makes no allowance for the relative
autonomy of cultural traditions. In sport, such
traditions, from improvised street games to being a
dedicated soccer supporter, are handed down from one
generation to another, and have never been completely
assimilated into the commercial sports spectacle.

To illustrate the relative autonomy of sports culture
and its history, and to underline its primarily accommodative nature, I shall survey briefly the rich variety
of interests and identification around four sports of
particular appeal to male working youth - speedway,
road racing (motor-cycle racing), boxing and football.

In the inter-war years motor sports held an extraordinary fascination for 'England's best sons', who
found themselves out of place in post-great-war
bourgeois society. For ex-public-school romantics like
Henry Segrave and the Campbells, motor sports were the
'last great adventure' in a middle-class world dedicated
to work, routine and limited achievements. The real
pride of the bike rider was 'that he no longer counts
as an end in himself, but only if he sacrifices himself
completely to the Great God of Speed.... I had pushed
my go-cart into the eternal stream, and it went faster
than the ones that are pushed cross-stream or upstream',
wrote T.E. Lawrence in 1928, recalling his fantastic
adventures as Lawrence of Arabia. Back in London, in
despair, he would try to find a substitute for the
'self-satisfaction' of being a secret agent of British

imperialism influencing the course of world history,
and found he could only get it out of 'hot speed on a
motor bike'. (5) And in the 1930s, the White City
speedway track in London boasted the incognito visits
of one of its most fervent aristocratic admirers, the
future King George VI.

The story of how motor bikes rose from such illustri-
ous patronage to become the supreme post-war symbol of
disaffected, rebellious youth without a cause need not
concern us here. The past two decades, however, have
seen a rise in the juvenile standard of living, and a
rapidly expanded market for relatively cheap, reliable
Japanese bikes. The bike sub-culture ghettoes, created
in the 1950s and 1960s still survive - bands of
provincial Hell's Angels still defy the moral standards
of the 'grey flannel dwarf' society. But their over-
publicised activities are very much a sideshow to the
main bike scene. For today, motor-cycle sports in
Britain command the allegiances and mobilise the
aspirations of quite massive sections of 'respectable'
lower-middle-class and working-class youth.

The popularity of off-road, countryside-based
disciplines such as motor-x (scrambling), trials, enduro,
and drag racing have all grown dramatically in recent
years, while big meets in the road race Grand Prix or
British League speedway calendar can attract audiences
running into tens of thousands.

SPEEDWAY

Speedway is Britain's second-biggest spectator sport
(next to football). It is also, surprisingly, its
most popular summer sport. From March to October, on
over forty tracks up and down the country, it is a
weekly way of life for many.

The rules of speedway are very simple. 'Up to four
riders race to execute at speed a series of tight turns
on a loose surface for three or four laps of an enclosed
track'. To the uninitiated speedway can seem repetitive
and monotonous. The bikes are all identical (Czech Jawa
500s or British Weslakes - no gears or brakes, controlled
entirely from the throttle). They are like bats in
cricket, merely tools. Technical advances are discounted.
To anyone interested solely in bikes, speedway must be
especially boring, since the machines bear no relation
to anything one can ride on the road.

But this uniformity of machinery and race format means
that speedway is a deliberate test of rider skill, a pure

demonstration of the technical expertise of riding.
Although organised in this country much like soccer,
with league and cup competitions, individual excellence
is paramount. Bluey Wilkinson, Ove Fundin, Split
Waterman, Barry Briggs, Ivan Mauger, Ole Olsen – it is
great foreign riders, rather than the English teams they
rode for, that are remembered and become legend. The
speedway racer, whether native or foreign, is essentially
a lone star. That special mix of 'bottle' and manual
dexterity with which he masters both machine and
opposition is especially appreciated by working–class
audiences. Before the war support for 'the game' centred
on London, Birmingham and Manchester. Today, followers
are scattered around numerous small provincial towns, as
well as cities. Kings Lynn, Exeter, Swindon, Poole,
Norwich and Ipswich all have strong teams, loyally
supported. On away–match visits they will often be
accompanied by quite fanatical groups of supporters
complete with their own songs, chants and colours. Yet
fighting between rival fans is virtually unknown. This
has not always been the case. The immediate post–war
years were a freak boom time for speedway. In 1946 a
staggering six million attended meetings. In the early
1950s, sections of the huge crowds of fifty or sixty
thousand who flocked to the White City or Belle Vue had
a reputation similar to part of the soccer crowds today.
Teddy boy gang warfare, the odd fatal stabbing with a
flick knife – such incidents became associated with
speedway in the 1950s, just as skinhead aggro became
associated with the soccer 'ends' of the late 1960s.
But the teddy boys never seized the speedway stadium
as their public platform, a visible stage, as the skins
were to do behind the goals at football. Of course,
they were not helped by the media, who have always tended
to ignore speedway. But also speedway, then and now,
is predominantly a family entertainment which attracts
a great many women of all ages and lots of children.
Today, some of the descendants of those early hellraisers
of the 1950s can be seen, at Hackney stadium in the
east end of London for example, rocker mothers and
fathers, with their children, side by side with groups
of new rockers, punks, and leather kids. Speedway may
be repetitive as a spectacle, but this is more than
compensated for by the friendly, family atmosphere that
prevails at meetings, out of the glare of the big
sporting commercial interests and sensation–hungry
television cameras. It is a sport, as one writer has
noted, 'lacking in cynicism, snobbishness, free of
gambling' (6) and one might add, free of aggro. The

speedway stadium is one place at least where working-
class youth and parents find common ground and display
a visibly peaceful co-existence.

GRAND PRIX

Road racing is the only other motor sport that rivals
speedway for mass popularity. Grand Prix (World
Championship) meets at Silverstone, Brands Hatch or
Oulton Park, can attracts crowds of 150,000. Most fans
own bikes and over half will travel to the meets on
them. Often they camp out overnight. The vast huddle
of bikes, sleeping bags, tents and trailers, ensures
that the atmosphere before a big race is more like an
open-air rock music festival than a sports event. Grand
prix racing is highly commercial. Every inch of bike,
track and rider is plastered with advertising signs.
Big meets are showcases for new products. Unlike
speedway, technical innovation is everything in road
racing, and the audiences' attention is on the machines
every bit as much as on the riders. Of course, much of
the appeal of Grand Prix racing to the young is at a
fantasy level. There is much identification, often
near-fatal over-identification, with the exploits of
Barry Sheene, Kenny Roberts, Randy Mamola and their
flying Yamahas, Suzukis and Hondas. And also close
communication between riders and fans. Race winners
often show off by 'pulling wheelies' in front of the
stands. But this is also a highly technically informed
crowd. Fan allegiance is to manufacturer as well as
rider. After all, the machines the stars ride are only
more expensive versions of what the fans ride on the
road. So big meets generate much sophisticated 'bike
talk'. Talk of disc valves, and piston rings, and the
relative merits of different machines, predominates.
   Like speedway, violence is the exception rather than
the rule at road race meets, although serious trouble
has occurred recently when drinks and hot-dog salesmen
and other bogus concessionaires have been suspected of
ripping off the younger fans. At the smaller meets at
club level, the majority of watchers are involved in
some way with the competitors. Here the self-organised,
co-operative, grass-roots base of the sport is evident.
Lending spares, advising novices, is all part of the
informal economy that surrounds and underpins the sport.
Many afficionados work in the trade, as mechanics,
garage hands, or with motor-cycle dealers, and are
encouraged to compete by their employers. Factory teams

compete regularly in moto-x. Motor-cycle despatch firms
sponsor their own teams of riders to compete at club
level. A high level of technical expertise is expected
by all concerned. Tinkering with a bike is not just for
the benefit of competition, or one of the more narciss-
istic instances of youth culture. It demonstrates a
mastery over the means of production. A lot of the
workers at Meriden bike co-operative were themselves
bikers. In the bike scene, the distinction between
the producer and consumer is broken down and becomes
part of the collective skill of motor-cycle maintenance.
Finally, to dispel any impression of bikers as grease-
covered, anti-social rebels without a cause, here is a
rough portrait of some enthusiasts...

Four or five lads, 18-22, medium-long hair, clean
shaven, favour denims or nylon paddock jackets when
not wearing their leathers. All live near each
other in some outer city suburb such as Eltham.
One of the group is a mechanic with a local cycle
dealer, the rest are in clerical work, or apprenticed
in one of the manual trades. All have steady jobs -
they have to have! Almost their entire disposable
income is spent on 200 Yamahas, if learners, or 400
Yamahas if not. These most-prized possessions will
be painted up as pseudo road racers. 'Hard' lads,
but not particularly disposed to demonstrating their
physical prowess. Instead it is drink and 'soft'-
drug-filled evenings listening to 'heavy metal' rock
music such as Deep Purple, Status Quo or Thin Lizzie.
Heavy drinking nights in the pub are mainly taken
up with swapping tales of hair-raising experiences
on the road. Weekends, they all go to the meets
together, 'the steady girl friend' on the pillion.
Bikers have a reputation for being hyper-sexist, and
even a girl's own not inconsiderable skill on a bike
does little to alter her essentially one-down status
in this scene, as in so many areas of youth culture.
No sense here then, of any 'profane culture', that
'Wild Ones' image of the bike gangs of the 1960s,
terrorising the suburban world of dullness and respectability. All that has changed. Biking is a respectable,
thoroughly mainstream pursuit these days, with a hint
of smooth, up-market, working class heroes, as exemplified by Britain's former world 500cc champion Barry
Sheene.

In so far as the biking legions do represent a social
problem, a problem of 'deviancy', it is not because they
are running amock in gangs, but the hospital bills they
rack up. The risk of a motor-cycle rider being killed

or seriously injured is thirty times that for car
drivers. In all, road deaths account for nearly half of
all male deaths in the 15-19 age group and for more than
a third of all deaths among 20-24-year-olds. Many of
these casualties come from the ranks of the teenage
bikers.

THE FIGHT GAME

Professional boxing's gymnasia may be exclusively working-
class domains, but, like bike racing, support for, and
patronage of, the sport has more often resembled a
coalition that crosses class lines. In the early nineteenth century, an often uneasy alliance was forged
between 'fashionable' London society, the sporting element
among the provincial gentry, and the proletarian sporting
crowd, who combined to defend 'the noble art' against the
bourgeois advocates of sobriety and respectability. (7)
Latter-day middle-class campaigners for rational recreation
and the spirit of improvement can still be heard, condemn-
ing boxing as 'cruel', motor-cycle racing as 'dangerous',
and so on. (8) And the 'degenerate aristocrat' attach-
ments to these popular pastimes have also survived well
into this century. In the 1930s, a big boxing promotion
always boasted a glittering array of Lords, Ladies and
nouveau riche Gentlemen, seated at the ringside.
But it was not at the major venues but in the small
halls that boxing had its popular base in the inter-war
years. Small halls were the grass-roots of the professional game, where more than 3000 registered professionals
found employment - usually at a few shillings for a
night's work. Small halls were located in working-class
neighbourhoods with fighting traditions going back to
the turn of the century; the East End of London, for
example, with its long-established tradition of
disciplined pugilistic prowess. Here fighters were
recruited from the ranks of the poorest first-generation
immigrants, struggling to survive in this hostile
environment. Irish, Jews, blacks, all successively
threw up 'people's champions', whose braveries in the
ring were acclaimed in the pubs and streets of Hackney
and Whitechapel, not only as a way out of poverty for
tough young men, but also as a way of asserting the
physical integrity of the parent culture. In this way
old fighting codes would be linked into the harshly
money-oriented fight game, as well as being a means of
defence of minority groups in the neighbourhood.
Irishman against Jew; black against white; 'natural'

contests between aspiring champions from the same ethnic group. Through such shrewd matchmaking, the main small hall venue in the East End, Shoreditch Town Hall, acquired a reputation for 'value for money' that spread far beyond the immediate locality, and attracted a colourful, cosmopolitan crowd.

The following account, from a former patron, conveys the atmosphere of fight night at Shoreditch Town Hall as it survived after the war, and details something of the sporting underlife that has traditionally converged around boxing...

You'd look at the bill; - no way was there going to be good nice boxing. You'd go along, there was always nobbins* thrown in the ring. You would always see a great fight. The word got around. This was the place to go if you wanna see a real scrap. It was like a cockpit. Boxers used to say that there was no way that you could box in that ring. The crowds in the overhanging balconies used to force you to have a war.

You'd get people come out of the business world of the West End. Show business people, they've always been closely involved with boxing. Oliver Reed - he was a frequent visitor to Shoreditch. There was always personalities from the showbiz world. And famous sportsmen, too. As soon as the place got a reputation for a great fight night, people used to turn up.

Sometimes it was like a fashion parade. Very brassy. Peroxide blondes. The local businessman turning out with a bit of stuff. It was a way of showing off his girlfriend. A little bit flash. The villains? They were definitely at the ringside, no doubt about that, and everyone seemed to know it. It was all the nudge-nudge treatment in the seats around 'em.

In the 1960s, the Krays come down with their entourage. It was about twenty or thirty of 'em. The heavy mob. So it was said, they didn't pay. They just walked in an' sat down 'cos they hated the promoter. Nothing was said. Just walked in, defied 'im. Nothing was said. What could he do? Call the police? You just didn't do that sort of thing at Shoreditch Town Hall.

Gambling, it used to go on all the time. Between people, and you used to get bookies round the ringside

---

* Money tossed into the ring as a gesture of appreciation after a particularly good fight.

taking bets off East End businessmen. 'I'll have
4-1 on that one'.
Shoreditch Town Hall managed to survive until the end
of the 1960s, but by this time countless small halls had
closed down for good. The decline of the small halls
coincided with the post-war rise in working-class living
standards, the break-up of old neighbourhoods, and the
consequent loosening of ties between boxing and community,
so that recruitment into boxing itself was confined to
a diminishing number of old established fighting families.
Even the seemingly impregnable boys' club amateur
tradition was in danger of being left behind in the
slipstream of 1960s youth culture.

For the 300 odd professional fighters, most of them
part-time, that remained in the early 1970s, matches
could still be found in one of the many new dinner boxing
clubs that sprouted up in all the big cities, and have
gradually taken the place of the small halls. The Anglo-
American, The World Sporting Club, The Café Royal.
Harking back to the Gentlemen Only Sporting Clubs of the
Edwardian era, these Members Only affairs have a very
different atmosphere to Shoreditch Town Hall. Guests
seated around small tables, the air heavy with cigar
smoke. Silence during rounds. Polite applause between.
Dinner jackets compulsory and so on. But despite outward
social decorum, patrons tend to lack the impeccable
breeding of their Edwardian predecessors.

You dress up, it's a nice night out for the lads.
You feel you've got a bit of class by going to these
dos and dressing up in dinner suits and bow ties.
They're great places for entertaining business
clients, impressing people, you know, the business,
things like that. People would book a table and
they'd have friends and business acquaintances
around. They can sit back and have a nice evening.
Not particularly take much notice of the boxing.
A good excuse to do a bit of business and have a
piss up.
Dinner boxing clubs, then, cater for the new kind of
aristocracy of boxing patrons - the post-war generation
of self-made working-class businessmen, bookies, car
dealers, jewellers, scrap metal merchants. All the
class snobberies may reflect social aspirations, but
adherence to the fight game, with its echoes of rough
street-based culture, indicates their cultural separation
from respectable bourgeois society. Meanwhile, the hard
core of less-well-off fans are left well out in the cold -
by exclusive rates of club membership and exhorbitant
ticket prices. Ironically, although boxing has increased

its spectacular appeal as a mass spectator sport
(through international closed circuit TV promotions, the
return of Mohammed Ali, Fights of the Century and the
rest), the British boxing night as a regular, local,
proletarian public event has virtually died out.

In the past few years, however, there has been something of a revitalisation of the sport at its working-
class base. This has been partly due to the rise in
juvenile unemployment coinciding with the emergence of
fighters from the black community. Some, such as Maurice
Hope, from Hackney, hold world titles in the professional
ring, and so serve as examples for young blacks who are
forced to bear the brunt of the current economic
recession. Amateur boxing, too, has grown rapidly
recently.   (There are now over 30,000 young practitioners,
almost double the 1960s figure.)   But I would suggest
that today the code of amateur boxing, like Kung Fu,
Kendo, Karate, is being cultivated as an end in itself,
as just another fighting technique, rather than what it
had previously been in the working class, as a means of
social control. Nevertheless, this does show that,
despite big changes in the levels of material wealth of
working people, echoes of the old fighting codes still
exert an influence on working youth.

FOOTBALL

It would be wrong to conclude that sports crowds in
England represent the material premises for some kind of
proletarian solidarity, or to romanticise the more volatile
and spontaneous elements such as the soccer 'ends' as last
bastions of working-class culture against 'embourgeoise-
ment'. I have tried to show that sports culture is
accommodative - part mass therapy, part resistance,
part mirror image of the dominant political economy.
Yet unlike other aspects of the entertainment industry,
the sporting crowd remains an integral and increasingly
dominant instance of what is left of a distinctively
proletarian public realm under advanced capitalism. This
latter concept, which informs much of this account, has
been best defined in general terms as follows:

> If the workers' needs and interests are directly
> suppressed, if they are used only exploitatively, to
> maximise profit, rather than productively as a means
> of collective self-expression, then these interests
> and needs maintain themselves simply as living labour
> power, as raw material. In this quality, as extra
> economic interests, they exist in forbidden zones of

fantasy, beneath taboos, as stereotypes of the
rudimentary organisation of the basic conditions of
proletarian life. As such they cannot be further
suppressed. They also cannot be assimilated. In this
respect they possess two contradictory characteristics;
in firstly their conservatism, and in their subcultural
form. Secondly they comprise a block of real life which
opposes profit maximising interests. Capitalism cannot
destroy this block, but the proletariat cannot attack
society from within it. (9)

Such an analysis applies particularly acutely to the
place of British football in the (under)development of
working-class consciousness, but only by first introducing
the mediations which the recent social history of this
spectator sport imposes.

In the post-war years, for example, old working-class
neighbourhoods which had long been centres of support for
the big teams, have been broken up, whether through urban
redevelopment or through dramatic changes in local
patterns of employment. One important consequence has
been that the children of 'life-long supporters' no longer
grow up in the old city centres but in suburbs, overspills,
new towns - places that were never designed for anybody
who wanted to move out of a living room, let alone go to
a soccer match. Outer London suburbs such as Borehamwood
or Basildon, or the massive Chelmsley Wood estate near
Birmingham, were designed for the family, for internal
immigration, and there are no natural mass meeting places.

But for the young, at this stage of their lives,
cultivating the back garden in Chingford has not yet
become a convincing metaphor of territorial control, as a
communal substitute for real control of the environment.
So they come back - to the old parts of Birmingham, London,
Manchester, where the soccer grounds are located. 'In our
City Home', 'We are the North Bank', 'United', once more.
But such feelings are seldom articulated beyond the level
of mass chants. The youth soccer 'ends', for all the
fervour of their displays, remain imaginary attempts to
take over what in material terms does not belong to them.
'Q+P+R = MAGIC', one slogan runs. But no one can magically
appropriate what does not belong to them by virtue of their
working-class place in society. The Loft at QPR for
example, does not belong to the Shepherds Bush boys. It
belongs to the club chairman who holds directorships in
several other companies, quite apart from QPR. Indeed
soccer's bosses, while grateful to the passionate support
the young fans give to the team, not to mention the money
through the turnstiles, have always gone to great lengths
publicly to disown the 'ends'. And in response, 'end'

leaders, such as this 17-year-old Leeds United supporter,
consciously flaunt their credentials as organisers of a
vast underlife of young fans: quite beyond all forms of
official control.

THE BOARD OF DIRECTORS, shareholders, they don't know
what's going on.   They all watch the play in seats.
They can't see what's going on.   Manny Cussins (10)
got a big house and he's got money.   He don't know.
When he were young he might have been at boarding
school.   He weren't at a comprehensive.   He don't
know.   They're old as well, and we're all young.   They
don't understand.

POLICE don't know what's going on as well.   When
you've back streets the police can't control it as
much.   They only control it on main roads.   They
don't know about back streets.   They get it all
wrong.   They think all fighting's done where they are.
They don't know about where it really is.   Same with
NEWSPAPER REPORTERS.   They can't report it.   They're
all in wrong places.

EXPERTS say it started 'cos of bad housing, unemployment... that's why you get football violence.
That's a load of rubbish as well.   That's now't to
do with it.   When I've been to court, judges ... 'good
upbringing, why do you do it?'.   Everyone says same.
'You've got a good job, you've got good school records'.
They all say this.   'Why do you do it then?'   And they
think it's 'cos of bad housing.   When you go to court
they say, 'Why do you do it?'   And they're supposed
to know already!   They don't know!

The following is an opposing account, from a life-long
Manchester City supporter, a witness to this battle, as
it takes place on his terrace and in his community.   It
is neither more nor less typical of the experiences of
supporters in any great footballing city.   Such concrete
analyses, of a complex phenomenon, made from *within*
working-class culture, can provide the basis for a popular
political sociology of sport.

When did you first go to Maine Road?

About 1939, and I went sporadically through the war.
I used to go to watch from the scoreboard end for
years and years, before they built the new north stand.
I stood there for donkey's years behind the goal.   Now
the crowd go to Platts Lane to stand, which is down the
side.   I went with my big brother.   He's one of the
rare cases who defected.   He went over to the Reds. (11)
He went in the navy and came out corrupted. (laughs)
But all the rest of my family have always been City
supporters.

Up until the north stand was built when I used to
stand behind the goal, it was a very mixed crowd.
There was a lot of old blokes, and women, even some
elderly women. You all stood there together. You
knew everybody. You never saw 'em between games.
But we always stood in roughly the same place and we
knew the forty or fifty people around us 'cos they
were always there. The worst hazard of standing in
that crowd was someone pissing down the back of your
leg. But now it's getting a bottle on your head and
that's a different thing altogether. It takes the
fun out of it. (laughs)

I don't think it ever occurred to us to fight on
the terraces. I remember when I was 17, and my
brother, who was a big lad, bigger than me - and the
old fella's a bit smaller than both of us, and he was
stood in front of us. And got into an argument with
a bloke. It almost came to blows. So we stepped
forward and said ''ere, leave 'im alone like'. Now
that really stuck in my head. It was nothing! It
never came to blows or anything, but it came very
close to blows, and that was the first time I'd ever
really seen anybody come close to violence at a match.
It was years and years after before I saw any real
aggro. Yet the crowds then were as big as now if
not bigger. Violence was almost unknown. Of course
we used to fight in pubs. (laughs) I mean, I
remember the occasional punch-up with other supporters
in a pub, but it wasn't really related to the football.
It was more like 'this is our pub, what are you fellas
doing in here? Go back to Sunderland or wherever.'
But it wasn't regular by any means. It was just now
and again.

Above all, you went to see a good game of football.
I've seen times when the team's won, and I've been
sick at the terrible football they've played. I've
seen 'em lose and it's been such a superb game of
football that you didn't care. All right, it's better
your team win, but to see a good game of football is
more important to me than to see my team win. And
that's dying too. I don't think many people go with
that attitude any more - particularly the kids. There's
a lot of explanations, there's lots of frustrations....
Kids now have got a worse time than we had. The
families might be better off, but they have a worse
life I think.... Where they were born old neighbourhoods
of Manchester have been smashed up and their communities
scattered to the four winds. People move on to a new
estate. There isn't an established society there.

There isn't anything for 'em to fit into. The kids
come along - you got a couple of hundred teenagers
roaming a newly built area. And all they can do to
prove themselves is to be better vandals than anybody
else.

I mean some of them are amazing vandals. I work in
East Manchester, and the imagination of these kids -
it's incredible. At one stage they were actually
gaining on the building workers who were putting up
the estate.   By the end of the week there was less
built than there had been on the Monday. They wrecked
lifts, they burnt out their motors. They didn't
just smash them up. They would rig up scaffolding
and then switch the lift on, so that the cable would
break and the motor would burn out. And these were
bright, intelligent kids.

Why do they do it? Look at the concrete flats
outside 'ere! Can you imagine anybody looking at
them and getting a warm glow and saying 'that's home!'
We used to have that in the old - what they told us
were slums. I mean at least you felt you were home
when you walked down the street. You were somebody.
You got a place, you got an identity. Everybody knew
yer.

When I was a kid there was this old cripple who was
a rag and bone man. But we didn't make fun of him.
'Cos we'd grow up and he'd always be there. You knew
who he was. I wonder what happens to blokes like that
after the bulldozers come, and he's dumped in an area
with kids who didn't grow up with him ... a figure of
fun...

I grew up in Moss Side and it was a tough place
when I grew up, but there were certain codes. In the
area if anybody did a gas meter, you know, they might
as well go and live somewhere else, they were finished.
If they took an old lady's purse they were gonna get
their legs broken. 'Cos the community - the villains
and the real thieves in the community - had a certain
code. Maybe not a code that was acceptable to society
at large, but it functioned in this area. And if you
wanted to go and rob someone's house, you went to
Cheedle, or Gatley, or Didsbury, where there was
something worth taking, and no way did you rob a
working-class guy because he didn't have anything and
he was like you and that was very much a community-
imposed code. But of course that community was
destroyed, and those kinds of codes were destroyed,
and we've got a situation now where kids don't have
any code at all, don't have any loyalty at all, except

a very, very small group of mates of maybe a dozen.
And even within that group you know, they'll go and
grass on each other. Now when I was a kid, if anybody
had gone and grassed to the police they'd 've got the
next bus out of town, 'cos that was it. It was a
hard and violent community, but it had its code, it
had certain things you didn't do, and you didn't rob
old ladies, and you didn't do gas meters, and you
didn't grass on your mates.

Now I've got season tickets, for seats behind the
goal. I suppose that makes me some kind of millionaire.
But you get a good view of the game, and that community
feeling, you can still get a bit of that now, in the
seats. You've got to sit with the same people every
week. You do get to know them and you do get to know
the kids. There's whole families go into our Park
Lane stand. But twenty years ago, the thought of
sitting down to watch a football match would have
seemed ludicrous to me. I even had a mate who had
two season tickets - he was a night club owner - and
he always used to stand with us on the terrace, and
he used to give his tickets away to business acquaintances as a goodwill thing. He used to say, 'Ah, you
can't sit down to watch a match.' He's in his seat
now as well.

NOTES AND REFERENCES

1 For a critique of sport's 'repressive function as an
   ideological state apparatus', see J.M. Brohm, 'Sport:
   A Prison of Measured Time', London, Ink-Links, 1978.
   'Sport is a commodity sold along normal capitalist
   lines', p.51.
2 D. Robins, and P. Cohen, 'Knuckle Sandwich: Growing
   Up in the Working Class City', Harmondsworth, Penguin,
   1978, p.128.
3 C. Lasch, 'The Culture of Narcissism', New York,
   Norton, 1980. See Chapter 5 The degradation of
   sport.
4 Brohm, op.cit., p.47.
5 T.E. Lawrence, 'Letters', edited by D. Garnett, New
   York, Doubleday, 1939.
6 M. Rogers, 'History of Speedway', Ipswich, Studio
   Publications, 1978, p.8.
7 R.W. Malcolmson, 'Popular Recreations in English
   Society, 1700-1850', Cambridge University Press, 1973.
8 Edith Summerskill, 'The Ignoble Art', London, Heinemann,
   1956.

9 O. Negt and A. Kluge, 'The Public Sphere and Experience',
   quoted in 'New German Critique' no.4, Winter 1975,
   p.75.
10 Chairman Leeds United F.C.
11 Manchester United F.C.

I am indebted to Dick Pountain, Ken Burgess and Ric Sumner,
for their recollections of bike racing, boxing and soccer
respectively.

Chapter 7

On the sports violence question: soccer hooliganism revisited

Ian Taylor

In the week preceding my revision of this paper for inclusion in this collection, the question of soccer hooliganism was once again headline news in both the popular and quality press and on television. The newly appointed manager of Leeds United, Alan Clarke, was widely quoted as recommending that 'The most violent offenders should be flogged in front of the main stands before the start of a home game. I feel so strongly on this matter that I would volunteer to do the whipping'. ('Guardian', 25 November 1980)

On 4 December 1980 the Football Association released a paper on 'Crowd Disorders' which was certainly less dramatic than Alan Clarke's proposal, but which none the less proposed some severe curtailment of traditional practices at soccer games, including a prohibition on the sale of alcohol at grounds, a ban on international selection of players found guilty of misconduct and an end to 'excessive exuberance by players'.

The urgency with which these measures were forwarded was clearly informed by the continuing and rapid declines in attendances at soccer games during the early part of the 1980-81 season, (1) which several surveys had shown to be connected primarily to spectators' fears of violence at soccer games. (2) In the additional context of the massive increases in mass unemployment under the Thatcher government, reducing the ability of workers to pay existing admission prices, professional soccer began audibly to fear for its future.

Some of these developments are anticipated in the paper which follows, which is reproduced more or less as given at the Roehampton Conference. But my primary concern in the paper I gave then was not with futurism: I was rather concerned to re-examine and reinterpret some of the writing I had done on soccer hooliganism at the start of the 1970s (Taylor 1971a, 1971b). In particular, my concern was to try to locate the growth of violence in the most popular sport of the British working class in the particular explanatory context provided by contemporary theories of the state and of class. So I was and am trying to show that *conventional* attempts to speak of sports and violence are ultimately incoherent, because the object to be explained is *not* 'violence-in-sport' itself, but the deterioratiòn in class relations in Britain and the changes that have been occurring in the form of the state.

That said, I still want to note that violence in sport in general, and hooliganism around soccer in particular, are by no means phenomena of contemporary British class society alone. There has been widespread concern in North America over the use of violence by professional ice hockey players, (3) and the use of violent tactics by soccer players has also been identified (and connected to spectator violence) by the bodies controlling European soccer. (4) Spectator violence around soccer has of course been given some responsibility for the outbreak of war (between Honduras and El Salvador, in 1970), (5) and is quite widespread throughout third-world societies, especially in Latin America (where it has a different significance in terms of the class relations to the significance it has in European societies). Spectator violence around soccer has even been reported in the Soviet Union. (6) There have also been reports in Britain of spectator violence 'spilling over' from soccer to cricket; whilst American commentators have written of changing forms of behaviour in that society's equivalent game form of baseball. (7) The phenomenon of 'sports violence' is widespread. I would still want to insist, as I do in this paper, that the various examples of 'the' phenomenon are actually expressions of very different, real, social relations in each of the societies in which they occurred. We can put the point even more finely: a particular spectator sport may have a very different historical and class significance in different sets in social relations, as indeed does soccer in Britain and North America at the present time (cf. Roadburg, 1980). Any analysis of sports-violence must pay attention to the specific, social, historical significance of a sport and any violence emerging around it. My concern in the paper that follows was and is to make that argument clear in the particular case of soccer hooliganism in Britain; and in that respect to identify errors and misleading elements in my own (and other people's) writing on the topic conventionally thought of as being about sport, on the one hand, and violence, on the other.

With the possible exception of this last FA document, each official initiative on soccer hooliganism during the last decade has been portrayed by the authorities, and often by the media, as a planned and coherent response to the problem, and as a first step in winning the war against soccer hooliganism. But read historically, each initiative can be seen to have been provoked by individually serious incidents; and a recital of the recent history of these incidents strongly suggests that 'the problem' has been noticeably unaffected by the escalation in the use of penal measures. Recollecting the history from 1974 onwards, these incidents have included (in April) the invasion of the Manchester United ground just prior to the end of their final game of the season against Manchester City (subsequent to a goal which ensured United's relegation); the first death in the history of soccer hooliganism (of 17-year-old Kevin Olson, at a Second Division game in Blackpool, in August, from a stabbing); and the riot of Tottenham Hotspur fans in Rotterdam after 'the Spurs' had been beaten in the UEFA Cup Final in May. In 1975, a similar 'riot' amongst British fans occurred on the continent of Europe when Leeds United were beaten in the Final of the European Cup, the major European tournament at club level. In 1976, further deaths occurred of young fans (in August, of a Glasgow Celtic supporter, subsequent to a game in Arbroath); and in September, a young Millwall supporter, found dead on a London railway track after a fight with a supporter of a rival London team, West Ham United). In 1976 and 1977, a series of massively violent incidents occurred at games involving Manchester United; and in 1977, the achievement of this violent reputation by the fans of 'the Reds' was challenged, in particular in similar incidents involving fans of Chelsea, Millwall and other teams in the English and Scottish League.

By 1978 and 1979, indeed, several more English and Scottish League clubs had developed violent reputations, which their 'fighting gangs' were no doubt concerned to maintain. The repertoire of some of these groups now extended far beyond the 'taking of the ends' and the property vandalism of the 1960s to involvement in National Front-inspired attacks on blacks (especially in south and east London), to terrorising bus crews and the staff of the London Underground (both of which public service occupations are very heavily black), to destroying the interiors of public houses and shops in the vicinity of soccer grounds, in city centres and near railway stations.

1980 was the year of the riot by English football

supporters during the European Championship in Italy, a
riot which may have been precipitated by the generally
nationalistic sentiments surrounding this tournament, but
which certainly was a clear expression of hooliganism as
a product and expression of the conditions of working-
class youth *in Britain*. There were also reports in 1980
of British Movement recruitment drives outside the Leeds
United ground, and confirmed accounts of bands of skinhead
supporters of the Movement waving swastikas, attacking
opposition supporters and local blacks alike, at West
Ham, Millwall and Brentford. There were also continuing
incidents of more conventional forms of violence,
including (in September) the invasion and occupation of
the playing pitch at Oldham by Sheffield Wednesday fans,
and the murder of a Swansea supporter by a visiting
Crystal Palace fan ('Guardian', 25 October 1980).

By the late 1970s, in other words, the holding of a
soccer match was close to becoming an occasion of fear
and anxiety throughout significant sections of local
working-class populations themselves. Violence in the
working-class neighbourhoods surrounding the soccer
grounds was no longer thought to be a possibility mainly
in local pubs and shops: it was a generalised possibility
in the environs of the soccer ground. Working-class
soccer supporters themselves could no longer even
contemplate a visit to away games with equanimity: the
personal safety of away supporters going to and from
League games, especially to the popular ends, often
depended on the availability of police escorts. So
violence around soccer was and is an integral and even
primary element in the generalised sense of unease and
anxiety over crime and violence that has become a part of
the reality of working-class life over the last decade.

We should anticipate some of our later remarks by
noting that this new reality of life for the working
class was systematically ignored or misapprehended by
liberal and social-democratic politicians and academic
commentators. Most of these groups obtained support
from liberal sociologies of crime and deviance in their
belief that the picture of soccer violence presented in
the press was a product of exagerrated and stereotypical
reporting, a part of 'moral panic' in which social
problems were amplified through a process of ideological
sensitisation. But the new reality of life for working-
class populations *was* taken seriously and given an
explanation in popular terms by the New Right leadership
of the Conservative Party, in its successful development
of a complex 'law and order ticket' from 1977 onwards,
and especially in the course of the General Election
campaign in 1979 (Taylor, 1980).

We shall return to the question of the New Right and
the form of the state (and state discipline) a little
later. Some comments are necessary, however, on the
character of the press reportage of soccer hooliganism
since 1961, since, as nearly all sociologists still
correctly insist, social problems like soccer violence
are known to many people only through the treatment they
received in the media.

THE MASS MEDIA'S TREATMENT OF SOCCER VIOLENCE

We have already suggested that a cycle of stimulus and
response was observable in both governmental and mass-
media reactions to the development of soccer violence
in Britain. Each new incident was taken by the media in
general (from popular newspaper to highbrow weekly
magazines) as evidence of the need for a new initiative
which was almost invariably described as 'a clampdown';
and each new initiative was a panacea which obviated
the need for more 'extreme measures'. So, for example,
calls for the use of the stocks (made by Lady Emmet of
Amberly in the House of Lords on 7 October 1976) or for
football hooligans to be sprayed with indelible dye (a
suggestion put by a Labour MP, Mr Arthur Lewis, in 1977),
could in this way be described as 'batty' (the adjective
used about Mr Lewis from another ageing Labour MP, Mr
Marcus Lipton, in the liberal 'Guardian' newspaper)
('Guardian', 13 April 1977). The effect of these
exchanges, however, was one which increasingly legitimated some form of *penal* response within existing social
arrangements, rather than calling forth the need to
subvert the social arrangements themselves; since the
question was framed, from the outset, as a question about
the *control of the hooligans themselves*. Observations
about the general poverty and dislocation of life in
contemporary working-class community in Britain, however
insightful or inspired, were irrelevant to the demand
for the restoration of control and order in such communities.
    The cycle of stimulus and response within which
official responses to football violence was formulated
also served to focus attention on the areas in which
action could immediately be taken. (17) Actions which
might be useful, from the point of view of social
democrats, in tackling the deepening nexus of deprivation
in the inner cities and in the ghetto areas from which
rank-and-file supporters might come, or in reversing the
upward spiral of youthful unemployment, were, in this

respect, not strictly or immediately relevant. Far Right
conservative measures, like the re-introduction of the
stocks, whilst acceptable in the sense of being
'practicable' without involving fundamental economic or
social change, tended to be given prominence in the
committedly right-wing newspapers ('Daily Telegraph' and
'Daily Mail'), but to be ultimately eschewed on condition
that the existing apparatus of penal discipline was used
with an appropriate severity. (18) Thus, whilst the level
of policing and the severe sentencing of soccer fans
increased, this intensification of penal discipline as a
political solution to soccer violence was also necessarily
accomplished with a due regard to the necessity for some
social consensus. The pressure exerted by press treatment
of incidents of soccer violence was exerted primarily on
liberals and social democrats, in the form of a demand
that they recognise youth violence as evidence of a need
for the *penal discipline* of *individuals*, and that they
suspend or bracket their other 'humanitarian' or (long-
term) reformist concerns. This consensus around the
need for a penal response to soccer violence was in part
a product of the demand for immediate and practical action,
with the practicability and immediate availability of
other measures (to combat unemployment, or to bring about
fundamental changes in the life chances of rough working-
class youth, etc., etc.) closed off in advance. In this
way, both the liberal and conservative press in Britain
wrenched soccer violence out of the social relations in
which it has been generated, and, without being avowedly
'political', made penal discipline the obvious and
necessary measure. They left untouched the question of
when it would be appropriate to address the humanitarian-
ism and reformist concerns of liberals and social
democrats.
     Press reportage of the struggle against soccer
hooligans successfully performed some other major
ideological projects. In particular, it had to react
to the claims of state authorities that they *could* deal
with the problem of soccer violence (and violent youth
generally) whilst also acceding to the commonsensical
view that 'the youth are getting more troublesome,
violent, difficult, etc. ...' The liberal media seemed
to achieve this task by taking on the role of a neutral
arbiter between the state control agencies, and 'the
people', who claimed that things were getting worse. This
was most notable in the many television documentaries
which were produced throughout the 1960s and 1970s on
soccer violence; (19) as well as in the 'in-depth
analyses' of the quality liberal daily and weekly press.

It was indeed precisely in this use of 'expert' evaluation, and distancing from a particular viewpoint, that the *liberal* media made their claim to 'balance' and neutrality. The answer in each individual article or television programme was to some extent produced in advance by the choice of experts, but it was also 'genuinely' dependent on the ability of the expert to persuade his audience and/or his questioner. (20)

The conservative media were not so sanguine. For them, the answer to the ideological conundrum was that youth *are* getting worse (because 'authority' continues to be soft, etc.) but that youth could none the less be *controlled* by the proper use of coercion. The problem was that liberal and social democratic agencies continued to be committed either to the treatment of recalcitrant individuals or to improving their life chances. The pursuit of these other goals weakened the effective pursuit of social control over troublesome and un-socialised youth. The key to the deteriorating situation was therefore to shift the responsibility for the exercise of social control to the forces of law and order (police, prison, probation service), and to cease conflating social control with the project of social reform. As soccer violence continued and developed throughout the 1970s, the conservative press in Britain increasingly effectively argued this case *as the case of the people*, directed against the 'experts' in the quality press and, especially, the reformers associated with the state social welfare institutions. So that, in general terms, the *real* anxieties of working-class populations at the decline in their standards of community were taken up and levelled at social democracy and its post-war pretensions of a re-constructed social order; and the specific instance of violent attacks by soccer hooligans on the working class's own community on a regular weekly basis was taken, repeatedly, as confirmation of the people's own need and demand for a return to law and order. The most predictable of headlines in the popular press on days following major soccer games were demands for state action to 'smash these thugs', 'stamp out violence', 'thump and be thumped' or even 'cage the animals' ('Sun', 4 October 1976, Sheffield 'Star', 1 December 1972, 'Daily Express', 25 November 1976 and 'Daily Mirror', 21 April 1976). And the reality of popular experience of soccer violence in 1979 ensured that this particular penal connection, for all that it was connected into a right-wing attack on the welfare state and on permissiveness, was much more resonant in the working-class community than the responses we have outlined from the liberal press and 'consensual' television documentaries.

We need to emphasise that both the conservative and liberal press developed their ideological paradigms on soccer violence (a) without reference to the massive material changes that had been occurring in the economic and social experience in the situation of working-class youth in Britain in the last thirty years, and (b) within the context of a journalistic language that almost guaranteed the playing out of violent response to the (unspoken, unproblematicised) experience of a readership that includes the working-class youth themselves.

Mass-media accounts of youthful activity in general have remained silent, for example, on the virtual collapse in the juvenile labour market that began in the late 1960s and early 1970s. (21)   They continue to remain silent now on the future employment possibilities of the reserve army of youth, and they tend to deal with working-class youth culture as a whole (from punk and skinhead culture for whites to Rastafarianism for blacks) as having significance only for fashion shows and consumerism, where their real connection is to futures of worklessness and social desperation. (22)

When the news media did report youthful activity and especially soccer hooliganism, they reported *major incidents* of violence rather than the broader economic context of worklessness or waged labour and the specific biographical context of the individuals involved in violent incidents. As in their reportage of demonstrations and political events, the media displayed a fixation with 'violence' and were silent on the larger significance and meaning of such incidents.

So the 'thugs' in the reports of soccer violence were highly stereotypical figures, presented without any personal history in school, in the declining housing market, in the labour market or in a class society. The closest they got to humanity was when their ages and occupations (which were frequently non-existent – they were described simply as 'unemployed') appeared in subsequent reports of courtroom appearances, in the week following arrest. The media's account of soccer violence was actually curiously static throughout the 1960s and 1970s. The account offered by the popular press in particular, was primarily articulated around a stereotypical picture of the growth of 'thuggery' and 'violence' in society, 'explained' by reference to the emergence of a stylised and moronic hooligan, contrasted to an equally stylised image of a 'family audience' for football (Whannel, 1979).

The use of stereotypes as an explanation of the activities of hooligans is perfectly mirrored by the

popular press's use of what Stuart Hall calls 'a language
of violence'. The treatment of soccer violence in the
British press has been characterised by an 'editing for
impact', characterised by: 'graphic headlines, bold type-
faces, warlike imagery and epithets, vivid photographs
cropped to the edges to create a strong impression of
physical menace, and the stories have been decorated with
black lines and exclamation marks' (Hall, 1978, p.26).

The embrace of this form of language by the press is,
however, general to its reportage of sport: it is *the*
general form of discourse in the back pages of the popular
newspaper. The game itself is increasingly reported in
such terms. Hall notes the continuity between a story
headed 'FANS GO MAD' in the 'Sunday People', on 3 March
1977, and a story on the following page about a tackle
on a Birmingham City half back, Howard Kendall, by Jeff
Nulty of Newcastle, under the lead headline 'C-R-U-N-C-H'.
The language of violence extends in the same edition even
to discussions of clubs over transfers of players, or
between managers and coaches. And since the back page in
the popular press is an 'alternative front page', which
is for many readers the starting point of the paper (and,
for many, the only worthwhile part), it is not difficult
to see the importance of this editing for impact. What
is for male working-class youth its own, relatively
autonomous 'life world', soccer, the people's game, is
increasingly depicted as being a world in which 'violence'
is a means both literally and metaphorically to goal.
As Hall observes:

> If the language of football reporting is increasingly
> the language of thrills and spills, hard tackles and
> tough games, of struggle, victory and defeat, studded
> with images drawn from the blitzkreig and the military
> showdown, it is not so difficult to understand why
> some of what is going on on the pitch, and recorded
> with such vivacity in the newspapers, spills over
> onto the terraces. Here the line between the sports
> reporter glorying in the battle on the pitch, and
> expressing his righteous moral indignation at the
> battle on the terraces, or between the managers who
> drill and rehearse their lads in tough and abrasive
> styles of play, but who think their faithful and
> involved fans should be birched or caged in or hosed
> down ('DRENCH THE THUGS' - 'Mirror' 4.4.77) - is a
> very fine and wavery one indeed (Hall, 1978, p.27).

So the language of the popular press is one which
encourages its largely working-class readers to think of
their sport not simply as a 'man's game', but specifically
as a display of controlled and militaristic discipline.

It then identifies hooligans, in effect, as immature
recruits, who need to have their natural taste for
violence more effectively controlled by the application
of a proper discipline. The language of violence works by
analogy and suggestion to encourage an explanation of
soccer hooliganism as resulting from a breakdown in the
proper, natural and *controlled* exercise of violence by
working-class males.

So the account of soccer hooliganism in the popular
media is one of significant silences (on 'social context'
and personal biography) and presences (the breakdown of
the appropriate disciplining of violence). It is an
account which also finds a place in the so-called quality
media, albeit with some competing or countervailing
interpretation of a more liberal (usually pluralistic)
character. It is an account which has had its own
determining effect in the cycle of incidents and official
responses to soccer hooliganism, which we discussed in
the last section: it is therefore an integral part,
itself, of the phenomenon of soccer hooliganism in Britain.

SOCIOLOGY AND SOCCER VIOLENCE

Sociologists do not have the mass audience commanded by popular
journalists, but in post-war 'social democracy' they may
have had a more significant influence over official
opinion. On the question of youthful behaviour in general,
and working-class youth sub-cultures in particular, liberal
sociology has been extremely vocal, and has certainly
prevented simplistic accounts of youthful behaviour as a
collapse of 'authority' from becoming generally acceptable.
In relation to soccer violence, in particular, sociology
has been generally progressive in standing out against
more outlandish psychological and even physical explanations of soccer violence, (23) and also against the
attempts that have been made to account for juvenile
delinquency as an 'effect' of exposure to television. (24)
It is not clear, however, whether 'sociology' itself can
really claim to have provided an alternative explanation
of all that requires to be explained in this field.

Specifically sociological accounts of soccer violence
in Britain may be said to fall, basically, into five
categories: (i) sub-cultural theories of youthful fashion
or style, (ii) theories of changes in the structure of the
game, (iii) social anthropological theories of ritual
violence, (iv) labelling theories and (v) more or less
empiricist amalgams of the above. Each of these theories
is capable of providing a critique of the limitations in

theories of violence as being the results of the physical
or psychological possession of individuals, the spread
of some contagion in a crowd, or the effects of watching
certain kinds of television. But they are lacking in
other crucial respects.

(i)   Theories of sub-cultural style

According to Clarke, Hall, Jefferson and Roberts (1975),
working-class youth sub-cultures in general should
primarily be understood in terms of the particular style
which they generate and sustain. These styles are
symbolic of the ways in which each youthful cohort of the
working class has attempted to resolve the dual structural
problems it must encounter, of subordination to adults
and subordination in the class structure. So each of the
post-war youth sub-cultures (the teddy boys (1953-7),
mods and rockers (1964-6), skinheads (1967-70) and,
latterly, in rapid sequence, glamrock, punk rock and
new wave) is best understood as an

> attempt at a solution to ... problematic experience:
> a resolution which, because pitched largely *at the*
> *symbolic level*, was fated to fail. . The problematic
> of a subordinate class experience can be 'lived
> through', negotiated or resisted; but it cannot be
> *resolved* at that level or by those means (Clarke et al.,
> 1975, p.47 my emphases).

The styles adopted by youth sub-cultures are in this
sense 'imaginary' or indeed 'magical' attempts to resolve
material (or structural) problems.

So the skinheads, for example, developed a style
which, in its use of clothing style (boots, workmen's
jeans, and rolled-up sleeves, etc.) and its core values
(sexism, racism, toughness, self-reliance within a group),
was a caricature of the working-class community,
increasingly destroyed by the post-war housing redevelopment and by massive changes in the internal structure of
the industrial workforce. It was an attempt at the
'magical recovery of community' (Clarke, 1975). The
mods of the early 1960s, on the other hand, developed a
style involving brush-cut hair, smart clothes and a
general sharpness, which symbolised their exploration of
'upward options' in the class structure; a move out of
the 'rough' working class. Each of the post-war youth
sub-cultures developed styles that symbolised the
particular strategies that were developed to combat the
double subordination experienced by working-class youth
in particular historical periods; and a 'reading' of the

style will therefore be a powerful indicator of the particular stresses and strains being experienced by those youth groups.

There is no doubt that the 'reading' of sub-cultural *style*, advanced by Clarke and the sub-cultures group at the Centre for Contemporary Cultural Studies at the University of Birmingham, is an important advance on earlier, more formal observational accounts of youth sub-cultural formations in Britain. But it *is* a reading of the more visible, 'violent' and therefore spectacular sub-cultural adaptations of youth: and it has been criticised, rightly, for its silence on the situation of the mass of working-class youth, only a minority of whom make firm sub-cultural adaptations, but many of whom do get involved, periodically, in soccer violence, and in the 'clampdowns' that follow on from moral panics in the media. There is also an associated tendency to posit what Simon Frith has called 'a false freezing of the youthful world into deviants and the rest' (Frith, 1978, p.53). Evidence suggests that the vast bulk of British youth 'pass through groups, change identities and play their leisure roles for fun' (Ibid.).

It is also a form of analysis that is relatively silent on the source of stylistic adaptations. The teddy boys' styles were clearly derived from a very different source to those of the bike-riding rocker ten years later, though many would argue that the social composition of the group was similar. In other words, the reading of style tends to be descriptive and celebratory, almost across the board: an important failing at a moment of increasing congruence between some youth sub-cultures in the rough working class and the youth groups of the National Front and the British Movement.

But, thirdly, as Simon Frith has observed, there is a tendency for sub-cultural analysts to articulate their account of youth around the symbol, or around the sub-culture itself, rather than to see the youth question as a displacement of a broader dynamic of the relation of the classes (a displacement at both the behavioural and ideological level). The behavioural point may be more clear in North America where the reproduction of class relations, and the need for the policing of class relations by the state, is routinely accomplished, as it were, 'on the street corner', in the public, political concerns over the delinquencies of the black or white, unemployed or underemployed, but always troublesome 'corner boy'. North American class relations have reproduced, with some regularity, a large reserve army of youthful labour, an increasing proportion of which was

until recently kept out of the labour market by being allowed
to go to college, but a significant proportion of which was
'left behind' at the street corner, as a potential source of
trouble in local civil society. The Schwendingers have shown
the centrality of this continual reproduction of the youthful
reserve army to the high rates of delinquency in North
America, whether of what early sub-cultural theorists
called an 'expressive' or an 'instrumental' variety
(Schwendinger and Schwendinger, 1976). The ideological
displacement which is accomplished in both North American
and British society is to make the youth question the
central conceptual problematic (as a problem of socialisation, discussed de-contextually, or as a constantly
occurring clash of the generations): class is displaced
into generation.

In Britain, which unlike North America was until the
early 1970s an economy with low juvenile unemployment,
the mass of working class were relatively effectively
incorporated by the disciplines of the workplace. It was
in the 1970s, as unemployment amongst youth began to
approach North American levels, that violent adaptations
began to spread beyond the small minorities of the class,
and that 'violence' (rather than particular styles) came
to be perceived in the class as a response to deepening
structural problems. In their continuing concentration on
youth cultural style and on the cultural expressions
surrounding youth, even the most radical and sensitive
of sociological accounts (like that provided by the
Birmingham Group) have tended to remain too silent on
the dynamic of political economy and the labour market.
One consequence is that they are able only to *describe*
the different cultures and styles. They are not really
able to speak of them evaluatively, in terms of their
differing utility as 'magical' resolutions. Nor either
are they able to speak to the popular and right-wing
beliefs that youthful behaviours are actually getting
'worse'.

(ii) Theories of the game

Broadly speaking, attempts to explain soccer violence
as a function of features of the game itself fall into
two categories. In my own early writing, for example,
I placed considerable emphasis on changes in the social
organisation of professional football (and in particular,
the decomposition of the football club as a neighbourhood
institution of the class, with football being increasingly
reorganised, after the Second World War, as a locally

based national entertainment sport aimed at 'paying spectators') (Taylor, 1971a, 1971b). This thesis has been extended by Clarke, 1978.

In both these versions, and also in the work of journalistic commentators on soccer violence like Hunter Davies (1972), the examination of the history of relations between clubs and supporters tends to deteriorate into specious anecdotal debates ('were the clubs in the 1930s *really* experienced as democratic organisations to which all supporters belong?' etc.), in which the club is abstracted artificially from its surrounding social relations. It was no part of my original intention in the 1971 papers to argue that membership of the football club in the inter-war period was any more or any less 'ideological' than membership of any other institution that occupied a significant position in class experience in that period (whether that institution was a sporting institution for spectators (like the greyhound stadium) or for players (the billiard hall), or whether it was a leisure institution of the neighbourhood (like the pub). All these institutions were physical territories of the class, and part of the social relations of the class. They were a part of the ensemble of class relations. Similarly, the 'alienation' of the football supporter from his local club, in the 1960s and 1970s, was *not* unrelated to the overall alienation of fractions of the working class that resulted from changes in the structure of the labour market and the 'class map' generally, and, specifically, from the decomposition of working-class community.

Calls for the 'democratisation' of football clubs of the kind made by myself, and later by Hunter Davies, albeit made for a polemical purpose, have not met with an active response from professional football as a whole, despite token schemes for participation of youngsters in club training and related activities. Professional football is a part of local political economy, and, perhaps more importantly, local civic power: and is no easier target for *real* democratisation than the political economy and structure of power at the level of the state itself. Analyses of the violence amongst football spectators and diagnoses of a solution which have been focused on *the club* in isolation from the ensemble of class relations in which they are located have fallen into a form of idealist politics of the left, or even of the liberal centre. They have also been analytically guilty, as it were, of 'reifying' football's social significance in the relation, simply, of the *club* to the *spectator*.

A second form of analysis of soccer violence as a
function of the game itself is that which concentrates
on some physical features of the game; and, in particular,
the fact that the game is played in front of large crowds,
caught up in the excitement of the competition, and (as we
indicated earlier) increasingly exhorted to think of the
game in physically violent terms. This perspective has
been advanced, inter alia, by researchers working for the
police (Jones, 1969, 1970), by the Harrington Enquiry of
1968, by Trivizas (1980) and, to some extent, in the
eclectic Report of the Sports Council and the Social
Science Research Council , 'Public Disorder and Sporting
Events' which we will discuss later (SSRC, 1978). Each
of these reports places considerable emphasis on the
irrationality of human beings in crowd situations (the
collective behaviour thesis, which is also discussed for
sport in general, ultimately rather ambiguously, by
Smith, 1975). Put simply, 'people in crowds commit
offences they would never do as individuals' (Trivizas,
1980, p.287). In the case of British soccer, the crowd's
essential irrationality has been exacerbated by the same
social factors spoken of in sociological accounts of
changes in the game (the decline in attendance at football
since the 1940s has left the remaining supporters more
committed; the massive number of domestic European and
international games has introduced further trophies and
successes to be prized and given 'symbolic significance';
and television and press coverage has given the crowd a
sense of being 'on camera' or 'in the news'). The
abolition of the maximum wage (1961) and the introduction
of new forms of wage bargaining are said to have made
players more cynical in their quest for success, and
their use of violent tactics has been relatively badly
controlled by referees, who have not been given the power
and authority to control the increasingly instrumental
athletes in their charge. All of these changes in the
sociology of the game have acted as 'bad examples' to
the individuals who make up the crowd, and thus, it is
argued, there are fewer controls, in the form of customary
bonds tying spectators to the club (its tradition, values,
etc.), when a crowd begins to get out of hand.
    All of these social 'facilitators' may be aided,
however, by the presence of psychologically-disturbed
individuals in the crowd, who, for reasons which are not
explained, may act as leaders of groups in the crowd; by
the need of particular groups of supporters to uphold a
fighting reputation; by the results of games themselves
(in the context of long rivalries between clubs, especially
within localities) or by particular *incidents* within the
games themselves.

Whatever the balance of precipitating factors, it is
at this point that the 'contagion' which is a quality of
collective behaviour incidents starts to operate, and so,
the argument proceeds, the conditions become present for
violence in the crowd. Fights and pitch invasions are
likely developments: and a sequence is fulfilled, more
or less in the fashion described in the various collective
behaviour theorists (from le Bon to Ralph Turner and
beyond).

The originating source of these violent developments is
invariably seen as the irrational, primitive and more or
less pathological crowd. What is never stated, but is
always implicit, is that the crowd is very largely
composed of working-class youth - the 'dangerous classes'.
To place the fact of class at the centre of any explanation of crowd behaviour would require commentators to
address the significance of collective situations for
citizens of a class society who are made subordinate by
their age, status, race or gender. The focus on the crowd
is therefore a *displacement* of all these crucial divisions.

The problematic in accounts which focus on changes in
the game itself is localised around the crowd in the
specific sense of being localised specifically on the
question of 'crowd control'. There may be reference to
the ways in which changes in the broader community have
brought about significant changes in the relationship of
the football fan, the locality, the owners and managers,
and the players, but such analysis is usually made without
implications for real reform and change in the structure
of ownership and management of professional football.
It is only offered as a contribution to the new problems
facing established authority (from the police to the
Boards of Directors of individual League clubs) in the
pacification or segregation of troublesome fans. The
changes in the social context of the game have altered
the imperatives of social control.

Accounts which refer to these changes in the relation
of the crowd to organised, professional football tend to
have given support to architectural solutions to these
new problems of social control. The taken-for-granted
theory here is that the introduction of more seating in
football grounds would have a generally pacifying effect
on the pathological crowd, whilst the introduction of
purpose-built entries from the pitch would enable the
police to isolate troublesome groups and make arrests.
Further, the redesigning of entries and exits is thought
to be helpful in enhancing crowd safety and also in making
the crowd more available to control. (25)

It is not that these architectural proposals for the

restructuring of football stadia are undesirable (certainly the vast bulk of British football grounds are in need of basic renovation in the name of the general comfort of the 'paying customer'): they *are* worthwhile in themselves. But like all architectural applications to social problems (from the New Towns and high-rise flats of the early post-war period to inner city walkways in the 1970s), these 'solutions' may have unintended effects, precisely because they are not solutions to specific *social contradictions* in a class society. To alter (and improve) the physical environment of the majority of the crowd in football grounds, by modernising seating accommodation and introducing bars and restaurants, may only distance the club even further from its supporters at the popular ends, caged into cheap, traditional terrace-type standing accommodation. Such modernisation (at Chelsea, Manchester United, Sheffield Wednesday, Newcastle, and elsewhere) did not prevent these grounds from being at the forefront of 'crowd trouble' during the 1970s.

This argument cannot be extended here. But we can note that whilst some earlier work on changes in the game (like my own) tended to focus idealistically on the *club* (isolated from other social relations), there is also work which thinks of the game in terms of the *crowd* in its physical space. The first kind of work tends to lead to idealist pleas for the democratisation of professional football, and the second to implicit proposals for the continuing isolation and control of working-class soccer crowds. Both perspectives are blind to any larger understanding of the significance of football in the broader social relations of the classes and the state.

(iii)   Social anthropology and ritual violence

Closely connected with sociological and psychological work on collective behaviour and on the crowd are the social anthropological traditions of investigation into the nature of animal and human violence and aggression and also into group formation. Some of this work is usefully summarised, for sports of all kinds, in Smith (1975) and also in SSRC (1978), section 7.2.

There has recently been a rush of work into British soccer violence but also into other forms of youthful disorder, from writers using a particular mix of animal ethology, social anthropology and sociological empiricism (Marsh, Rosser and Harré, 1978; Marsh, 1978a). Our concern here will be with the application of this mix to soccer violence. (26)

Marsh bases his theory on close observational work undertaken on actually occurring behaviour at soccer grounds. When it is observed at this close range, he argues, football violence can be seen to be ritual violence; and a slowing-down of films of fights at football matches will also show, he claims, that the fist or the boot rarely hits home. According to Marsh, this ritualism was also characteristic of both early (folk) and modern (professional) forms of football playing and spectating; and he provides some interesting detail on the gestures, songs and crowd rituals of earlier forms of the game. The essential function, therefore, of what is now called 'aggro' is, and, importantly, in different forms always has been, a means of signifying membership of what Marsh calls 'micro-cultures', and thus a way of affirming the identity of otherwise amorphous 'cultural unities'. This observational lesson is then illustrated in historical times ('aggro in history') with particular attention being given to the symbolic struggles of the Blue and Green charioteers in the Roman and Byzantine circus (recently reported on by Alan Cameron in 'Circus Factions'); to duelling in seventeenth-century France and to the symbolic and instrumental violence of American culture in general (Marsh seems to be convinced of the *inherent* violence of the United States, which in its early settle-ment 'lacked a culture on which to fall back', Marsh, 1978a, p.82). Aggro in some form, however, is universal in all societies, in being a symbolic and ritual form in which real conflicts can be sublimated, or 're-represented'. Aggro is useful in maintaining a requisite level of dynamism in a culture, and thereby renovating the basis of cultural cohesion during periods of social change.

The Durkheimian cast of Marsh's explanation of 'aggro' is arrived at, in part, as a result of his attempt to construct a 'sociological' critique of the socio-biologists and cultural anthropologists for whom territorial struggles, and other instances of human aggression, are determined, specifically, by the fact of differential genetic endowments amongst the species. For Marsh, explanations of this order could only be true at the level of struggles over the most basic features of human existence. 'Once culture has taken over the role of transmitting life-styles and social values there is no reason to suppose that the genetic imprint will remain' (Marsh, 1978a, p.34). By the same token, animal studies are unhelpful in explaining what Marsh calls the 'secondary level of aggression management' - the ritual violence which exists in all cultural totalities (or societies).

The point about Marsh's excursion into cultural anthropology is that it constitutes an attempt to contextualise the 'moral panics' of the last fifteen years (over soccer hooliganism and associated instances of violence and vandalism) in a *theory* of the *fundamental character of the human species*. Aggro is a product of human beings' struggle to express identity, in forms of interpersonal ritual, the rules governing which are well understood at a micro-cultural level. Thus, there are good anthropological reasons to justify the adoption of a policy of non-intervention (or at least liberal treatment rather than punitiveness) vis-a-vis troublesome youth. Labelling theory's benign conclusions are given an anthropological justification. Attempts by 'society' to repress aggression ('to the extent that [the] useful function of aggression is negated') - of the kind that have been proposed by the magistracy, by the police and by the media in recent months, and years, as a way of 'dealing with the problem of soccer hooliganism' are unhelpful, for if aggression is repressed rather than 'socialised', it will merely be transferred on to other targets, and there will also be an accompanying destruction of 'the groups and micro-societies in which ritualised aggression is acted out'. The point here is that these 'groups and micro-societies' are man's own *natural solutions* (in symbolic form) to conflicts over material interest and human identity; they alone have the capacity to socialise and thus to contain the real potential for violence in the species which led Desmond Morris, in 'The Naked Ape', to speak of the inevitability of Armageddon.

We can usefully relate this exposition, and our criticism of this, to the accounts of soccer violence offered out by labelling theorists and by interactionists.

(iv)   Labelling theory and soccer violence

A significant number of the accounts of soccer violence written by both professional and amateur sociologists have utilised a more-or-less straightforward version of the notion of deviancy amplification derived from North American labelling theory of the early 1960s; or, alternatively, a slightly more 'theorised' framework derived from Stan Cohen's reformulation of this theory in his classic study of the mods and rockers (Cohen, 1972).

In the deviancy amplification version, the concentration is on the sequences of rule breaking, social reaction,

labelling and ostracism that occurred vis-a-vis youthful
disturbances of all kinds in the 1960s, and the particular
impact of this process of 'sensitisation' on the football
terraces. The sequence is seen to have been speeded up
by the emergence of the skinhead, whose behaviour and
presentation of self resulted in powerful reactions from
a broadly based 'social audience' of teachers, social
workers, police and magistrates, aided by the media
(Clarke, 1973). A spurious dramatisation is thought to
have occurred, whereby the wearing of the skinhead garb
was sufficient to excite the attention of 'agencies of
social control', and probably lead to arrest. A classic
cycle of stimulus and response was initiated, resulting
in the signalling of the original skinhead style (whose
adherents were by now firmly 'cast' as social outcasts)
as the uniform of committed deviants. Ultimately, the
'societal reaction to skinheads' was so all-pervasive
as to have produced, on the one hand, an alienated but
increasingly committed group of outcasts (who had now no
other option), and, on the other, the deterrence of the
mass of youth. The result, artificially, was to define
violence at soccer games as an activity of a 'hard core'
of committedly anti-social, untypical, and dangerous
youth (which, in turn, gave soccer violence a spurious
attractiveness to working-class adolescents seeking
adventure and diversion).

The slightly different account advanced by Stan Cohen
involves what might be called the 'recasting theory' of
youth culture. Here, the argument is that 'society'
continually creates new 'folk devils' over time, relegating
earlier devils to 'relatively benign roles in the gallery
of social types' (Cohen, 1972, p.200). For Cohen, the
production of youth as folk devils is in large part
explicable by the facts of the generational conflict
(that youth are relatively powerless, that they must
always attempt to establish identity, that their
attempts to break free of adult authority will result in
responses of moral indignation, etc.) as well as by
resentments provoked, in the 1950s especially, by the
partial emergence of possibilities of relative 'affluence'
for sections of working-class youth.

Both versions of labelling theory are in themselves
silent, however, on the questions addressed by our
earlier theories: the source and contexts of the initial
youthful adaptations. Indeed, they tend to imply (like
all labelling theory) that the initial behaviour is
irrelevant, arbitrary or, in Becker's term, 'random'; or,
even worse, a 'fad', fashion, or indeed imitation (in the
manner of other species). This would be a severe omission

in any period, but has become all the more severe with
the recent increases in recruitment into fighting groups
of Fascist organisations, and in the blurring of some new
wave music and fashion into the themes of Fascist
political culture.

Labelling theory also argues that the continuation of
soccer violence results from the continuingly over-
sensitive intervention of agencies of social control into
the activities of youth and argues for a policy of non-
intervention. This is also a policy implication of Peter
Marsh's social anthropological contextualisation of
labelling theory, where the insistence is on the *ritual*,
unreal, and functional character of the 'aggro' on the
terraces. In so doing, the labelling theorists and the
anthropologists desert the ground of social control
altogether. They argue, still, for 'radical non-intervention'. This is a crippling error, especially in the
current moment, with vast numbers of working-class people
being won, via populist political appeals, to parties of
the right in a desperate attempt to find a means for
guaranteeing 'order' and security in their personal lives
and living environments. It is also a major departure
from the classical concerns of liberals with the protection
of the lives and liberties of all sections of the broader
community, since many of the worst incidents around soccer
games, and in the weeks between soccer games, have
involved attacks on immigrants, women and the elderly,
and members of the fighting gangs' own community, the
working class.

Many of these attacks perpetrated by youths who are
affiliated with football's fighting gangs, are unreported
in the national press, and misleadingly or incompletely
reported in the local press. (27) This alerts us to
another of labelling theory's unfortunate effects. Almost
as a catechism, labelling theorists have written of the
role of the mass media in terms of the theory of
'deviancy amplification'. The press and television are
thought of as being over-sensitive to even the most
minute of incidents, and as tending to amplify it and
accord it a spurious significance. Individual crowd
happenings are written up spuriously as though they were
general to the crowd, or the terrace, and as if they were
occurring throughout the game.

Labelling theorists in Britain have however remained
silent in the face of recent accusations made by the
right vis-a-vis the role of the media in the reporting
of youthful delinquency generally, and soccer violence in
particular. According to Patricia Morgan (1978), Mary
Whitehouse and the National Union of Licensed Victuallers,

amongst others, the mass media have underestimated the extent
and the character of youthful violence in Britain in the
late 1970s. Little *direct* reportage is carried out in the
media on the violence that public transport workers are
experiencing from passengers on trains and buses, on the
violence that is occurring at certain discotheques and
night clubs, or on the violence in certain schools, since
none of these are routinely covered for stories by
reporters of the local or national press; they are not a
part of the routine division of labour of the newspaper or
radio and TV station. Sports reporters covering football
matches for newspapers, radio or TV have tended to report
incidents *inside* the football grounds, ignoring incidents
of interpersonal or property violence occurring before or
after the game, because they have not witnessed them. Thus,
there have been few reports in the national press in the
1970s of incidents between supporters on the route to and
from football grounds, in pubs or on public transport.

The New Right are therefore correct in identifying some
under-reportage of violence by the press. Confrontations
between fighting gangs prior to games, and subsequently in
the streets surrounding football grounds are now common
knowledge amongst football supporters at the popular ends:
these ritual confrontations are no longer confined to the
taking of the ends. There are also frequent major
incidents at Underground and railway stations throughout
Britain, especially on Saturdays, as groups of supporters
encounter each other en route to and from away games.

Some of these incidents are reported in the local press,
but there is a general silence in the national press, and
especially the popular press, towards the nihilism and
violence of white, male, working-class soccer supporters.
In part, this silence is obviously a product of the
conception which the popular press has of its audience,
which is a conception which would certainly include, and
even celebrate, the 'culture' of this section of the
class.

Labelling theorists and social anthropologists would
presumably still insist that reports of football violence
in the popular media are a product of exaggeration and
amplication. In so far as they do this, I would argue
that they lack any sense of the historical specificity
of soccer hooliganism. This is a paradoxical accusation
to make of Marsh's work, in particular, since Marsh does
base his argument in part on long 'sweeps' over existing
historical evidence. The problem is, indeed, that the
perspective advanced by Marsh is *so* general (the history
of the species) that it is incapable of addressing
particular historical moments in their social and

political specificity. Putting the criticism polemically,
it is an epochal conception of history which is coupled
to a conception of the social as man in relation to
'culture'. So no attention is given to the material basis
of historical development (man's struggle to produce) and
to the material character of the social relations which
result (the relations of classes). It fails to recognise
the relation between capital and labour as a general,
determinant structure, and it also fails to speak to
particular features of that relation (like the economic
and cultural crises of capitalist societies) in the present.
So the production of ritual violence is a constant
solution to a natural and continuing problem, common to
all societies; and, as labelling theorists observe, the
production of 'folk devils' like football hooligans is
also a constant process, irrespective of cycles of boom
and slump, crises of profitability, shifts between relations
of production, etc. Labelling is presented as a cultural
inevitability in all forms of social relations, albeit we
are all urged to be more tolerant, as an act of individual
empathy and historical sensitivity. We have already
suggested that this extension of tolerance is made the
more difficult by the concrete effects that football
violence, in its general contemporary form, is having in
working-class neighbourhoods, and also by the appropriation of the fighting gangs by movements of the extreme
right. Social contradictions of the kind now facing
working-class neighbourhoods in Britain cannot be resolved
by tolerant and sensitive management of a fractured
class: they have to be resolved at the level of the
structural contradictions of a class society, by policies
which reverse the accelerating economic, environmental
and social impoverishment of the mass of working-class
people.

(v) Eclecticism

In a recent revival of a form of empiricist sociology
familiar in the 1950s, the Social Science Research
Council and the Sports Council in a joint publication
have attempted to link sub-cultural theory, labelling
theory, animal ethology and social anthropology together
and to construct an explanation of disorder at sports
events (SSRC, 1978).
    This report was written by a committee, subsequent to
consultations with many social scientists, and, partly
as a result of this, but also out of an evident *a priori*
belief in the inevitable interplay of many 'factors' in

the constitution of any social phenomenon, the report
takes the form,more familiar now in North American social
science than in British, of a multi-factorial account, in
which the different and often contradictory accounts
offered by others are placed together in (sociologically
false) integration. The literature on theories of
aggression, on crowd behaviour, on 'culture', sport and
society lead into a 'possible synthesis' in which the
particular features of football as 'natural arena' for
the exercise of masculine qualities, for the creation of
group bonds and the development of localised forms of
social organisation are posited as the key to its contemporary importance. The report then proceeds to call for
a more cautious form of press reportage, 'a major new
programme' for the provision of facilities of leisure and
recreation, and research into the relation between football
hooliganism and the decline in attendance at football
matches, as well as into the provision of better information for police purposes on the relation between the types
of matches and the degrees of violent incident to be
expected.

    One of the most obvious features of this 'synthesis'
is that it appropriates almost all of the descriptive
elements in the other theories, but removes them from
the theoretical perspective in which they were originally
given meaning. Peter Marsh has indeed already complained
of the way in which his work on group formation and
ritual in 'the ends' was misappropriated without accurate
recognition of the liberal non-interventionism which he
derives from this work (Marsh, 1978b). The point is,
of course, that the SSRC report's eclecticism is
profoundly theoretical. It is a liberal social scientific
version of the popular demand for practicable action for
the control of youthful dissidence, through the informed
actions of the state, including, as it does, in the end,
a discussion of the existing state of the relevant
criminal law. The 'discussion' of existing literature
in the SSRC report is the moment where the Committee
deconstructs and then reconstructs the 'knowledge' that
has been produced by researchers working in the area of
soccer violence, in order to make this knowledge
(a) *commonsensical*, in the sense of being a support to
dominant forms of commonsense reasoning about violence
as a breakdown of control, (b) *practical*, in the sense
of giving support to *penal* and *legal* measures as if they
could provide solutions to *social* contradictions, and
(c) *liberal*, in the sense of trying to encourage the
state to make improvements in the leisure and work
situation of disadvantaged youth in general. The

problems in each of these 'positions' have already been
discussed earlier: common sense does not, by definition,
penetrate to the structural changes which have produced
the violence around football; penal measures may merely
fill the jails and detention centres, whilst intensifying
the confrontation between working-class youth and its
'sport', and the state may not any longer be able to offer
social-democratic subsidies for the relief of economic
and environmental deprivation (the state may indeed be
caught in an altogether different logic).   The problems
that existed in each individual account of soccer
violence are merely compounded by the *incoherent integration* of the different theoretical perspectives by the
SSRC and Sports Council committee.

SOCCER VIOLENCE, CLASS AND THE STATE

Existing sociological accounts of soccer violence - like
the journalistic reports they deplore - can all be indicted
for their tendency to extrapolate a single feature of the
phenomenon (its style, its ritual character, its essential
violence, its existence as a feature of 'the crowd', its
connectedness with the violent language of the media,
and/or its 'existential dependency' on the fact of
societal reaction) and to treat this feature in isolation
from the 'ensemble' of social relations in which they
occur.   Equally seriously, they can be indicted for the
assumption they nearly all share, namely that the object
of analysis is properly to be found in the 'soccer-violence'
couplet: that *this* is what is to be explained, via a
'theory of soccer' (the history and sociology of the
game etc.), via a 'theory of violence', or via a sociology
that 'integrates' the two.
    Even radical sociologies are guilty here of dealing
analytically primarily with soccer violence (even though
they may reference the violence as a symptom of the larger
ensemble) when the problem must be to theorise the significance of soccer violence in Britain (and sports violence
in general) as a displacement of the primary relations of
the class and the state.   This is necessitated not merely
by the fact that limits have been encountered within the
sociological accounts themselves, but also by the
increasing need for social commentators to make their
theoretical work responsible.   The developing economic and
social crises of Western society *force* recognition of the
fundamental and worsening inequalities of class in its
general and specific effects.   We have to develop analysis
that begins and ends with the fundamentals of class in its

simple and complex divisiveness, and which is competent
to recognise in events, like the soccer violence panic,
a particular kind of decomposition within a class at a
particular moment in the history of that class within one
nation state. It is a task which has been initiated in a
recent text by Dave Robins and Phil Cohen, who address a
wide variety of features of decomposition in the British
working class, from the physical character of its
neighbourhoods to the dislocations in its long-standing
sporting traditions of boxing and street-fighting; and
who begin the task of explaining the growth of nihilism
and racism in the white youth of that class (Robins and
Cohen, 1978). (28) It is a task which must be undertaken,
however, across the broad terrain of the existence of
that, or any other, 'working-class' experience.

To speak of the need for class analysis is not to
argue for a return to what C. Wright Mills called the
'labour metaphysic', or what others have called *ouvrierism* -
the romanticisation of 'the working class' as *the* prime
agent in history. It is to the credit of structuralist
writers like Althusser and Poulantzas that they have
alerted us to the need for a close analysis of the
developing contradictions *within* the class, as well as
across the 'class map' as a whole. Robins and Cohen's
account of the social composition of football gangs
(white, male, and from the disorganised sections of the
class) should remind us of the role of sexual, racial
and status divisions within the class, and also alert
us to the problematic question for capital of the reserve
army of labour in moments of economic recession and
decline. Is this reserve army to be thought of as a part
of the working class or is it 'objectively' destined to
become a constituent part of an enlarged under-class,
a lumpenproletariat controlled and policed directly by
the state rather than capital?

I would insist that the key to the current decomposition
of working-class spectator sport lies in the decomposition
of the working class itself. Sensitive analysis of this
development depends on a full understanding of the original
involvement of the class in popular sport, later developments in that relation, and the subsequent decline in
what in another paper I called the 'working class weekend'
(Taylor, 1976). (29) It is an analysis which is actually
obscured by formal sociologies which speak only of crowds,
sub-cultures and 'labelling' and by journalistic accounts
which deal with sport generally as if it existed in a
classless and uncontradictory vacuum.

The importance of this kind of class analysis, however,
is that it suggests a way out of the politically agnostic

and un-historical responses of labelling theory and
other schools of sociology to 'the crisis', and here,
specifically, the crisis in the lived experience of the
reserve army. Specifically, there *are* grounds for
believing that the lived experience of this 'under-class'
is one of material and psychic frustration and resentment
at the continued reproduction of inequality of material
and existential possibility. Recent developments in
Western capitalist societies seem to be consigning
increasing proportions of the working class to the
marginal reserve army of labour. The 'revolution of
rising expectations' which was cultivated in popular
ideology throughout the 1950s and 1960s has now decidedly
been put into reverse, as a result of a series of
successful ideological offensives by organised ruling-
class opinion. And these economic and ideological logics
are at work on a working class which no longer has access
to the traditional institutions (of community, street,
extended family and even church) which traditionally acted
as its most significant support in such moments of crisis
and transition. Explanations of this kind of 'moment'
are unlikely from a sociology set apart from the political
economy and the lived ideological relations of class.
    Most of the sociological accounts we have discussed
(and especially labelling theory) can be faulted for
their continuing reproduction of the language of
pluralist political science as a means of conceptualising
the way in which soccer crowds are actually controlled.
The general reliance is on something like Edwin Lemert's
notion of the 'societal control culture' as a means of
identifying the bodies with the responsibility for
defining, labelling and controlling soccer hooligans.
For Lemert, the societal control culture comprises:
'the various agencies, both private and public, which
society or the community has organized to aid, repress,
rehabilitate, or otherwise deal with its "problems"'
(Lemert, 1951, p.68).
    But, as Hall et al. observe (in an already classic
passage in their recent important collective work on
'mugging and law and order'):
    The 'control-culture' approach ... appears too
    imprecise for our purposes. It identifies centres
    of power and their importance for the social-control
    process; but it does not locate them *historically*,
    and thus it cannot designate the significant moments
    of shift and change. It does not differentiate
    adequately *between* different types of state or
    political regime. It does not specify the kind of
    social formation which requires and establishes a

particular kind of legal order. It does not examine
the repressive functions of the state apparatuses in
relation to their consensual functions. Thus many
different types of society-'plural' societies, where
some are more plural than others, or 'mass societies',
where power is alleged to be distributed between the
elites, or a 'democratic society' with countervailing
powers - all are made compatible with the concept of
a 'social control culture'. It is not a historically
specific concept. In short, it is not premised on a
theory of the state: even less on a theory of the
state in a particular phase of capitalist development -
e.g. class democracies in the era of 'late capitalism'.
(Hall et al., 1978, p.195)

The agenda for analytical work presented here is
formidable enough. But 'Policing the Crisis' goes beyond
this, and argues for the recognition that the institutional
apparatus of the state is the basis of an *ideological
structure*. The argument is initially put in an abstract
form:

the *conditions* for [capitalist] production - or what
has come to be called *social reproduction* - are often
sustained in the apparently 'unproductive' spheres of
civil society and the state; and in so far as the
classes, fundamentally constituted in the productive
relation, also contend over this process of 'social
reproduction', the class struggle is present in all
the domains of civil society and the State. It is in
this sense that Marx called the state 'the official
resume of society', the 'table of contents of man's
practical conflicts'.... (Hall et al., 1978, p.202)

and then, more directly,

the state [has] another and crucial aspect or role
beside the legal and coercive one: the role of
leadership, of direction, of education and tutelage -
the sphere, not of 'domination by force', but of the
'production of consent'. (Ibid.)

The state is seen, following Gramsci, as an apparatus
within which the exercise of both coercive and consensual
forms of power is articulated: both types of domination
being present in all social formations. But the
production of *hegemony*, which for Gramsci was the form
of class power that was legitimated primarily in popular
consent, was best achieved in the liberal-democratic
state with its elaborate apparatus of 'representation'
and the organisation of social interests via parliamentary
parties, pressure groups, 'independent' mass media, etc.
The achievement of hegemony (or the universalisation of
the *particular* interests of a class) depends on what

Gramsci calls 'the decisive passage from the structure to the sphere of the complex superstructures' or, in other words, the achievement of authority over civil society as well as over production. In this perspective, analytical work on the mass media or on the organisation of state welfare or, indeed, sport is important in uncovering the ideological connections upon which such hegemonic domination depends. In particular, it is through our examination of the activities of state authorities and the organisations (like the free enterprise media, or privately owned sports club) which are allowed existence within the formal, public arena of the state that we can begin to understand how a dominant class attempts, through the state, to take the side of the people, and, thus, to produce popular consent to its rule.

This version of state theory is not without its critics: it has been accused of a variety of analytical sins (like functionalism) and empirical mistakes (over periodicisation). But it is a theory of the state which makes sense of the extent to which the British state, in particular, increasingly attempted until 1979 to move into the direct position of control over the economic problems being experienced by British capital *and* into the direct control over social policy at large. For the particular 'conjunctural' situation of British capital is one in which hegemony has become more and more precarious, at the level both of the economy and of civil society. The progressive liberalisation that has occurred in Britain (as well as in other societies) *has* unpacked and dislocated the traditional and substantially unreformed relations of the classes, but this reform of civil society has not been accompanied by a successful reform of the traditional economic base. The post-war period of social reconstruction and its promise of a new age of affluence has been followed by a succession of currency crises, by regular and deepening cycles of boom and slump within the national economy and by the entrenchment of capital and labour in regular struggles over their share of profits in a context of continuing low wages and low industrial productivity.

Gramsci identified a situation of this kind as a 'crisis of hegemony', occurring

> because the ruling class has failed in some major political undertaking for which it had requested, or forcibly extracted, the consent of the masses.... A 'crisis of authority' is spoken of: this is precisely the crisis of hegemony, or general crisis of the State. ('Prison Notebooks', quoted in Hall et al., 1978, p.216)

For Hall et al. the British state has been in the throes of such a crisis since the end of the 1960s, and in particular since 1968, the year of 'the parting of the waters' (Ibid., p.240). The crisis in civil society is thought, also, to have had reached high tide in 1972, a year in which a Conservative Government's Industrial Relations Act was introduced and immediately and violently resisted by the organised trade union movement, and a year of general panic in the media, amongst headteachers, psychiatrists, police and other guardians of the social order, over 'pupil violence' in schools, 'violence' among adolescent girls and mugging in the streets (Taylor, 1981a, ch.1).

The point about such moments of moral panic for Hall et al. is that they are instances of the activities of the state itself (and not merely the over-anxious interventions of social control agencies, spurred on by moral entrepreneurs). They are part of the transformation of the state as an ideological structure (resulting from an internal recomposition of the social forces) in the direction of the coercive pole: towards the attempt to construct a consensus around the need for an authoritarian form of state. The 'law and order campaigns' of the 1970s are no simple repeat of the instances of right-wing moral enterprise or morally indignant societal reaction of the form familiar in the 1960s. They are a constituent element of the work that is required to reconstitute the relation of the state to civil society.

The emergence of this strong, authoritarian state in Britain precisely parallels the panics over soccer hooliganism *and* over youthful behaviour in general. The parallels are indeed so close as to invite further speculation, for it was in the year of political 'cataclysm' (1968) that the skinhead first emerged within the youthful cohorts of the class; and it was in 1972 (the year of entry into world recession and also of the Heath government's confrontations with the unions) that the 'threshold of violence' amongst working-class youth was encountered in the mass media. Once again, Hall puts the overall argument astutely:

> the sharp reaction against football hooliganism has been paralleled by a striking *toughening* in popular social attitudes - marked by a return to traditional standards and practices in education, a call for stricter social discipline, a stern defence of the family and traditional ethical and sexual codes, an abrasive stance towards anyone who is 'scrounging' on the welfare state ... support for tougher sentencing and policing policies and harsher prison regimes and

so on. This general background against all forms of social permissiveness has already produced active grass-roots campaigns of vigilance and discipline, attributing our economic plight to the weakening of our moral fibre as a nation - a theme which has become an active element in the mainstream of political life, as well as being taken up and exploited on the extremist fringes of the far-right. Though football hooliganism was certainly not dreamed up by a conspiracy of strict disciplinarians, the excuse it has offered for the airing of traditionalist remedies has played a significant part in the construction of a popular social consensus which ... can only be called authoritarian. (Hall, 1978, p.35)

I could not improve on this formulation, but I have consciously chosen in this paper to leave aside the revisions made to labelling theory formulations of the moral panic by theorists of the state and of ideology (like Hall) until after full discussion of real 'declines' in the relations of working-class youth with their class, the state and civil society generally. The law and order rhetoric of the far-right has an unambiguously ideological character and significance in terms of the reformulation of the 'struggle for hegemony', but it also has a *real* reference to actually occurring behaviours and also to felt deteriorations in the lived experience of the class itself. The responses of police and other state agencies *are* very often necessitated by members of the working class calling for protection, and who *are* more open to attack and victimisation because of the weakening of traditional support and protection of working-class family and community. The social relations on working-class estates and high-rise flats *are* such as to give a significance to the policing of working-class homes, which it did not even have in traditional working-class communities.

The appeal of 'Thatcherism' to the British working class, in 1979, rested in part on the promise it implied of some restoration of order to increasingly disorderly and frequently dangerous working-class neighbourhoods, a promise which Thatcherism tried to underline in its constant derogatory equation of social democracy and permissiveness. This ideological offensive against social democracy continues, and may indeed be a key element when the Thatcher government attempts to retain electoral power in 1984, at the next general election.

Failing any significant new interventions by the Labour Party into the fields of law and order and social policy, in order to disconnect the class from Thatcherite ideology, we may expect that the next few years will see a continuing elaboration of the coercive policies of government, and a further dismantling of Keynesian economic and social policies.   There are therefore no grounds for expecting any real structural change in the social context of professional soccer.   That is to say that professional football in Britain will continue to be patronised by two kinds of spectator: by supporters in the stands, paying higher prices for seated accommodation, access to refreshments and police protection; and by supporters at the popular ends, caged in and policed by special police squads.   Further violent incidents are inevitable, especially as a result of the entry of Fascist organisers onto the football terraces, and the degree of control by the police exercised around the grounds themselves will be useless in preventing the fighting gangs from predatory behaviour on public transport and elsewhere, away from the grounds.   The ultimate consequence may be the financial collapse of many professional football clubs, brought about by massive declines in attendance, resulting from the fears of working-class and middle-class spectators alike.

Such a collapse is no inevitable result of soccer's economic problems (soccer survived the recession of the 1930s in a very healthy state), nor is there much evidence that soccer has exhausted the *interest* of its audience (television-viewing figures are high, and the rapid development of soccer in North America is evidence of the intrinsic appeal of the game).   The recent development of other, competing sports and leisure-time activities in Britain could in principle be a source of inspiration to professional soccer (to innovate, involve its local community, think through the needs of its audience, etc.) rather than be a source of diminishing popular interest in soccer.   But these visions *are* idealist because they fail to recognise that the current problems of professional soccer in Britain are directly the product and expression of a major crisis in working-class experience, deriving in turn from a major ruling-class initiative to alter the character of capital-labour relations.   What makes the task of renovation in soccer impossible is the refusal of the established authorities who govern the longest-established and easily the most popular sport of the class even to recognise a simple connection.   The economic fate of professional football in Britain is inextricably bound up with the economic and social destiny of the British working class as a whole.   Any successful resolution to the problem of soccer hooliganism must therefore depend on

political and economic policies which create real social
order in working-class life, and not on the elaboration
of penal measures for sections of that class by an
authoritarian state. There are few signs of any such
policy coming from the existing government or opposition
in Britain at the end of 1980, and no spark of recognition
of that as the problem from the headquarters of the
various organisations involved in the mass spectator sport
of the working class.

NOTES

1 At the end of the 1980-1 season it was revealed that
   attendances at English League games had fallen to
   21,907,569, a drop on the previous season of $2\frac{3}{4}$
   million. This total compares with 41.2 million in
   1948-9 and 30 million in 1967-8 (Football: our most
   popular sport, 'New Society', 23 October 1980). The
   loss of spectators between 1979-80 and between 1980-1
   represented a loss of about £6 million in 'gate money'
   and an unknown loss of other income from advertisers
   or sponsors (cf. Taylor, 1981b).
2 A Marplan survey published in the 'News of the World'
   in August 1980 (of 622 who 'expressed an interest in
   football') found that the former supporters who did
   not watch any football during the 1979-80 season
   blamed 'violence at the ground' in 48 per cent of
   cases; 15 per cent blamed 'family commitments' and
   13 per cent expensive admission charges (quoted in
   'New Society', 23 October 1980).
3 Ice hockey may be the 'joker in the pack' in
   discussions of violence around sport, since there is
   a long history of violent incidents amongst both
   players and spectators, *pre-dating* the covering of
   the sport on the mass medium of television. Michael
   Smith, and others, have discussed the instance of
   the Montreal hockey riot in March 1955 (Smith, 1975;
   Lang and Lang, 1961). Some indication of the
   severity of the situation in professional ice hockey
   may be gained from the fact that the sport's troubles
   are now receiving coverage in the British press.
   A good example is the piece by David Lacey on the
   New York Rangers-St Louis Blues fixture of March
   1973 (Slap shot league, 'Guardian', 20 March 1979).
4 Major discussions took place, for example, into
   'indiscipline among players and spectators' at the
   congress of the European Union of Football Associations
   (UEFA) held in Edinburgh in May 1974 (consequent on a
   fall in attendances at European tournament soccer games
   during 1972 and 1973) ('Guardian', 23 May 1974).

5 The 'soccer war' between El Salvador and Honduras
   was precipitated by spectator riots during the three-
   match regional finals of the World Soccer Cup in those
   countries in June 1970. For discussions of the role
   of soccer in the maintenance of social relations in
   two Latin American societies, Brazil and Mexico, see
   Lever (1969) and Taylor (1970).

6 A syndicated report in British newspapers in 1975
   indicated that riots had recently occurred in games
   in Nalchick (in the North Caucasus), in Dushanbe
   (capital of Tadzhikistan) (when the home side, Pamir,
   were losing to the Red Army club of Rostov) and at
   the Radzan stadium in the Armenian capital of Yerevan,
   whose home side Ararat had just won the Soviet Cup.
   Even in 'more well-behaved' Moscow, the authorities
   use uniformed troops to keep order during games (and
   even in the 100,000 seat Lenin stadium (Hooliganism
   hits soccer in Russia, 'Star', Sheffield, 26 September
   1975).

7 Violence amongst football spectators has been the
   subject of an increasing number of journalistic
   reports and assessments. Cf. The ugly sports fan,
   'Newsweek', 17 June 1974, pp.93-5, and P.S. Greenberg
   and Clark Whelton, Wild in the stands, 'New Times',
   vol.9, no.10, 11 November 1977.

8 In particular, there is evidence of pitch invasions
   by fans in both Scotland and England in the years
   immediately after the First World War. In Scotland,
   many of the soccer fans were members of 'brake clubs',
   whose commitment to violent support of their teams
   was at least as great as the fighting gangs of the
   1970s. Members of the 'brake clubs' were known for
   their wearing of steel helmets painted in club
   colours and for their use of weapons retrieved from
   the Great War. Cf. correspondence from T. Paris
   et al., 'Sunday Times', 6 April 1969.

9 One high point of this crowd 'tactic' was the
   invasion of the Newcastle United playing pitch by
   supporters of Glasgow Rangers, on 21 May 1969.
   This 'occupation' of the pitch occurred as a result
   when 1,000 Rangers fans realised that their team
   was likely to be eliminated from the Inter-Cities
   Fairs Cup competition (Newcastle had just scored
   their second goal, with ten minutes left of normal
   time). Newcastle was again the scene of a pitch
   invasion in March 1974, when home supporters moved
   on to the playing area after Nottingham Forest
   went into a 3-1 lead in an FA Cup-tie. After
   resumption of play, Newcastle scored three goals to

'win' the game 4-3; but the game was later declared void and replayed.

10   The Lang Report was preceded by an unofficial enquiry by a team of psychiatrists from Birmingham, published in 1968. The Harrington Report, presented to the Minister of Sport in that year, was a characteristic example of psychiatric positivism, with its primary concern being to differentiate the (arrested) hooligan from the non-hooligan in terms of the possession of certain individual psycho-pathological characteristics. Cf. discussion in Taylor, 1971a, 1971b, and Ingham, 1978. The Report seems to have been a largely *individual* initiative, and to have had no major significance for state policy at the time.

11   The ad hoc accounts in the press of the origins of the skinhead ranged from the assertion that the skinhead 'uniform' was a development of naval uniforms (and thus a phenomenon of the south coast of England) to the view that the skinhead style was an imitation of contemporary American teenage styles. The considered view - that the style was complex, but largely a caricature and celebration of the blue-collar worker - was only to emerge a little later. For a fuller discussion, see Taylor and Wall, 1976.

12   This major difference in the analysis of the skinhead is caught in the contrast between what can now be seen as a *premature* but far-sighted analysis of the potentialities of rough working-class youth's narrowing range of options by John Hoyland (1969), and the attempt of Project Free London (a middle-class anarchist group) to link into skinhead culture, in the free leaflet, Up theirs (Agro Pilot Issue, December 1969).

13   On 20 September, 1969, a trainload of Tottenham Hotspur supporters who 'had become destructive' were turned off a train at Flitwick and left to walk the remaining fifty miles to London. As a consequence of this incident, the Home Office announced that there would henceforth be 'stewards' on all trains carrying fans to football games, and the circulation of a code of good practice for supervising supporters on trains (Home Office Press Notice, 20 November 1969).

14   On 19 September, 1973, the Minister for Sport under the then Conservative government, Mr Eldon Griffiths, announced that the recommendation of the Wheatley Enquiry would only be enforced in the case of grounds capable of holding 10,000 or more spectators; and that the first grounds to be modified for safety

purposes would be those used for international,
English First and Second Division and Scottish First
Division Matches (68 in total). Even they 'would be
put to no unnecessary expense' ('Star', Sheffield,
19 September 1973).

15 Notable for a time amongst the clubs who tried to
'involve' their young supporters were Coventry City
(with their Sky Blues Club), Sheffield United, and
Notts County. Many of these youth organisations are
now defunct; and the short history of these initiatives
requires research and analysis. The democratising
gestures of the club managements were in many cases
compromised by the attempts of the club to involve
local police in 'making contact' with local working-
class youth.

16 These conferences included the national conference
organised by Glasgow Corporation in November 1972,
and a series of conferences organised by other local
authorities and by police organisations throughout
the 1970s.

17 The demand for immediate practical action in combating
social problems is central to the Western professional
journalist's preference for commonsense solutions to
problems and also to the social policy programmes
of the New Right. The avowed atheoreticism of both
these constituencies is underpinned by a profound,
and unstated, belief in the tenets of nineteenth-
century liberalism updated and revamped in recent
years to enable attacks on social-democratic state
interventionism. In criminology, the clearest
exponent of New Right 'common sense' as a means of
attacking social democracy is J.Q. Wilson (1975).

18 In practice, state responses to soccer violence in
Britain during the 1970s did not simply involve the
use of existing penal disciplines. They have
contributed to the continuing use (and revival) of
institutional measures, like the Attendance Centre,
the Remand Centre, and the Detention·Centre, which
were scheduled for attrition or abolition (in the
Children and Young Persons Act of 1969); and they
were also in part responsible for the re-introduction
'experimentally' of the military glasshouse version
of the Detention Centre by the Conservative government
in 1979. Arrested soccer hooligans may also be a
significant proportion of the youthful populations
of the 'secure units' (lock-ups) in the Community
Home System, where places increased from 60 (in 1969)
to 6,000 in 1977, and are likely to escalate further
(cf. Taylor, 1981a).

19   There have been innumerable documentaries of this sort
     on soccer violence, on British television, in the
     last ten years. I have personally participated in
     half a dozen, including a 'Man Alive' special on
     BBC-2 in November 1974 and a Scottish Television
     special in November 1976. On each of these occasions,
     the agenda of the programme has been set in terms of
     an initial evaluation of the 'seriousness' of the
     issue, with an implicit bias against any participant
     who wanted either to deny its seriousness or to
     place its seriousness in an explicit context (for
     example, the contemporary situation of working-class
     youth). The third stage of each programme (guaranteed
     in advance by the inclusion of police officers,
     representatives of football clubs, etc.) was an
     evaluation of existing, *practical* policy alternatives.
20   The existence of this area of 'freedom', within which
     all is dependent on the experience or agility of the
     expert, gives individuals who are experienced in the
     implicit rules of television debate (like professional
     politicians of high-standing) very considerable
     advantage. Cf. the examination of the rules underlying
     party-political exchanges in current affairs television
     by Hall, Connell and Curti (1976).
21   Between 1969 and 1973, the percentage of the total
     numbers of unemployed in Britain aged 19 or under
     increased from 10.4 per cent to 14.3 per cent, and
     a Department of Employment Study in 1974 projected
     that the percentage of under 20s in the labour force
     would decline from 8.6 per cent in 1971 to 4.6 per
     cent in 1991. (The 1921 figure had been 18.7 per
     cent.) Most of these pessimistic estimates are
     currently being revised, downwards, in the context
     of the recession, and recognition of the likely
     impact of the new micro-technology.
22   Although 'worklessness' is the key to the current
     crisis of working-class youth in Britain, it is clear
     that there is a broader withdrawal of legitimacy for
     'liberal-democratic' politics taking place (resulting
     from the continuing reproduction of the inequalities
     and amorality of anachronistic forms of class relation
     in that society). The 'nihilism' of punk is economic
     only in the final instance; and clearly constitutes
     at one level a deep attack on the double-standards
     and the pretence of British middle-class society.
23   The authors of the Harrington Report of 1967 were
     apparently convinced that soccer hooligans were
     possessed by a psychological syndrome produced by
     contagion in crowd situations, and evidenced by a

glazed expression on faces. They were later to
witness the same expression on the faces of anti-
American demonstrators in Grosvenor Square in 1968.
In one move, they were able to invalidate the social
or political meaning of soccer violence *and* the
Grosvenor Square demonstrations of the late 1960s.
(Did the football fury syndrome hit Park Lane?,
'Sunday Times', 28 June 1968). In 1972, Derek Bryce
Smith, in the 'British Medical Journal', wrote that
there was a serious possibility that 'abnormal
behaviour' (like soccer violence) was associated with
'elevated levels of neurotoxic compounds picked up
in the normal course of life' (lead, and other forms
of environmental pollution) (Could pollution send
fans wild? 'Guardian', 29 May 1972).

24 Cf. in particular the critique of the work of Belson
on the alleged relation between television and
delinquency by Murdock and McCron (1979).

25 Some of these concerns were specified in the Wheatley
Report, in 1972, and later in the McElhone Report
of 1977.

26 This next section draws upon a recent review article
(Taylor, 1979). A more extended examination and
critique of Marsh's work on ritual violence is
available in Murphy and Williams (1980).

27 A good example of this phenomenon of under-reportage
was the silence of the national press as to the
character of the crowd disturbances that occurred
early in the League Cup quarter-final between West
Ham United and Tottenham Hotspur on 2 December 1980.
Eye-witness accounts confirm that the disturbances
involved fighting gangs of West Ham supporters
brandishing Fascist insignia attacking nearby
Tottenham supporters, on the grounds that they were
Jewish.

28 For a frightening analysis of racial violence, and
its press reportage, in the East End of London, see
Bethnal Green and Stepney Trades Council (1978).

29 This kind of analysis has been attempted for popular
leisure activity in the US by Alt (1976).

REFERENCES

ALT, J. (1976), Beyond class: the decline of industrial
labor and leisure, 'Telos', vol.28 (summer).
BETHNAL GREEN AND STEPNEY TRADES COUNCIL (1978), 'Blood
on the Streets', a Report by Bethnal Green and Stepney
Trades Council on Racial Attacks in East London.

CLARKE, J. (1973), Football hooliganism and the skinheads,
Occasional paper, Centre for Contemporary Cultural
Studies, University of Birmingham.
CLARKE, J., HALL, S., JEFFERSON, T. and ROBERTS, B. (1975),
Subcultures, cultures and class, in S. Hall and T.
Jefferson (eds), 'Resistance through Rituals: Youth
Subcultures in Post War Britain', London, Hutchinson.
CLARKE, J. (1975), The skinheads and the magical recovery
of community, in S. Hall and T. Jefferson (eds), op.cit.
CLARKE, J. (1978), Football and working class fans:
tradition and change, in R. Ingham (ed.), 'Football
Hooliganism: The Wider Context', London, Inter-Action.
COHEN, P. (1976), Cognitive styles, spectator roles and
the social organisation of the football end, 'Aspects of
the Youth Question' (318a Mare St., London E2): Working
Paper no.6.
COHEN, S. (1972), 'Folk Devils and Moral Panics: The
Creation of the Mods and Rockers', London, McGibbon & Kee.
DAVIES, H. (1972), 'The Glory Game', London, Weidenfeld &
Nicholson.
FRITH, S. (1978), 'The Sociology of Rock', London, Constable.
GREENBERG, P.S. and WHELTON, C. (1977), Wild in the stands,
'New Times', vol.9, no.10, 11 November.
HALL, S. (1978), The treatment of 'football hooliganism'
in the press, in R. Ingham (ed.), op.cit.
HALL, S., CONNELL, I. and CURTI, L. (1976), The 'unity'
of current affairs television, 'Cultural Studies', vol.9,
pp.51-94.
HALL, S. and JEFFERSON, T. (eds) (1975), 'Resistance
Through Rituals: Youth Subculture in Post War Britain',
London, Hutchinson.
HALL, S., CRICHTER, C., JEFFERSON, T., CLARKE, J. and
ROBERTS, B. (1978), 'Policing the Crisis: Mugging, the
State and Law and Order', London, Macmillan.
HOYLAND, J. (1969), The skinheads: a youth group for the
National Front?, 'Black Dwarf', 30 August.
INGHAM, R. (1978), A critique of some previous recommenda-
tions, in R. Ingham (ed.), op.cit.
INGHAM, R. (ed.) (1978), 'Football Hooliganism: The
Wider Context', London, Inter-Action.
JONES, M.N. (1969, 1970), Soccer hooliganism in the
Metropolitan Police District, Management Services
Department Reports 8/9 and 19/70, (unpublished).
LANG (1969), 'Report of the Working Party on Crowd
Behaviour at Football Matches' (Chairman: Sir John Lang),
London, HMSO.
LANG, K. and LANG, G.E. (1961), 'Collective Dynamics',
New York, Crowell.
LEMERT, E.M. (1951), 'Social Pathology', New York, McGraw-
Hill.

LEVER, J. (1969), Soccer as a Brazilian way of life, 'Trans-Action' (December), reprinted in G.P. Stone (ed.), 'Games, Sport and Power', New Brunswick, N.J., Trans-Action.

MARSH, P. (1978a), 'Aggro: The Illusion of Violence', London, Dent.

MARSH, P. (1978b), A critique of the Sports Council/SSRC Report 'Public Disorder and Sporting Events' in R. Ingham (ed.), op.cit.

MARSH, P., ROSSER, E. and HARRE, R. (1978), 'The Rules of Disorder', London, Routledge & Kegan Paul.

MORGAN, P. (1978), 'Delinquent Fantasies', London, Maurice Temple Smith.

MUNGHAM, G. and PEARSON, G. (eds) (1976), 'Working Class Youth Cultures', London, Routledge & Kegan Paul.

MURDOCK, G. and McCRON, R. (1979), The broadcasting and delinquency debate, 'Screen Education', vol.30 (Spring), pp.51-68.

MURPHY, P.J. and WILLIAMS, J. (1980), Football hooliganism: an illusion of violence? Unpublished paper, University of Leicester, Department of Sociology.

PEARSON, G.(1976), Paki-Bashing in a North East Lancashire Cotton Town: A Case Study and its History, in G. Mungham and G. Pearson (eds), 1976.

ROADBURG, A. (1980), Factors precipitating fan violence: a comparison of professional soccer in Britain and North America, 'British Journal of Sociology', vol.31, no.2, (June) pp.265-76.

ROBINS, D. and COHEN, P. (1978), 'Knuckle Sandwich: Growing Up in the Working Class City', Harmondsworth, Penguin.

SCHWENDINGER, H. and SCHWENDINGER, J. (1976), Marginal youth and social policy, 'Social Problems', vol.24, no.2, (December), pp.184-91.

SMITH, M.D. (1975), Sport and collective violence, in D.W. Ball and J.W. Loy (eds), 'Sport and Social Order: Contributions to the Sociology of Sport', Reading, Mass., Addison-Wesley.

SOCIAL SCIENCE RESEARCH COUNCIL/SPORTS COUNCIL (1978), 'Public Disorder and Sporting Events: a report by a joint council of the Sports Council and the Social Science Research Council, London, Sports Council/SSRC.

TAYLOR, I. (1970), Social control through sport: Soccer in Mexico, unpublished paper presented to BSA Annual Conference.

TAYLOR, I. (1971a), Soccer consciousness and soccer hooliganism, in S. Cohen (ed.), 'Images of Deviance', Harmondsworth, Penguin.

TAYLOR, I. (1971b), Football Mad - a speculative

sociology of soccer hooliganism, in E. Dunning (ed.),
'The Sociology of Sport', London, Cass.

TAYLOR, I. (1976), Spectator violence around football:
the rise and fall of the 'Working Class Weekend',
'Research Papers in Physical Education', vol.4, no.1,
(August), pp.4-9.

TAYLOR, I. (1979), Two new departures in the analysis of
youth violence, 'British Journal of Criminology' (July),
pp.270-8.

TAYLOR, I. (1980), The law and order issue in the British
and Canadian General Elections of 1979, 'Canadian Journal
of Sociology', vol.5, no.3, pp.285-312.

TAYLOR, I. (1981a), 'Law and Order: Arguments for
Socialism', London, Macmillan.

TAYLOR, I. (1981b), Professional Sport and the Recession:
The Case of British Soccer, paper given to the 1st
Regional Symposium of the International Committee for
the Sociology of Sport (28 May to 1 June, Vancouver).

TAYLOR, I. and WALL, D. (1976), Beyond the Skinheads:
some notes on the emergence of Glamrock Cult, in Mungham
and Pearson, op.cit.

TRIVIZAS, E. (1980), Offences and offenders in football
crowd disorders, 'British Journal of Criminology', vol.20,
no.3 (July), pp.276-88.

WHANNEL, G. (1979), Football, crowd behaviour and the
press, 'Media, Culture and Society', vol.1, no.4,
(October), pp.327-42.

WILSON, J.Q. (1975), 'Thinking about Crime', New York,
Basic Books.

Chapter 8

Sport and drugs

Martyn Lucking

I would like to start by defining the meanings of the two
words 'sport' and 'drugs'. The 'Oxford Dictionary' states
that a sport is an amusement, diversion or fun, and that
a sportsman is a person who regards life as a game in
which opponents must be allowed fair play. You may take
the latter how you like in the context of international
sport today, but the gist is that the fun should be fair.
  A drug is a substance, either organic or inorganic,
which can influence metabolism within an organism. It
would seem that on the face of it fair fun would have
little to do with meddling with metabolism. Regrettably,
so far have some sports been removed from fun and
fairness, that it is now *almost* obligatory for leading
athletes to interfere with their very biochemistry and
structure, by means of drugs, in order to achieve
excellence.

LAWS OF DRUGS IN SPORTS

The Olympic Movement, through the International Olympic
Committees, have definitely ruled 'thou shalt not'. The
use of drugs by Olympic sportsmen and sportswomen is
forbidden. The laws are unequivocal and the penalties
for contravening them are clear. Likewise, governing
bodies of sports have no doubt that the use of drugs to
influence sports performance is unfair and reprehensible.
They at least want the fun to be fair.

BANNED DRUGS

The International Amateur Athletic Federation have drawn
up a list of banned drugs which, if an athlete is found

taking them, would incur penalty. (1) The list is long
with many equally long and almost unpronounceable names,
but can be categorised under the following headings:
(a) Psychomotor stimulant drugs - Amphetamines, etc.
(b) Sympathomimetic amines - Ephedrine, etc.
(c) Miscellaneous central nervous stimulants - Strychnine,
     etc.
(d) Narcotic analgesics - Morphine, etc.
(e) Anabolic steroids - Dianabol, etc.
This list is already out of date.

     The following drugs which are not currently on the
banned list, but are currently in use to assist sports
performance or to lessen the likelihood of detection,
will probably be added when the extensive groundwork
discussions and research necessary for international
agreement have been completed:
(f) Diuretic compounds - Frusemide, etc.
(g) Aldosterone inhibitors - Spironalactone, etc.
(h) Beta blocking agents - Inderal, etc.
(i) Cortic steroids and their derivatives - Hydrocortisone,
     etc.
(j) Sex hormones - Testosterone, etc.

USE OF DRUGS IN SPORT OVER THE LAST 25 YEARS

I think that it would be fair to say that in the 1950s the
use of drugs to influence sporting achievement was
confined very largely to certain professional human
sports where the stakes were high and the pressures
great, and to animal racing as with horses and dogs.
The sport which seemed most ready to use drugs at that
time was cycling, especially the longer-distance type of
race such as the Tour de France, where a cyclist built up
increasing fatigue which one night's rest was not sufficient
to restore. Cyclists were using the stimulant drugs, in
particular the amphetamine - or purple heart type of
compound - which have the effect of heightening awareness
and counteracting the effects of fatigue. Morphine and
its derivatives have a similar action initially, having
the advantage of producing a sense of euphoria which
combines nicely with the analgesic (or pain-relieving)
property, to allow an athlete to endure the agony of the
last hour or so at a stage before the sedative effect
comes on lulling the athlete into a deep sleep. Furthermore, he will awaken refreshed the following day for the
next gruelling stage. The disadvantage of morphia is
the need to time the administration accurately in an
event taking several hours. If the drug is administered

too soon the euphoric effect will have given way to
sedation before the finishing line is crossed and here
there could be disastrous results.

Curiously and conversely, drugging in horse and dog
racing is not usually to enhance the performance, but
rather to slow the animal down. In this way a favourite
in a race can be nicely 'nobbled' and put out of the
running, whilst a less-fancied member of the field, with
a more favourable betting price, is enabled to do better
than if the favourite was running under normal circumstances. Doping in horse and dog racing is nowhere near
the spectacular problem it used to be - or so one gathers
by its rarity as a headline nowadays. It seems that the
racing fraternity has largely come to terms with drugs
by a sophisticated and thorough system of policing and
checking and severe penalties.

Twenty-five years ago the amount of drug-taking in
amateur sport was minimal. The odd person would try the
effect of a stimulant to enhance a performance when they
were getting stale, or a clay pigeon or rifle shooter
would use alcohol or some other anti-anxioltic to steady
his aim. Sport for the amateur in the 1950s was more
the fun that it was supposed to be and the pressures to
cheat were less.

During the late 1950s a more sinister type of drug
administration was being pioneered. Not much was said
or published about it, but there were comments to the
effect that certain Eastern European female athletes
had a remarkable resemblance to men. The sex test was
introduced to determine that athletes were in fact the
sex they purported to be. In 1962 some five well-known
Eastern European women athletes declined to submit to
the sex examination and walked out of the European Games.
Could it have been that these 'ladies' were showing
secondary male sexual characteristics as the result of
drug administration? Certainly, at this time, male
athletes were beginning to use male hormone derivitives -
or anabolic steroids - to enhance the effect of their
training. By 1964 the practice was probably widespread
in American universities and also in Eastern Europe.
With each succeeding major international event after
that, the practice of anabolic steroid administration
increased without bounds. I can well remember a good
friend whom I had known for several years as a competitor,
and by whom I had never been beaten, almost overnight
increasing in size from seventeen to twenty-one-plus
stones, and increasing his shot-putting performance from
around 56 feet to 64 feet. The effect was dramatic: it
was almost as if a 'Michelin Man' had been blown up - but
made not just of fat, but of useful muscle.

Initially in the United Kingdom, where sport was still commonsensically fun and fair, the practice was regarded with disbelief and accompanied by protestations that anabolic steroids could not have this effect anyway. Later, the reality of the situation became more apparent, and efforts were made (a) to put sex hormone derivitives on the banned drug list and (b) to determine an effective test to detect the drug administration.

Thanks largely to the efforts of Professor Arnold Beckett of Chelsea College and Professor Raymond Brooks of St Thomas' Hospital, effective tests were developed, so that by 1976 testing for anabolic steroids was an accepted policy and used in the Olympic Games in Montreal. Eight athletes were found to have a positive test result. All major games subsequently have been tested for anabolics, and with each one a crop of 'positives' found, not just in what are known as the 'heavy events' (weight-lifting and throwing), but recently in middle-distance runners also.

I mentioned before that I regarded the advent of the use of sex-hormone derivitives as more sinister. Perhaps not more sinister in some senses than the use of opiates, but nevertheless engineering sexual characteristics to achieve strength and aggression is sinister, and smacks somewhat of superman. Furthermore, hormone engineering has not been limited to achieving strength and aggression, but includes the control of the onset of puberty of gymnasts. A slender, light, pre-pubertal figure is more advantageous to a girl gymnast than that altered by the broadening at the pelvis and breast development of puberty.

With each successive year newer applications of drugs to influence sporting achievement are being found. Improved control of 'competition nerves' results from the use of beta-blocking agents – drugs which block the beta effect of adrenalin. Cortisone-type drugs are being used to help to overcome the stress of extreme exhaustion. Diuretic drugs are being used to help eliminate other drugs from the body to avoid detection. It seems that where there is a drug with a potent action it will be used to see what effect it will have on training, performance or recovery.

TYPES OF DRUG TAKING

I subdivide drugs into those taken at the event and those taken during preparation. I have touched on most of these during the former brief outline of developments during the last twenty-five years.

Drugs used at the event

1   Stimulants
Amphetamine-like drugs. Action: to increase alertness
and offset fatigue by affecting the central nervous
system. Side effects: addiction and hypertension.

2   Stimulants and sedatives
Opiate derivatives. Action: powerful analgesics with
euphoric stimulatory stage followed by sedation. Side
effects: nausea, vomiting and respiratory depression,
strongly addictive.

3   Anti-anxiolytics
Multitude of drugs including such preparations as
barbiturates, the benzodiazepine group (Valium, Librium),
alcohol and beta-blocking agents. Action: to lessen or
eliminate the nervous tension and anxiety associated
with competition.

4   Cortico-steroids
Cortisone type drugs are being used to help the body
overcome stress. The normal reaction of the body to
stress from exertion, illness or psychological factors
is to increase the normal secretions of the adrenal
cortex. Action: it is reported that cortico-steroids
are being used to assist the normal production of the
adrenal cortex in the stress of extreme exertion and to
aid subsequent recovery. Side effects: there are
multiple hazardous side effects including thinning of
skin and bones with subsequent brittleness, hypertension,
muscle weakness and dystrophy, diabetes, increased
susceptibility to infection, suppression of normal
endogenous cortico-steroid production.

Drugs used during training

Sex hormone derivatives
Anabolic steroids. Compounds derived from the male
hormone testosterone with maximal anabolic properties
and minimal virulising properties. Action: (a) it is
believed that when taken by a fully trained athlete
together with an intensive power-orientated exercise
programme and a high protein intake these drugs will
give an added boost to both body weight-gain and muscle
power, (b) they give the athlete a sense of well-being
and increased aggression to train harder, and (c) they
improve the recovery rate from training schedules,

thereby enabling more work to be done. Administration:
by tablet or longer acting injection. Side effects: liver
toxicity and liver tumour (oral drugs only), virulisation
in females, hypertension, fluid retention, interference
with adrenal cortex secretion, acne, nausea, hypercholer-
sterolaemia and possible increased incidence of coronary
thrombosis.

Testosterone. The male hormone itself has the same
action as the anabolic derivatives but more powerfully
so. The side effects are largely the same, but more
pronounced.

DETECTION OF DRUGS

This has become a science in itself, thanks largely to
the efforts of Professors Raymond Brooks and Arnold
Beckett.

All detection is done on urine samples, by mass
screening for all drugs with radio immunoassay and then
specific identification by gas chromatography. These
tests are carried out by a special department - the Drug
Control and Teaching Centre at Chelsea College under
the supervision of Dr D. Cowan. With the guidance of
this department it is hoped to set up laboratories
worldwide to enable testing to be done close to the
athlete.

Professor Beckett supervised drug testing at the
Winter Olympics at Lake Placid and at the Summer Olympics
in the USSR, 1980. It is imperative that testing is
done absolutely accurately and that standard procedures
are adhered to so that there is no doubt left for
dispute. Hence the need for properly supervised
specialist laboratories to carry out this work.

As previously mentioned, testing has been done at all
major international sports meetings for many years and
these tests have included the detection of anabolic
steroids since 1976. Testing was introduced at major
domestic meetings in the United Kingdom in 1978 and this
has meant that UK athletes have been subjected to testing
more frequently than their foreign counterparts during
the last two outdoor athletic seasons. However, despite
this, the use of drugs to influence training has continued
because the testing is only being done at major events
and it is possible to leave off drug administration for
sufficient time to allow it to be eliminated from the
body and yet allow the increased strength to be maintained.

SPECIAL REFERENCE TO SEX HORMONES AND THEIR DERIVATIVES

To those closely connected with international-class
athletics the advent of the use of anabolic steroids to
influence training has been as significant as the advent
of weight-training and interval-training.

Most athletes reaching this level of competition will
have very likely used them or have made a conscious
decision to jeopardise their chances in competition by
refraining. Nevertheless, there is a scarcity of evidence
to support the widely held belief in the efficacy of
these drugs. The problem here lies in the fact that drug
administration is illicit, therefore it is pursued in a
clandestine way. Very few practitioners of their use are
willing openly to admit to the fact, and even less willing
to subject themselves to scientific analysis for the
purpose of publication. Hence, much of what is known of
the use of these drugs is hearsay and speculation.

Some attempts have been made to analyse scientifically
the expected benefits and side effects of anabolic steroids
in volunteers but have failed to show any real benefit
above that of placebo. One significant trial was done on
well-trained experienced weight-lifters by Freed, Banks,
Longson and Burley at the University of Manchester in
1975. (2) I stress the words well-trained and experienced.
I also stress that the trial was conducted when the
weight-lifters were taking in a high protein diet. It
seems that these two factors are a prerequisite to obtain
the super benefit anabolic steroids are purported to give.
This paper did in fact show that there was a significant
increase in strength as a result of the anabolic administration. A further trial, not against placebo or on a
double blind basis, by Johnson in 1969, (3) did show
benefit, but others have failed to confirm this. Indeed,
one trial using placebo has shown this alone to be very
effective. (4) All this adds to the confusion, but does
not apparently deter the athlete from using drugs.

Observers of the United Kingdom domestic athletic scene
over the last two outdoor seasons will have noted a fall
in standards in the two heavy events - shot and discus.
It will be remembered that it is during these years that
testing has been carried out at major domestic events.
Hence the likelihood of detection has increased and one
would suppose the use of anabolic steroids during the
summer period therefore decreased.

In Britain one suspects that it is only the leading
athletes with an international ambition who are tempted
to use anabolic steroids. Hence, in events such as shot
or discus, probably only the top four to six athletes

would, in fact, use them. In plotting a graph to illustrate
the trend in standards it would be reasonable to expect
that the top ten in an event would illustrate the general
trend. In the accompanying graphs I have taken the average
of the top ten in the ranking lists for that year in each
event. I doubt whether more than five of these would in
fact be using drugs, and probably less, so that the average
would, if anything, tend to disguise any fall in overall
performance when those few drug-takers cease to take drugs.
Nevertheless, it will be seen that the standard in the
shot and discus show a marked fall, which is not reflected
in high and long jumps.

Again, taking the top three United Kingdom athletes in
the AAA Championships for shot, long jump and three miles
it will be seen that, whereas the three miles shows a very
undulating picture, long jump shows an undulating overall
improvement, shot shows a dramatic increase with an equally
dramatic decline coinciding with the years of increasing
and then decreasing use of anabolic steroids.

I cannot pretend that these graphs prove anything.
There are obviously several factors to be taken into
consideration. Nevertheless, it would seem that some
factor has influenced the rise and fall in the standards
of the shot and discus which is not apparent in other
events and the rise and fall is coincident with the rise
and fall in the probable use of anabolic steroids. Further
analysis of the statistics over the next few years would
perhaps be more revealing. However, the inference is
there, and it is a pointer towards the efficacy of
anabolic steroids in the heavy events.

The main problem now with the detection of anabolic
steroid use is that the administration is away from the
scene of competition. Thus athletes are still able to
use them without fear of detection so long as they stop
a judicious time prior to a major event. This will
inevitably reduce the effectiveness of the drug, but
does not stop the administration. It is reported that
certain athletes are getting over the problem of needing
to stop drugs by switching from anabolic steroids to
pure testosterone just prior to major events. The
rationale behind this is to avoid the long-term use of
the more harmful testosterone but to obtain the maximum
anabolism and aggression from the more potent drug just
at the time of the event. Administered testosterone is
undetectable since it is indistinguishable from that which
is naturally secreted in males. Hence, to solve the
problem it is necessary first, to test athletes during
the training period, and second, to determine whether
testosterone has been administered.

It is considered probable by Professor Brooks that it
will become possible quantitatively to determine levels
of the pituitary hormones - the follicle-stimulating
hormone and the luteinising hormone - which are reciprocally
affected by levels of circulating male hormone, and to
arrive at a circulating level of these hormones to be used
as a base line to indicate whether or not additional
significant male hormone has been administered. If this
becomes the case, it will then become possible to
determine whether supportive testosterone is being, or
has been, used.

Spot testing of athletes away from the events during
training presents a mainly administrative problem which,
if overcome in motivated athletes and countries, could well
be abused in those who wished to cheat the system. To this
end the International Athletes Club (IAC) of this country
has initiated a two part programme (a) to test out the
mechanism of spot-testing athletes at random in the
community and (b) to initiate international debate and
hopefully action along these lines on a world scale.

At this stage, nearly half-way through the IAC's spot-
testing experiment, it can be said that it will probably
be possible to carry out such testing at random. The Club
has some twenty-eight active international athletes who
have volunteered to make themselves available for spot-
testing at their homes, places of work or training. As
central organiser, I have contacted doctors and nurses
in the areas in which these individuals live, seeking
their co-operation to do spot-testing at minimal notice
at my request. Athletes are being given less than
twenty-four hours' notice that a test is to be carried
out. This is to obviate the possibility that orally
administered drugs can be eliminated from the body by
forced wash-out if longer notice is given.

The system is that a box containing two specimen jars
be sent to the athlete's collector asking for a sample
of urine to be provided within the next week or so at
the collector's convenience. The collecter then contacts
the athlete by telephone, or first-class letter,
informing him that a test is required at a specific time
within 24 hours of the initial contact.

At the time of the collection the athlete and his room
are inspected to ensure that no false specimen is
produced. The specimen is then passed into one jar and
split in front of the athlete into two separate containers.
Each is placed into a padded envelope, sealed by wax and
signed by the athlete. The second specimen is needed to
test in the event of a breakage, spillage or positive
test being challenged. The two padded envelopes are then

replaced in the box and posted as soon as possible by
first-class mail to the Drug Control and Teaching Centre
at Chelsea College.

So far the co-operation of the collectors (all working
voluntarily on remote written instruction from the
organiser) and the athletes has been excellent. The tests
are being done promptly, averaging about 10 hours from
the time of contact to the time of the production of the
specimen. The specimens are arriving the following day
at Chelsea College in good condition.

It appears, then, that it will be possible to do spot-
testing in this fashion with well-motivated athletes.
The IAC have drawn up a complex list of rules and regulations designed to control possible abuses in the
collection procedures by deliberately not being available,
producing false specimens and so on. It is felt that
with adequate efficient administration and penalties
for non-co-operation a spot-testing scheme could be a
distinct possibility.

The IAC presented the final results of this experiment
at an international conference in 1981 with the object of
stimulating international action along these lines. (5)
Any international spot-testing scheme would require firm
rules and regulations to be agreed by all countries
participating in major athlete events. There would need
to be suitable international cross-checking to ensure
that the spot-tests were being carried out properly.
There would need to be adequate safeguards to prevent
non-availability of athletes or visa obstruction to an
international spot-test collection, with severe penalties
to those countries which may seek to obstruct the spot-
collections in any way.

It looks as though it will be possible in the future
to introduce adequate national and international testing
throughout the year, provided there is the political
will to do so. The technology of testing will become
sophisticated enough to be able to detect the administration of all banned drugs and hormones. The 1970s have
seen a great change in the struggle to come to terms with
drugs cheating in sport. I anticipate that the 1980s
may well see a virtual elimination of the current widespread abuse.

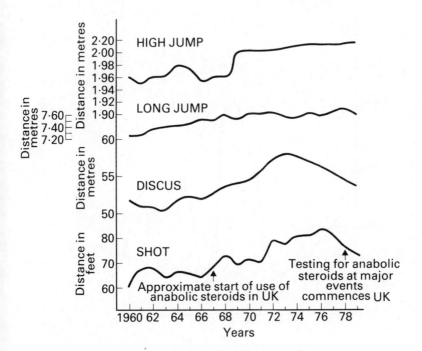

UK average of top 10 rankings

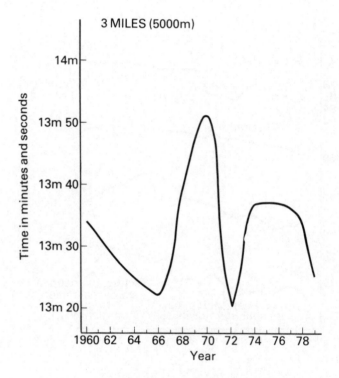

3 miles (5000m) - average top 3 UK athletes AAA champion-ships

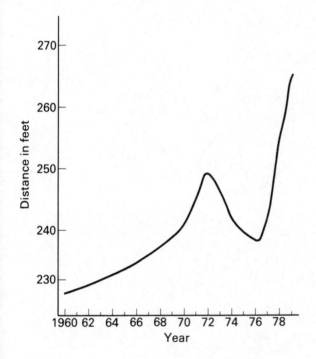

Javelin average top 3 UK athletes AAA championships

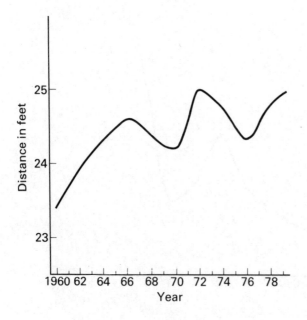

Long jump average top 3 UK athletes AAA championships

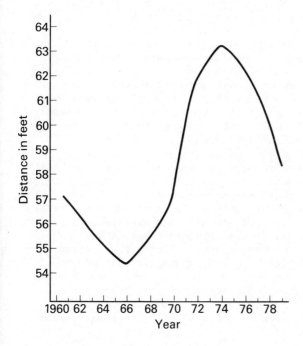

Shot average top 3 UK athletes in AAA championships

NOTES

1   'Doping Control Regulations' - a booklet published
    by the International Amateur Athletic Federation.
2   David L.J. Freed, Anthony J. Banks, Donald Longson
    and Dennis M. Burley, Anabolic steroids in athletes -
    cross over double - blind trial on weightlifters,
    'British Medical Journal', 31 May 1975.
3   L.C. Johnson and J.P. O'Shea, 'Science', 1969.
4   G. Ariel and W. Saville, 'Medicine and Science in
    Sports', 1972.
5   The 'International Conference on Sports Medicine' was
    held in Utrecht, the Netherlands, in March 1981. For
    a full account of the results see Martyn Lucking,
    Experimental random spot testing for drugs in
    sportsmen, 'British Journal of Sports Medicine',
    vol.15, no.1, March, 1981.
        28 active international athletes agreed to be
        available for random spot urine collections at
        their homes, places of work and training. Suitable
        briefed collectors were arranged to conduct the
        spot collections and forward the specimens for
        analysis. An average number of 3.4 collections
        per athlete were made in the 9 month period of the
        trial. Overall there was a failure to collect a
        percentage of 14 during the winter months and 54
        during the summer months. The average time interval
        between initial contact with the athlete and
        collection was 11 hours 50 minutes. It is
        concluded that random spot collections of urine
        from active athletes in training is possible and
        practical. Improved collection rates could be
        achieved by additionally spot collecting at
        athletic events during the summer and by using
        regionally based mobile collectors responsible for
        several athletes.

Chapter 9

Sport and communism - on the example of the USSR

James Riordan

I INTRODUCTION

Any comparative analysis of sport runs the risk of comparing like with unlike. No development of sport can be fully understood apart from a country's size and traditions, climate and culture, military and international considerations, social and economic needs, as well as the ideals of a political order. There is therefore no *single* model of capitalist or socialist sport, however similar may be many of the structural features. It would be as mistaken to posit the British and Soviet models as representative of capitalist and socialist development as it would to export them unadapted. Both of course have been tried.

That is not to say that certain fundamental characteristics are not common to sports development in the West and the East: in countries like Britain, the USA and Canada on the one hand, and the USSR, China and Cuba on the other. In liberal capitalist development, sport came to be regarded typically as the concern primarily of the individual; in state socialist development, it came to be regarded as the concern primarily of the state. The distinction is important because it provides an insight into the role of sport in social development and into conflicting conceptions of sport as a 'cultural-universal' or 'developmental-specific modern phenomenon'. It is important, too, for an understanding of the place of sport not only in capitalist and socialist societies, but in those that follow - i.e. in the modernising societies of Africa, Asia and Latin America.

This paper examines sports development largely on the example of the USSR with which the author is familiar.

II   SOME THEORETICAL CONSIDERATIONS ON SPORT AND COMMUNISM

At the time Marx was writing, metaphysics was in the grip
of a dualism that separated mind from matter and, under
the influence of Christian theology, often exaggerated a
distinction into an antagonism; in such a world view,
body and soul were seen as warring parties with the body
cast as the villain of the piece, (1) Marx rejected the
dualist philosophy and stressed that not only was there
an intimate relationship between matter and mind, but that
the former largely determined the latter. In his view,
political and social institutions and the ideas, images
and ideologies through which people understand the world
in which they live, their place within it and themselves,
all ultimately derived from the 'economic base' of
society – the class relations into which people had to
enter with one another in order to produce. This fundamental Marxist tenet contains certain implications for
sport.

First, since the human psychosomatic organism develops
and changes under the influence of external conditions,
including the social environment, subjection to physical
exercise not only develops that part of the body to which
it is directed, but also has an effect on the body as a
whole – on the personality. A strong bond exists between
social and individual development and between the
physical and mental development of the individual.
Societies are likely to seek to shape this development.
Marx himself had looked forward to the education system
of the future that would 'combine productive labour with
instruction and gymnastics, not only as a means of
improving the efficiency of production, but as the only
way to produce fully-developed human beings'. (2) This
would seem to imply that physical culture should be
treated on a level with mental culture in socialist
society both for the all-round development of the
individual and, ultimately, for the health of society.

Second, sport being part of the social superstructure
and therefore strongly influenced by the prevailing
relations of production (not something 'in itself' and
so divorced from politics) – though with some temporal
independence of the economic base – a society's pattern
of sport will ultimately depend on the specifics of that
society's socio-economic foundation, its class relationships. Moreover, says Marx, 'with a change in the
economic foundation, the entire immense superstructure is
more or less rapidly transformed.' (3) The nature of
sport can therefore be expected to alter with any change
to a new socio-economic foundation. Figure 1 is an

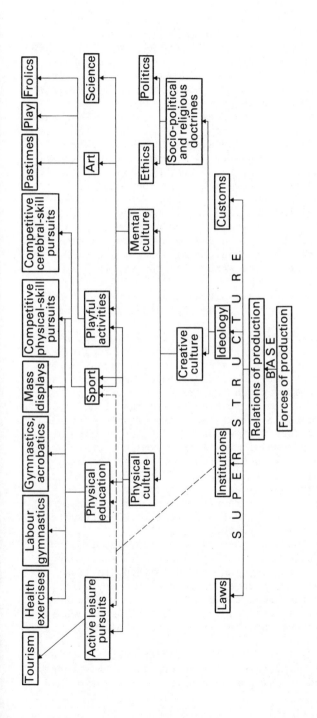

Figure 1   A Marxist view of the place of sport in society

attempt to portray a Marxist view of the component parts of sport and their interrelationship.

Third, the acceptance of a dualist metaphysic, a sharp separation of body and mind, had often led to a concern with things of the mind at the expense of bodily activities. Marx emphasised that practical activities have a decisive impact on all human development in the broadest sense. None more so than work, through which people could change themselves as well as Nature:

> Labour is, in the first place, a process in which both man and Nature participate, and in which man of his own accord starts, regulates, and controls the material reactions between himself and Nature. He opposes himself to Nature as one of her own forces, setting in motion arms and legs, head and hands, the natural forces of his body, in order to appropriate Nature's productions in a form adapted to his own wants. By thus acting on the external world and changing it, he at the same time changes his own nature. (4)

This proposition implies a strong link between work and such other bodily activities as physical exercise and games-playing.

Whether games-playing contained its own justification within itself or whether its value was to be sought in ulterior ends was not a question specifically raised by Marx. The Marxist vision of the future, however, does seem to imply that work and physical recreation will merge, or that work will be elevated to the plane of recreation by the removal of the yokes of specialisation and compulsion. But Marx evidently did not envisage recreation under communism as simply games - rather as a fusion of work-like activities with play. In this, he affirmed a principal criterion of playful activities, namely, that they were freely chosen and are pursued for their inherent pleasure rather than for practical results. This is a view that was later to be reiterated by Trotsky who maintained that

> The longing for amusement, distraction, sight-seeing and laughter is the most legitimate desire of human nature. We are able, and indeed obliged, to give the satisfaction of this desire a higher artistic quality, at the same time making amusement a weapon of collective education, freed from the guardianship of the pedagogue and the tiresome habit of moralising. (5)

To sum up, Marx provided few clear-cut guidelines on sport or physical culture. On the one hand, he stressed the interdependence of work and physical recreation and,

on the other, he saw the playful use of energy as contri-
buting to the enrichment of the personality, or self-
realisation. The same might be said of Lenin. That is
not to say, of course, that there is no consistency in
the writings of Marx or Lenin, no *Marxism* or *Leninism*. A
Marxist-Leninist interpretation of culture, mental and
physical, including a belief in the interdependence of
the mental and physical states of human beings, provides
a general framework within which physical and mental
recreation is viewed in all socialist states. It should,
however, be noted that aphorisms drawn from and myths
about Marx, Lenin, Mao, etc., in regard to physical culture
have been taken to justify policies at particular stages
of development and need not be taken as creative Marxist
thinking (indeed, they have sometimes replaced it).

III   SPORT IN SOCIALIST DEVELOPMENT

It was thought natural by some after the Russian Revolution
of 1917 that a fundamentally new pattern of recreation
would emerge, reflecting the requirements and values of
the working people and the new socialist state. In the
melting pot of ideas and theories that existed in the
USSR during the 1920s, many influential people sharply
contrasted the new 'proletarian physical culture' with
competitive sport.
    The strongest proponents of physical culture were the
'hygienists' who were mainly medical personnel concerned
about the need to raise health standards, to eliminate
disease and epidemics. The extent of their influence may
be judged from their virtual control over the government's
Supreme Council of Physical Culture, the Health Ministry,
the institutes of physical culture and the 'sporting'
press.
    To the hygienists, sport implied competition, games
that were potentially injurious to mental and physical
health. Such pursuits as weight-lifting, boxing and
gymnastics were said to be irrational and dangerous, and
encouraged individualist rather than collectivist
attitudes and values. They frowned upon the 'record-
breaking mania' of contemporary sport in the West, and
they favoured non-commercialised and non-professional
forms of recreation that dispensed with grandstands and
spectators. Doubts were cast upon the social value of
competitive sport - above all, on attempts to attain top-
class results. As a future Soviet President Kalinin was
to put it:
    Sport is a subsidiary affair and should never become an

end in itself, a striving to break records.... Sport
should be subordinate to communist education. After
all,, we are preparing not narrow sportsmen, but
citizens of communist society who ought to possess
primarily a broad outlook and organisational ability
as well as strong arms and a good digestive system. (6)
Not all supporters of the hygienists, however, were
opposed to every form of competitive sport. Nikolai
Semashko, Chairman of the Supreme Council of Physical
Culture, who was himself a doctor and concurrently also
People's Commissar for Health, argued against restricting
physical culture to narrow medical confines and against
banning competitive sports: 'If you keep the populace on
the semolina pudding of hygienic gymnastics, physical
culture will never gain wide currency.' Competitive
sport was, he believed, 'the open door to physical
culture.... It not only strengthens the various organs,
it helps a person's mental development, teaches him
attentiveness, punctuality, precision and grace of
movement, it develops the sort of will-power, strength
and skill that should distinguish Soviet people'. (7)
Moreoever, although he wrote the following lines before
the full-scale campaign for 'socialist competition' had
been launched to accompany the industrialisation drive,
he clearly anticipated the regime's support for competition: 'Competition should serve ultimately as a means of
involving people in building socialism. That is how I
look upon competitive sport and competition generally.
(8)
     Another widely influential group in 'sport' during the
1920s was the 'Proletarian Culture Organisation'
(Proletkul't). The Proletkultists demanded the complete
rejection of competitive sport and all organised sports
that derived from bourgeois society, as remnants of the
decadent past and emanations of degenerate bourgeois
culture. A fresh start had to be made through the
'revolutionary innovation of proletarian physical
culture' which would take the form of 'labour gymnastics'
and mass displays, pageants and excursions. Gymnasiums
and their 'bourgeois' equipment would be replaced by
various pieces of apparatus on which young proletarians
could practise their 'labour movements'.
     While the hygienists had admitted the possibility of
the usefulness of some bourgeois sports, the Proletkultists
made no such concessions. To many Proletkultists, the
recourse to 'bourgeois' institutions such as sports seemed
a compromise, a withdrawal from already conquered
positions. Lenin criticised them, pointing out the need
to draw on the cultural heritage of the past and to base

further development on everything valuable. that had been
accumulated by mankind up to the Russian Revolution:
'What is important is not the *invention* of a new proletarian culture, but the *development* of the best forms,
traditions and results of *existing* culture from the
viewpoint of Marxist philosopny.' (9)   Other critics
maintained that there were no such separate entities as
bourgeois and proletarian sports; there was, rather, a
bourgeois and a proletarian *attitude* to sport, a bourgeois
and proletarian *spirit* of competition.   Sporting attain-
ments were, they asserted, necessary for inspiring young
people to fresh successes in sport - which were, in some
way, a measure of the country's cultural and technical
development.   This point of view was given the official
stamp of approval in the Party's famous resolution on
physical culture in 1925, which stressed that

   physical culture must be considered not simply from
   the viewpoint of public health and physical education,
   not only as an aspect of the cultural, economic and
   military training of young people.   It should also
   be seen as a method of educating the masses (inasmuch
   as it develops will-power and teamwork, endurance,
   resourcefulness and other valuable qualities).   It
   must be regarded, moreover, as a means of rallying
   the bulk of workers and peasants to the various
   Party, Soviet and trade-union organisations, through
   which they can be drawn into social and political
   activity.... Physical culture must be an inseparable
   part of overall political and cultural education,
   and of public health. (10)

The years of experimenting and searching in the 1920s
reflect a contradiction fundamental to the period:
between the subjective desires to shape society according
to ideological preconceptions and the objective lack
of the material conditions for implementing ideals.   There
can be little doubt that because they were not based
on the reality of the USSR's situation some immediate
aspirations, including those of the hygienists and
Proletkultists, were utopian and unrealistic.   Even so,
the questions they raised are important and relevant to
any assessment of the role of sport in socialist society
for, as the actual development of sport showed, sport
became geared far more to practical needs than to ideological considerations.

   It was against the background of world and civil war,
economic and political breakdown, that the Bolsheviks
had to introduce a new system of sport after 1917.   The
first steps to be taken were by no means obvious, for
there was no pattern to follow; the change-over from

criticism of capitalist institutions and the sports of
Western industrial states to practical action in an
80 per cent-peasant, overwhelmingly illiterate society
presented immense problems and dilemmas. In fact, like
everything else, sport during the first few years came
to be subordinated to the needs of the war effort. All
the old clubs and their equipment were commandeered and
handed over to the military training establishment
Vsevobuch, whose main aim was to supply the Red Army with
contingents of trained conscripts as quickly as possible.
One means of achieving this was to carry out a crash
programme of physical fitness for all people of recruit-
able and pre-recruitment age.

In line with the policy of combining military drill
and weapon-handling with political and general education
in elementary hygiene, it was also decided to co-ordinate
the activities of Vsevobuch with those of the Commissariats
of Education and Health. In the opinion of the head of
Vsevobuch, Nikolai Podvoisky, it was impossible to bring
the Civil War to a successful conclusion or to start to
build socialism without a large-scale campaign to
improve physical fitness and health. (11) A second major
consideration then (after military training) was *health*.
Having inherited a country with an inclement climate,
whose population was more than three-quarters illiterate,
where disease and starvation were common, and where most
people had only rudimentary knowledge of hygiene, the
Soviet leaders appreciated that it would take a radical
economic and social transformation to alter the situation
substantially. But time was short, and able-bodied and
disciplined men and women were vital, first for the
country's survival, then for its recovery from the
ravages of war and revolution, for industrial development
and defence against further probable attacks.

Regular participation in physical exercise was to be
one, relatively inexpensive but effective, means of
improving health standards rapidly and a channel by
which to educate people in hygiene, nutrition and
exercise. One indication of the health policy being
pursued was the campaign during the Civil War under the
slogans 'Help the Country with a Toothbrush!', 'Help
the Country by Washing in Cold Water!' and 'Physical
Culture 24 Hours a Day!'. With the influx of masses of
peasants into the cities (bringing with them rural habits),
the significance of health through physical exercise took
on a new dimension. The ignorance that was the cause of
so much disease, starvation and misery - and which
hampered both military effectiveness and labour productivity - was to be combated by a far-reaching programme of

physical exercise and sport. And if the material facilities
were lacking, then people were urged (by Podvoisky) to make
full use of 'the sun, air, water and natural movement -
the best proletarian doctors'. The therapeutic value of
sport was also widely advertised in the intermittent
three-day anti-tuberculosis campaigns of the late 1920s.
It was, further, not thought incongruous to put out a
poster ostensibly advertising sports, yet featuring a
young man with a rifle and toothbrush above the slogan
'Clean your Teeth! Clean your Rifle!'.

But sport was not confined to improving physical
health; it was regarded as important in combating anti-
social and anti-Soviet behaviour in town and country.
If urban young people, especially, could be persuaded to
take up sport and engage in regular physical exercise,
they might develop healthy bodies *and* minds. Thus, the
Ukrainian Party Central Committee issued a resolution in
1926 expressing the hope that 'physical culture would
become the vehicle of the new life ... a means of
isolating young people from the evil influence of the
street, home-made alcohol and prostitution'. (12) The
role assigned to sport in the countryside was even more
ambitious: it was

> to play a big part in the campaign against drunkenness
> and uncivilised behaviour by attracting village youth
> to more sensible and cultured activities.... In the
> fight to transform the village, physical culture is
> to be a vehicle of the new way of life in all measures
> undertaken by the Soviet authorities - in the fight
> against religion and natural calamities. (13)

Sport, then, stood for 'clean-living', progress, good
health and rationality and was regarded by the Party
as one of the most suitable and effective instruments
for implementing its social policies.

The far-reaching aims envisaged for sport may be
illustrated by the early concern that physical culture
should make some contribution to the social emancipation
of women - in Soviet society generally, and especially
in the Muslim areas where women were effectively excluded
from all public life. The bodily liberation and naked
limbs (and faces!) along with the self-acting, competing
'image' associated with sport were not accepted without
a struggle: 'I would call our first sportswomen real
heroines. They accomplished great feats of bravery in
liberating women from the age-old yoke of religion and
the feudal-bey order.' (14) Even in the European areas
of the country, the women's emancipation-through-sport
policy was presented as both feasible and effective.
For example, in a letter to Podvoisky through the medium

of 'Pravda' in 1922, the first women graduates from the
Central Military School of Workers' Physical Culture
wrote: 'You understood how important physical culture is
for women and you tried to impress its importance upon us
women, among whom there is so much passivity and conservatism, the results of age-old servitude, both economic and
social.' (15)

The physical culture campaign could only catch on, in
the view of the authorities, if the emotional attraction
of *competitive sport* were to be utilised to the utmost.
Contests began to be organised during the 1920s from the
lowest level upwards, culminating in the All-Russia Pre-
Olympiads and the First Central Asian Olympics of 1920.
Sports were taken from the town to the countryside, from
the European metropolis to the Asiatic interior, as an
explicit means of involving as many people as possible in
physical exercise and organised sport. A third explicit
function of sport then was *integration*. The significance
of the First Central Asian Olympics, held in Tashkent
over a period of ten days in early October 1920 (i.e. even
before the Civil War was over!), may be judged by the fact
that this was the first time in history that Uzbeks,
Kazakhs, Turkmenians, Kirgiz and other local peoples,
as well as Russians and other European races, had
competed in any sporting event together (as many as
3,000 participants altogether). As was made clear later,
the authorities regarded sport as an important means of
integrating the diverse peoples of the old Russian empire
in the new Soviet state: 'The integrative functions of
sport are very great. This has immense importance for
our multinational state. Sports contests, festivals,
spartakiads and other types of sports competition have
played a major part in cementing the friendship of Soviet
peoples.' (16)

To sum up, there existed during the 1920s a widespread
adherence to the notion of *mens sana in corporo sano*, a
feeling that physical culture could somehow be used, along
with other policies, to combat socially and politically
undesirable phenomena. It was also a valuable means of
promoting national integration and military training.

By the end of the 1920s, the scene was set for the
implementation of an industrialisation programme that
was to hurl the whole of the country into a gigantic
campaign to 'build socialism', then to lead to the
forcible collectivisation of agriculture and to transform
the USSR from a backward agrarian into an advanced
industrial economy - all on the nation's own resources.
The implications for the sports movement of these
processes were extremely important, for it was in the

1930s that the pattern of Soviet sport (and of most other
socialist states) as we know it today was basically formed
and its main role and functions set. By the end of the
1930s, the main organisational pattern had already been
established - with its sports societies, sports schools,
national fitness programme (the GTO) and the uniform
rankings system for individual sports and proficient
athletes. The Soviet society of the 1930s differed from
that of the preceding period in seeing the flourishing
of all manner of competitive sports (soccer, basketball,
volleyball) with mass spectator appeal and the official
encouragement of leagues, stadiums, cups, championships,
popularity polls, cults of sporting heroes - all the
appendages of a sub-system designed to provide general
recreation and diversion for the fast-growing urban population.

Millions of people, uprooted from centuries-old
traditions, were pitched into new and strange environments;
the newcomers to industry joined factory clubs and looked
to them for the recreation they had previously enjoyed in
an open-air rural setting. Since urban conditions were
spartan and deteriorating, sports served many townsfolk
as an escape from the drudgery of their domestic and work
environments. The many sports contests of the 1930s were
intended, too, to create and reinforce a 'togetherness',
to evoke feelings of patriotism, and to demonstrate to
people at home as well as abroad how happy and carefree
life was under socialism. It is significant that sports
rallies often accompanied major political events or
festivals (May Day, Anniversary of the Revolution Day,
Constitution Day). In this way, sport became a means of
linking members of the public with politics, the Party
and, of course, with their leader.

Furthermore, a relatively close link was re-established
in the 1930s between sport and the military. It stemmed
partly from the conviction of the need for a state
surrounded by unfriendly powers to be strong militarily
and constantly on the alert. This conviction became
widespread in the 'besieged fortress' atmosphere of the
1930s, encouraged by the rise of Fascism in Europe. Sport
openly became a means of providing pre-military training
and achieving a relatively high standard of national
fitness of men and women for defence. Several sports
with potential military application - e.g. shooting,
skiing, gliding and mountaineering - came to be dominated
by servicemen. The two largest and most successful sports
clubs in the USSR were those run by the armed forces and
the security forces: the Central House of the Red Army
(today the Central Sports Club of the Army - TsSKA) and

Dinamo respectively. And, after 1931, the GTO national fitness programme was expressly intended to train people, through sport, for work and military preparedness - the Russian acronym GTO standing for Gotov k trudu i oborone (Ready for Labour and Defence).

The war years (1941-5) cannot simply be seen as a wasted interlude that retarded the Soviet sports movement. They had certain consequences, some intangible, but none the less far-reaching, whose effect was evident for many years ahead. For a start, the war convinced the authorities that they had been absolutely right to 'functionalise' sport, to control it from the centre, and to make country-wide physical fitness a prime target.

With the conclusion of the war and the setting of a new national target - to catch up and overtake the most advanced industrial powers (and that included catching up and overtaking in sport), the Soviet leadership felt it possible to demonstrate the pre-eminence of sport in socialist society. Given the limited opportunities elsewhere, sport seemed to offer a suitable medium for pursuing this goal. This was an area in which the USSR did not have to take second place to the West.

With the central control of sport and the utilitarian-instrumental role assigned it, it is natural that the pattern of foreign sports competition involving the USSR should follow the course of Soviet foreign policy and display clearly differentiated contours in regard to the geo-political situation of different countries. With the completely new balance of power that developed after the Second World War (the creation of a group of socialist states, the emergence of newly independent Afro-Asian countries, and the nuclear stalemate) the Soviet leadership assigned sport such tasks as winning support for the communist system, encouraging friendly, commercial and good-neighbourly relations with the USSR, and achieving unity within the socialist bloc. It evidently considers that sports emissaries can sometimes do more than diplomats to recommend a political philosophy and way of life to the outside world.

To sum up, the Soviet leaders would seem to have opted for the following in developing forms of sport, particularly since the late 1920s:

First, using sport as a means of obtaining the fit, disciplined and co-operative workforce needed for attaining economic and military strength and efficiency - in particular in order:

(i) to raise physical and social health standards - and the latter meant not simply educating people in the virtues of bodily hygiene, regular exercise and sound nutrition, but also overcoming unhealthy deviant, anti-social (and therefore anti-Soviet) conduct: drunkenness, delinquency, prostitution - even religiosity and intellectual dissidence;

(ii)   to socialise the population into the new establishment system of values.   Character-training, advanced (so the Soviet leaders seem to have believed) by sport, in such values as loyalty, conformity, team-spirit, co-operation and discipline, may well have encouraged compliance and co-operation in both work and politics;

(iii)   to encourage a population, in transition from a rural to an urban way of life, to identify with wider communities, all-embracing social units such as the workplace, the town, the district, the republic and, ultimately, the entire country.   By associating sport (like other amenities) organisationally with the workplace, the Party leadership and its agencies could, moreover, better supervise and 'rationalise' the leisure-time activities of employees.

Second, linking sport ideologically and even organisationally with military preparedness; the reasons for this 'militarisation' of sport must be sought in:

(i)   the leadership's fear of war and its conviction of the need to keep the population primed to meet it;

(ii)   the all-pervasive presence throughout society of military and security forces, necessitated by the imposition from above, should enthusiasm from below flag, of 'socialist construction' upon a tired public. This 'presence' had been the norm in Russian society before the Revolution in sport as elsewhere;

(iii)   the fact that, in a vast country with problems of communication, lukewarm (at best) popular attitudes towards physical exercise and few sports facilities for most of the Soviet period, military organisation of sport was actually an efficient method of deploying scarce resources in the most economical way and using methods of direction which were, perhaps, more effective coming from paramilitary than from civilian organisations.

Third, in a vast multinational land that has witnessed disorientingly rapid change, sport extended to and united wider sections of the population than probably any other social activity.   With its broad relevance to education, health, culture and politics, and its capacity to mobilise people (predispose them towards change), sport has uniquely served the state as a vehicle of social change and national integration.   Moreover, it has served a public that has, in a short span of time, lived through such shattering events as two world wars, three revolutions, a civil war, rapid industrialisation, forced

collectivisation of agriculture, purges and mass terror.
In this society, hard work, discipline, self-censorship
and periodically necessary acute readjustments may well
have needed a counterpart in sport, offering as it does a
particularly rewarding area of relaxation, diversion and
recreation.

Many of the processes described above in relation to
the development of the USSR have been experienced in other
socialist countries, and their sports organisation has
shown several similarities with that in the USSR. One
reason for the latter is, of course, that they have all
(including China) been strongly influenced by the USSR
in their attitudes to, and organisation of, sport: sport
is state-controlled, encouraged and shaped by specific
utilitarian and ideological designs (it is certainly not
a matter merely of 'fun and games' or the 'garden of
human activities'). A more fundamental reason for the
similarity of sports development in the socialist
countries, however, is likely to be that, with just a
couple of exceptions (Czechoslovakia, German Democratic
Republic), they are all modernising, developing countries
based at least initially on a mainly peasant population.
No leisure class has existed to develop sport for its
own disport; in any case, sport (with its potential for
social change) has been regarded as too important to be
left to the whim of private clubs with restricted
entrance, commercial promoters, circus entrepreneurs
and foreigners (as it was in China, Cuba and Russia).
Thus, in China, sport has been employed quite explicitly
to help build up a backward nation: for health, hygiene
and defence; it would seem to be an integrating factor
in a multinational country and to contribute to the
promotion of patriotism. In the German Democratic
Republic, where other channels have been closed, sport
would seem to have helped attain a measure of recognition
and prestige for the regime, both at home and abroad.
In Cuba, success in international sport has helped nurture
and satisfy patriotic pride in the face of boycott and
subversion; it has also helped divert potential popular
discontent with declining living standards, rationing
and austerity. (17)

IV   SOME CONCLUSIONS ON SPORT IN SOCIALIST DEVELOPMENT

The state-centralised control of sport in socialist
states has prevented commercial exploitation of mass
spectator sports for private profit and the playing of
particular sports in which actual or simulated violence

predominates; it has also inhibited the extremes of
hooliganism, corruption and commercialism associated with
a number of sports in the West.

All the same, there are today features of organised
sport strikingly common to both socialist and capitalist
societies. There are, of course, the very sports themselves. Together with these sports goes an elaborate
system of government sports departments, giant amphi-
theatres, officials, trainers, semi- and full-time
professional players, sports journalists and so on - even
gambling establishments (for horse racing, for example).
A similar sports ideology in East and West cultivates
irrational loyalties and ascribes similar prominence to
the winning of victories, the setting of records and
the collecting of trophies. Indeed, the 'citius, altius,
fortius' design has nowhere such an elaborate supporting
system as in the socialist countries for spotting,
nurturing and rewarding sports talent, with the aim of
establishing world sporting supremacy.

Despite these practices, communist leaders have
consistently affirmed their allegiance to Marxism-
Leninism in general, and their adherence to a number of
Marxist goals in respect of recreation in particular,
emphasising the provision of sport for all and the need
specifically to enable all citizens to be harmoniously
developed, to combine 'spiritual wealth, moral purity
and perfect physique'. (18) Such affirmations notwith-
standing, official practice would seem to have diverged
from official theory and the forms of recreation which
have developed in socialist societies have not coincided
with the predictions of Marxist writers about the playful
activities in the society of the future.

As far as the Soviet Union is concerned, reasons for
the divergence may be assumed to parallel those in other
areas of life. In the early post-revolutionary period,
genuine efforts were made by certain future-oriented
groups to move in the direction foretold by Marx and
Lenin, but civil war and national poverty made them
impossible to bring to fruition. From the late 1920s,
command over the repressive apparatus, disposal of
material resources and sources of information were in no
real sense under popular control but in the hands of
members of the leading group in the ruling party which,
in the absence of help from a revolution in the industrial
West, was pursuing a policy of building a strong nation-
state power-base, using these instruments of power.

Some Marxists might argue that the fetishisation of
recreation, in the form of competitive sport (which
offers vast opportunities for manipulating people's minds)

in the socialist states, is one of a number of temporary
'defects' of a society *in transition* to communism, 'still
stamped with the birth-marks of the old society from whose
womb it emerges'. Such 'defects' might be regarded as
inevitable as long as the individual still remains subordinate to the division of labour, as long as labour is
primarily a means of livelihood, as long as the forces of
production are at too low a level to permit the all-round
development of the individual - i.e. as long as the
socialist states remain 'at the first stage of communist
society'.

We might speculate further on whether, given Russia's
overall backwardness in 1917, any road to socialism other
than a path of prolonged bureaucratically enforced
development was possible, whether Soviet society is yet
ripe for genuinely socialist or communist human relations
(including those of free recreation) and whether, indeed,
the original social goals can have remained uncontaminated,
in the minds of any leaders, by the class or caste
differentiation actually involved in the process of
bureaucratic state-socialist construction. It is here,
perhaps, that we should seek the key to an understanding
of the fetishism of sport that developed in the USSR.
Whereas in Western society, the fetishism of sport was
a consequence of this field of human action (like almost
all others) offering the possibilities of profit-making -
and turning out, characteristically without any conscious
purposive intent, to be a highly appropriate means of
distracting the populace from class-conscious politicisation - in Soviet society it characteristically resulted
from centralised planning and administration designed to
subordinate areas of social life such as sport to the
political and economic tasks of building a strong state.
The distinction is important in terms of the potential
dynamics of the two systems.

Today, the inheritors of the sports system that
evolved during the Stalin years must find themselves in
a quandary: to what extent should they break with the
past? How sharply and through what new forms should
necessary change be brought about? In the field of
culture, and specifically of recreation, how could they
dismantle the various by now well-entrenched fetishised
institutions and values? The task is circumscribed
partly by the fact that today sport is evidently regarded
as an important weapon in the rivalry between what the
Soviet leaders may see as the two opposed world systems -
capitalism and Soviet socialism. The international
situation is just one of a number of objective constraints
(that also include domestic, economic, cultural and

political factors) on leaders attempting to realise their
desires - which are likely to be by no means uniform or
clearly perceived. To make two extremal assumptions about
the leaders' desires, one may be against fundamental
change, the other may be in favour of introducing full
communist relations. Whatever course of action is
pursued, the *subjective will* of the leaders is bound to
be constrained by the *objective possibilities* of the
situation.

It is hardly surprising, then, that the actions of the
leadership should appear contradictory: on the one hand,
it reinforces the fetishism of sport by its increasing
stress on international success in sport and on the
training of even faster, stronger and more skilful
professional sportsmen (e.g. through its twenty-six sports
boarding schools) in an ever-growing range of sports,
while the false consciousness of the mass of people is
reinforced through a cultivated obsession with mass-
produced, media-oriented spectator sports. On the other
hand, the leadership is increasing the amount of free
time available to people, providing an ever-wider range
of amenities and equipment for people to pursue the
recreational activities of their choice, is encouraging
people to be active participants rather than passive
spectators, and is increasing opportunities for individuals
to enjoy recreational activities in a non-institutional
setting (such as fishing, hiking, rock-climbing, boating,
pot-holing, horse-riding, hang-gliding, skin-diving,
water-skiing, etc., all of which are rapidly increasing
in popularity in the USSR).

It is too early to prophesy which trend will prevail.
There has so far been no obvious sign in the field of
recreation of a movement towards transparent, demystified
social relationships. At the same time, no fundamental
obstacles, such as commercialism, exist to prevent
recreational activities in the Soviet Union from being
liberated from fetishism and manipulation so that they
would become freely chosen and pursued for their inherent
pleasure rather than for utilitarian ends. Some Marxists
would argue that profound cultural-revolutionary changes
of this sort could be brought about, in Soviet conditions,
by comparatively minor political changes (new men at the
top); others would incline to the view that the present
course is more systemic, all possible candidates for the
leadership having common class (or quasi-class) relations
to the means of production different from the masses and
so resulting in a vested interest in the status quo.

Whatever the interpretation of past events or the
perspectives for future development, there can certainly

be no doubt about the absolute positive material gains of
the population of the old Russian Empire in the sphere
of recreation since 1917. It is also in many ways better
off in this respect than the public in the West. Most of
the Soviet urban population can today pursue the sport
of their choice, using facilities free of charge through
their trade union society. Sports are not, as they were
before the Revolution, in the hands of foreigners,
commercial promoters, circus-entrepreneurs or private
clubs with restricted entrance. Unlike some Western
sports clubs, Soviet sports societies do not discriminate
in regard to membership on the grounds of sex, nationality
or social background. Even sports involving expensive
equipment are open to anyone who shows natural ability
and inclination. Lastly, there has been an undeniable
consistent aspiration and effort in the USSR, as in all
socialist states, to make sport culturally uplifting,
aesthetically satisfying and morally reputable which,
given all the necessary qualifications, has set a tone
of altruism and devotion in sport in which there is much
which cannot but be admired.

NOTES AND REFERENCES

1   See J. Riordan, Marx, Lenin and physical culture,
    'Journal of Sport History', 1976, no.3, pp.152-61.
2   K. Marx, 'Capital', vol.I, Foreign Languages
    Publishing House, Moscow, 1961, pp.483-4.
3   K. Marx, A Contribution to the Critique of Political
    Economy, in L.S. Feuer, 'Marx and Engels. Basic
    Writings on Politics and Philosophy', Glasgow,
    Fontana, 1969, p.85.
4   K. Marx, 'Capital', op.cit., p.177.
5   L. Trotsky, 'Problems of Everyday Life', New York,
    Monad Press, 1973, p.32.
6   M. Kalinin, 'O kommunisticheskom vospitanii', Moscow,
    1962, p.17.
7   M.A. Semashko, Fizicheskaya kul'tura i zdravo-
    khranenie v SSSR, 'Izbrannye proizvedeniya', Moscow,
    1954, p.264.
8   N.S. Semasho, 'Puti sovetskoi fizkul'tury', Moscow,
    1926, p.14.
9   V.I. Lenin, 'Leninsky sbornik', vol.XXXV, Moscow,
    1945, p.148.
10 'Izvestiya tsentral'novo Komiteta, RKP (B)', Moscow,
    20 July 1925.
11 N.I. Podvoisky, 'O militsionnoi organizatsii
    vooruzhonnykh sil Rossiiskoi Sovetskoi Federativnoi
    Sotsialisticheskoi Respubliki', Moscow, 1919, p.41.

12   'Teoriya i praktika fizicheskoi Kul'tury', vol.12, 1972, p.13.
13   Ibid.
14   'Fizkul'tura ı sport', 1970, no.6, p.5.
15   'Pravda', 22 June 1922.
16   'Teoriya i praktika fizicheskoi kul'tury', 1975, no.9, p.9.
17   See J. Riordan (ed.), 'Sport Under Communism. Sport in China, Cuba, Czechoslovakia, German Democratic Republic and USSR', London, C. Hurst, 1978.
18   Programme of the Communist Party of the Soviet Union, in 'The Road to Communism', Moscow, 1961, p.567.

Chapter 10

The politics of sport and apartheid

Peter Hain

> We are a free people playing an amateur game and we
> have got the right to play where we like ... as sure
> as hell we can play our game in South Africa.

> British athletes have the same rights and the same
> responsibilities towards freedom and its maintenance
> as every citizen of the United Kingdom ... for British
> athletes to take part in the games in Moscow this
> summer would be for them to seem to condone an
> international crime.

The first of these statements was made by one-time rugby
referee, Denis Thatcher, in support of the British Lions
rugby tour to South Africa in 1980; (1) the second by
his wife, Margaret Thatcher, Prime Minister of Britain.
(2) Expressed within several months of each other, they
contain contradictory views on the relationship between
sport, politics and morality - a relationship which has
become increasingly controversial in recent times and
which it is necessary to explore in order to establish
the parameters of an analysis of sports apartheid.

POLITICS AND SPORT

The cry of 'keep politics out of sport' has struck a
deep chord in Britain and indeed throughout the Western
world. It has received strong support from those many
citizens for whom sport is an all-consuming interest;
the Dutch international footballer, Johann Cruyff,
expressed a typical view when he remarked: 'I don't
care about politics. The impact of soccer is much
healthier and deeper than politics.' (3) However,
right-wing politicians especially have also taken up the

cry - although it was striking how abruptly those
political figures, who for decades had criticised
opponents of white South African participation in international sport, suddenly discovered the abiding virtues
of mixing politics and sport over the 1980 Moscow
Olympics. Their conversion was quite moving.

In reality, of course, moral and political views
cannot be divorced from sport because sport does not
occur in a vacuum but is an integral part of life.
Thus, the cry to 'keep politics out of sport' is based
upon a romantic caricature of the real nature of sport:
it is tantamount to saying 'keep life out of sport'.
To support this argument, we only have to look at the
way sport has become 'political' in situations which
attract little controversy.

Nobody seemed to mind President Nixon's use of 'ping
pong diplomacy' in 1971 to smooth the way for political
rapprochement with China. Nor were there any strident
voices raised against the 'basket ball diplomacy' between
the USA and Cuba in 1977. Yet it would be difficult to
imagine a more blatant use of sport for political ends:
table tennis and basket ball tours being employed quite
literally as tools of international diplomacy.

The fact is that historically sport has always been
intertwined with politics. A supreme example was the
1936 Berlin Olympics which furnished the Nazis with a
valuable propaganda victory and enabled them to present
a false facade of fraternity to the rest of the world:
while being wined and dined by Nazi officials, politicians
and journalists at the Games ignored Nazi rearmament and
the brutal suppression of the Jews. (4) Such was the
insensitivity of leading sports officials at the time
that the then President of the American Olympic Committee,
Avery Brundage, was able to remark of those pressing for
a boycott of the Berlin Games: 'Certain Jews must now
understand that they cannot use these Games as a weapon
in their boycott against the Nazis.' (5) That he was
later to be one of white South Africa's firmest
supporters in the 1960s in his capacity as President of
the International Olympic Committee is perhaps appropriate.

Other examples demonstrate that the suggestion that
the mixing of politics and sport is somehow a new phenomenon is quite misleading. As sport has become more
important - and the Olympics after all is probably *the*
most important single event linking the countries of the
world - and as sports events have attracted growing
business interests, so the role of politics has been
heightened. But to acknowledge that is quite different

from arguing that there was some golden age of 'pure' sport, unsullied by the 'cynical' machinations of politicians. Even the 1976 controversy over Taiwan's participation and ultimate exclusion from the Montreal Olympics had a forerunner. In 1908, at the Olympic Games in London, Britain demanded that the Finns march under a Russian flag at the opening ceremony because a trade pact had just been signed between the UK and Russia!

More recently, in 1973, the French government cancelled a sports tour to Australia after the Australian government had vigorously objected to French nuclear tests in the Pacific and, in January 1977, Kenya broke all sporting links with neighbouring Tanzania as relations between the two countries hit a new low following a dispute over the airline, East African Airways.

Such brazen instances of government interference in sport are complemented by the wider impact of national sporting performance on governments. Italy's poor showing in the 1966 World Cup caused questions to be asked in cabinet. And the sports-mad Australians were so demoralised in 1976 by their worst Olympic performance in 40 years that newspaper commentators wrote seriously of a 'national identity crisis' (6) - even a vital cabinet meeting on the budget was recessed so that Ministers, apparently hopeful that the political situation could be defused by a victory in the 1500 metres swimming event, could watch Australia's chief gold medal hope in action on television.

Of course success has political repercussions too. Harold Wilson was fond of reminding the public that England won the 1966 World Cup while he was in charge of the nation (actually, England lost it in 1970 while he was still Prime Minister - a factor touched upon half-seriously by pundits analysing Labour's 1970 election defeat). After England's famous 1966 victory, Britain's exporters reported an upsurge in the popularity of British goods overseas. Similarly, Sunderland's surprise victory in the 1973 Football Association Cup Final was a great boost to the town's depressed economic morale.

Nowhere is the political backdrop to sport more clearly illustrated than in the very structure of international sport itself which mirrors the structure of international capitalism. Most international sports bodies were formed at the turn of the century, when classic imperialism was at its height and when the Third World was under colonisation by the West. The individuals who founded these sports bodies came largely from the West - and then from a restricted class within Western societies: they were usually 'gentlemen', aristocrats

or financiers. Today's international sports bodies are
thus rooted in the imperialism of that period.

Most international sports bodies for instance have had
undemocratic constitutions, giving control to countries
such as Britain and the USA, the International Olympic
Committee being an interesting case in point. Whereas
the Olympic movement as a whole consists of about 140
member countries with National Olympic Committees, only
70 have now been granted full member status of the IOC;
the remainder have no voting or representative rights.
The maldistribution of votes is clear from the fact that
out of 85 voting members of the IOC (some countries having
more than one vote), over 50 come from Western Europe,
the white Commonwealth and the USA. Currently, for
example, Britain, the USA, West Germany, Italy, France
and Australia have the same number of votes (12) as the
whole of Black Africa. This undemocratic structure is
compounded by the fact that the IOC consists of *individual*
voting members who are elected after selection and
nomination by the IOC's executive. They are regarded as
the IOC's ambassadors in their countries rather than as
representative national delegates. Thus, an IOC member
can be opposed by his own country's National Olympic
Committee yet still retain his seat as its 'representative'
(as has happened with Kenya). And despite South Africa
being first suspended in 1964, and then expelled from the
Olympics in 1970, a white South African has remained on
the IOC as a full member.

Other sports bodies which parallel the undemocratic
structure of the IOC include the International Lawn
Tennis Federation and the International Amateur Athletics
Federation.

SPORT AND POLITICAL PROTEST

The political roots of sport therefore lie deep. But to
acknowledge this requires a major dilemma to be resolved:
must the umbilical cord which unites sport and politics
always provide a channel for sport to become a vehicle
for political protest? The answer brings directly into
focus the issue of apartheid in sport.

For we need to draw a firm line between those countries
which have objectionable political systems, and those
which *also* introduce discrimination into the organisation
of their sports system in a way that injures the very
essence of sporting ethics. Only South Africa does this.
It is only under apartheid that there is a formal and
automatic barrier against sportsmen and women on racial

grounds. Even though sport and politics are connected
in every country, only South Africa allows its particularly obnoxious system totally to dominate its sport.

This is not equally true of say Russia: Jews for
example can and do participate in Russian sports teams,
from club to national level, as do non-communists. That
does not make Russian political oppression any more
palatable: it simply means that there are no specifically
sporting grounds for objecting to sporting links with
the Soviet Union - or Chile or any other Fascist regime,
for that matter.

To oppose international sports participation by white
South Africa is therefore a matter of fundamental *principle;*
with other tyrannies, it is a matter of *tactics*: will
such opposition assist the cause of human rights or not?
It is a question which requires each case to be assessed
carefully on its merits. For to do otherwise, to protest
on every sporting occasion, against every country in
which human rights are under attack, would literally bring
international sport to a grinding halt.

The case for selectivity and for a sparing employment of
protest against sporting events is therefore a strong
one, not least because if sport automatically became a
target for political pressure regardless of the circumstances, then international sport would be destroyed, and
the frequency of such protest would render it less and
less effective. There is, in addition, a need to clear
away the cobwebs of hypocrisy and double standards which
envelope the whole issue. There *was* a strong case for
backing the boycott of the Moscow Olympics, well before
the invasion of Afghanistan, on the grounds that the
Soviet Union continued mercilessly to repress internal
dissent. But the campaign launched by President Carter,
and taken up with such verve by the British government
under Mrs Thatcher's personal direction, quickly
degenerated into a front for cold-war posturing and
cynical political manoeuvring. If the Afghan invasion
was the sole pretext for the boycott - and no Western
government had backed the boycott before Russian sub-
jugation of the Afghans occurred - then surely there was
a case also for expelling or suspending the USA in 1968
for its 'international crime' of invading Vietnam to prop
up a puppet regime there? Indeed, what about American
participation in the 1972 Olympics whilst the rape of
Cambodia was continuing? Should Mexico have played host
to the 1968 Games whilst hundreds of students were shot
dead during demonstrations outside the stadium? Should
Argentina have been allowed to stage the 1978 World Cup
when the country's jails were overflowing with political

prisoners and the society dominated by a repressive Junta?
Should the Scottish football team have played in 1977 in
the very stadium which the Chilean Junta had used as a
concentration camp?

These questions are not easy to resolve and ultimately
depend upon the weight of opinion on a given issue at a
given time. However, we are entitled to be spared the
kind of self-righteous posturing exhibited by the Carter/
Thatcher axis over the Moscow Olympics when their previous
support for human rights issues in sport had been singularly absent.

RACE AND SPORT

The one area where matters ought to have been crystal clear
is over the relationship between racism and sport. For
here there is such a clear violation of the fundamental
principle of sport that merit should alone be the criterion
for opportunity or success. One of the classic examples
was the Nazis' exclusion of even world-class Jewish
sportsmen and women from the German national teams. The
usual excuse given by Nazi officials was one which has
echoed through South African sport since the Second World
War. As Ritter von Halt, the Nazi sports leader, put it:
'The reason that no Jew was selected to participate in
the Games was always because of the fact that no Jew was
able to qualify by his ability for the Olympic team.
Heil Hitler!' Thirty years later, a white South African
sports official employed that kind of sophistry which
the Nazis would have admired when he sought to dismiss
queries about the absence of Blacks in his country's
swimming team for the Olympics: 'Some sports the African
is not suited for. In swimming the water closes their
pores and they cannot get rid of carbon dioxide, so they
tire quickly.' (7)

Sport for the Nazis, as for white South Africa, was
a vehicle to assert the mythology of racial superiority.
Conversely, it has also been an escape route out of the
ghetto for Blacks in the USA, for example, where there
is a long tradition of individuals excelling at sport,
notably boxing, and thereby raising their living standards
and social status, if only for a limited period. There
is an equally long tradition of white society in America
patronising black sportsmen as 'honorary whites' who
could bring national prestige whilst the racism inherent
in the country's social system remained intact. It was
that contradiction which the black American athletes
Tommie Smith and John Carlos tried to expose in their

famous 'Black Power' salute at the Mexico Olympics in
1968 as they were presented with their winner's medals.
They were revolting against the role of the 'Uncle Tom
athlete' (8), as John Carlos made clear after their
demonstration: 'We are sort of show horses out there
for the white people. They give us peanuts, pat us on
the back and say, "Boy you did fine".' (9)

The American experience in fact could be echoed in
South Africa in the future, for there is clear evidence
that white South Africa's sports and political rulers
are embarking upon a limited strategy of absorbing
certain black sports officials and sportsmen and women,
where previously they were rigidly barred from major
sports opportunities.

SPORT IN SOUTH AFRICA: THE BACKGROUND

To understand what is happening in the complex, shifting
sands of sport in South Africa today, we have to go back
to 1970. Up until that time, white sports spokesmen
made no attempt to apologise for the exclusion of Blacks
from 'national' teams. They were quite uncompromising
about the existence of apartheid in sport. Blacks would
not actually be prevented from participating in sport
but they had to do so within their own separate sports
organisations and would not be permitted to represent
their country. No mixing between the races would be
allowed in sport, and attempts by black people to resist
this were opposed by the apparatus of South Africa's
police state: black sports officials were issued with
banning orders, imprisoned and harassed by the security
services. (10)

But internationally the pressure was building up.
From the late 1950s, when Bishop Trevor Huddleston alerted
public opinion to the existence of racialism in South
African sport, the spotlight was increasingly on South
Africa. Inside the country, black sports bodies had
stepped up their activity, many of their leaders being
forced into exile from 1964 onwards as they were prevented
from organising internally. It was principally their
persistent lobbying under the leadership of the South
African Non-Racial Olympic Committee, SAN-ROC, which
forced the suspension of South Africa from the Olympics
in 1964. Protest was by that time achieving a momentum
on a world scale, for example in New Zealand which had
traditional commonwealth ties with white South Africa,
notably through rugby and cricket. (11) But it was
perhaps the 'D'Oliveira affair' which first placed the

issue seriously on the world stage and triggered off an
international reaction. Basil D'Oliveira, a South
African cricketer of Cape Coloured descent, had been
forced to go to England to further his cricketing career
and was eventually selected for the England team.
However, the South African government vetoed his late
selection for a tour there in 1968 and, amidst general
outrage, the English cricket authorities cancelled it.
(12)

   The D'Oliveira controversy laid the foundations in
Britain for massive demonstrations during the 1969-70
tour of the Springbok rugby side which was literally
placed under siege. Despite the players actually voting
to go home half-way through the tour, it staggered on to
the end, with matches being heavily disrupted and militant
demonstrators infiltrating the players' hotels and their
coach. But then, in May 1970, a planned cricket tour to
Britain was called off under the threat of massive
disruption from the organisers of the campaign that had
plagued the rugby tour: the Stop the Seventy Tour
movement. (13)

   1970 proved to be a catastrophe and ultimately a
turning point for white South African sport. Besides
the success of militant demonstrations in Britain, she
was finally expelled from the Olympics and from Davis
Cup tennis, suspended from athletics and barred from
gymnastics. Soon she faced virtual blanket isolation
from world competition. Even conservative Australia -
previously a steadfast ally - cancelled a projected
cricket tour in 1971 after demonstrators had heavily
disrupted a rugby tour the same year. (14)

   Apartheid's rulers faced a crisis, the magnitude of
which it is hard to comprehend without direct knowledge
of the sportsmania which grips the white community.
A boycott, as the black newspaper, the Johannesburg
'Post', argued, on 24 May 1970, 'hits South Africa where
it hurts most - in the sports breadbasket, and we all
know that you don't muck about with South African sports
and sportsmen, particularly if South Africa happens to
be good at it.' So sports-starved Whites looked to
their government for an initiative.

   It came on 22 April 1971 when the prime minister,
John Vorster, unveiled his new 'multi-national' sports
policy. In essence it meant that the different racial
groups in South Africa - Whites, Africans, Coloureds
and Asians - would be allowed to compete against each
other as four separate 'nations' within the country, but
only in major 'international' events with foreign
participants. This apparent concession merely expressed

the logic of apartheid which states that racial groups
should develop separately - provided of course that the
Whites remain in overall control. Crucially, Vorster
added: 'I want to make it very clear that in South
Africa no mixed sport shall be practised at club,
provincial, or national levels.' (15)

Thus, in the 'South African Games', held in Pretoria
in March-April 1973, South Africans competed together,
not in integrated teams, but as four separate 'nations',
in the presence of international sportsmen. And when
the British Lions rugby side toured the country in mid-
1974, while the vast majority of their matches were
played against white sides (including of course the all-
important Tests), two were played against a 'Bantu XV'
(Africans) and a 'Coloured XV'.

However the 'multi-national' policy did not bring the
fruits that the government had anticipated. Far from
relieving international pressure, South Africa's remorse-
less drift into isolation continued. Even less prominent
sports like hockey, squash, snooker and netball joined
the queue of sports from which she was excluded.

By the mid-1970s it was evident that a different
approach was necessary - always provided however that
the roots of sports apartheid remained intact. So
began a new phase which we shall characterise as a 'co-
option' strategy. Under it, white sports bodies, tacitly
encouraged by the then sports minister, Dr Piet Koornhof,
found it necessary to embark on a process of co-opting
those black sports groups who showed willing. By this
process it was hoped to both preserve the power structure
of white sport and present an image of integration.

Not all Blacks have been amenable to such co-option,
however. For besides the dominant white sports bodies -
the ones which traditionally have enjoyed exclusive
recognition and therefore contact with international
sports organisations - there are two different kinds of
black sports body: the racially exclusive black bodies
which confine membership to Africans or Asians or
Coloureds (i.e. they do not permit mixing even between
the different ethnic groups amongst Blacks as a whole);
and the 'non-racial' bodies which have members drawn
from all the black racial groups and a small, though
growing, number of Whites.

This 'tri-partite' structure is expressed in virtually
every sport within South Africa. The non-racial bodies
on the whole represent the majority of Blacks in each
sport, and contemptuously dismiss the blacks-only bodies
as 'stooges' or 'Uncle Toms', not surprisingly for the
latter mirror in their racial exclusivity the essence of

apartheid, and have thus been more readily co-opted.

RUGBY

In rugby, for example, where the South Africans achieved a breakthrough with a tour to Britain by a mixed 'Barbarians' side in October 1979 and then with the British Lions tour to South Africa in mid-1980, this tri-partite structure is clear.

The Barbarians side was sponsored by the white South African Rugby Board (SARB) of Dr Danie Craven, and consisted of eight Whites, eight Coloureds and eight Africans. SARB provided the Whites in the touring party, the Coloureds were drawn from the Coloureds-only South African Rugby Federation (SARF) and the Africans from the Africans-only South African Rugby Association (SARA). The latter two, SARF and SARA, are affiliated to SARB - but only on a subservient basis. For SARB as a 'national' umbrella body also has affiliated 22 white provincial units who thus out-vote the black 'national' bodies by 22 to 2. Furthermore, the black organisations were not allowed to enter teams into the Whites' premier inter-provincial rugby competition, the Currie Cup, because they were 'not good enough'. Yet, when it comes to a tour like the Barbarians or the visiting British Lions, they become 'good enough' to be selected. Thus it can be seen that the prime object is to win over international opinion rather than honestly to modify rugby at ground level domestically.

Significantly, SARA and SARF between them represent under 10,000 black rugby players, concentrated in the Cape province. The vast majority of Blacks - nearly 50,000 - belong to the non-racial body, the South African Rugby Union (SARU). It has rejected overtures from SARB on the grounds that only a genuinely non-racial, democratic and unified structure for rugby would be acceptable, whereas SARB was simply seeking to encapsulate Blacks. SARU was therefore not involved in the Barbarians tour nor would it in any way play host to touring parties such as the Lions. It condemns SARA and SARF as 'collaborators' and, like its sister non-racial bodies in other sports, has supported international boycotts of South African sport, believing that only through such a strategy have the Whites been forced to change and will future changes be achieved. SARU is affiliated to the non-racial umbrella group, the South African Council on Sport. It is the national spokesman for the non-racial sports bodies and rightly regards

itself as the authentic voice of sport in the country,
being the only one genuinely committed to non-racialism.
SACOS is in turn linked to the South African Non-Racial
Olympic Committee which has been such a successful
international lobbyist against white South African sports
participation, and is also an associate member of the
Supreme Council for Sport in Africa, the voice of black
Africa in sport.

Recently, as international pressure has forced changes,
SACOS has become more influential and powerful, the South
African government being in a dilemma over its response
to this: the normal reflex action of the government would
be to suppress such an opponent outright, but the international sensitivity of the sports issue has forced it to
tread more carefully.

APARTHEID IN SPORT TODAY

So, within South African sport, there is a whole layer of
predominantly black sport that has never been recognised
by the outside world (or rather the Western nations who
dominate most world sports federations) and still refuses
to compromise until all vestiges of racialism have been
removed from the sports system.

For, despite claims to the contrary, apartheid still
rules the roost in South African sport. There have
certainly been changes, brought about as a result of
world pressure. By South African standards, these changes
have been significant - in many respects unthinkable prior
to 1970. But by world standards they have been entirely
superficial. The sports system has been given a facelift,
with racial restrictions being relaxed in certain limited
senses and usually during prestige events likely to
attract international attention. At club level, however,
where fundamental change must occur if it is to have any
meaning for most sportsmen and women, restrictions have
hardly eased at all. As a government MP said, in South
Africa's House of Assembly on 21 May 1979, 'Integrated
clubs and integrated sport constitute far less than
1 per cent of the total sport activities in South Africa.'
With the exception of those clubs affiliated to the non-
racial bodies, virtually all clubs in all sports are
racially exclusive, and school sport is if anything even
more rigidly segregated. Thus, whilst a certain flexi-
bility is permitted at national level, this is not the
case locally - a dichotomy which holds the key to understanding the contemporary development of South African
sport. The official attitude is that whereas the

national level can be controlled and contained, matters could get out of hand in a way that could so easily spill over into the whole of society if integration started seriously to occur locally.

It is also necessary to appreciate that, although there is no law *specifically* prohibiting mixed sport on South Africa's statute books, there are a string of apartheid laws and regulations which actually make multi-racial sport illegal, just as they restrict any other aspect of life in South Africa.

For example, the Urban Areas Act 1945 controls black sports facilities and restricts their use by permit. The 1950 Group Areas Act segregates the population – sportsmen and women included – and in October 1973 the Sports Minister issued Proclamation R228 under the 1950 Act which enabled multi-racial matches to be banned on private grounds as well. The Proclamation was brought in specifically to prevent the Aurora Cricket Club, in Maritzburg, Natal, from playing multi-racial games. The Club had been formed early in 1973 by a group of black and white cricketers, breaking new ground in the process. In the event no prosecution was launched using the new regulation, prudence presumably dictating that the government refrain from using its new power – although members of the Special Branch at one stage took names of players and spectators and prepared a report for the Attorney-General.

Other laws such as the Reservation of Separate Amenities Act 1953 and the 1928 Liquor Act prevent the integration of ground and club facilities for refreshments, seating, toilets and dancing. In August 1979, the Wanderers Club in Johannesburg was restricted to admitting Blacks as 'honorary members' because full membership would have contravened the law in respect of club facilities. In May 1979, Cape Town's international rugby stadium, Newlands, also announced that the law prevented it from integrating facilities, while in March 1980 black spectators and athletes were barred from the opening of a new running track in Oudtshoorn in the Cape Province because it had no provision for separate toilets.

Black African sportsmen and women are also governed by Pass Laws which restrict their movements as citizens and prevent them travelling freely to 'away' matches, or on tours. Every black has to have special permission entered on his pass book to reside in an area for more than 72 hours, such permission being dependent upon official discretion. Significantly, the onus is on the individual to prove that he is legitimately outside his home area, so that at any time a black sportsman could be arrested, held in police cells, and required to prove he has been away for less than 72 hours.

Although many of these laws can be and are increasingly circumvented by obtaining permits from the relevant government department, discretionary power over the issue of permits enables control to be exercised by the authorities. Thus, matches between 'stooge' black groups and Whites are automatically cleared for permits, or alternatively granted special 'international licences' on the basis that different 'nations' are competing. Moreover, whilst the government has been increasingly prepared to turn a blind eye to the flouting of the law by sports groups - especially when foreign teams are involved - a full range of racialist legislation and regulations remains in force and can be applied at any time it is deemed appropriate. The result is regular incidents such as the one in February 1978 when a multi-racial soccer match in Pretoria was forcibly broken up by police and the participants threatened with prosecution under both the Group Areas Act and municipal bye-laws. Until such legislation is repealed - at the very least in so far as it impinges directly upon sport - then claims that apartheid is on its way out of sport will remain entirely spurious.

This is underlined by the experience of non-racial sports officials and sportsmen who have faced both intimidation by the security services and actual prosecution. For example, Morgan Naidoo, president of the non-racial South African Swimming Federation, was issued with a banning order in 1973 - that is, he was not allowed, inter alia, to meet with more than one other person or to attend public places, thus stopping his work as a sports official until the order expired in 1978. Passports have been denied to leading black officials on non-racial bodies, such as Hassan Howa and M.N. Pather, President and Secretary of the South African Council on Sport, preventing them from presenting their case abroad. (By contrast, black sports officials co-opted by the Whites are able to travel freely, sometimes at the authorities' expense.)

Even Whites who join the non-racial bodies do not escape attention. Thus, the former white Springbok triallist, 'Cheeky' Watson, who in 1977 resigned from SARB and joined the non-racial SARU, has been arrested several times, solely for the 'crime' of entering the black township of New Brighton outside Port Elizabeth in order to play for his new non-racial team in the local Kwaru league. (Whites need permits to enter black areas and he was refused one.) He was severely reprimanded by

white rugby officials such as Danie Craven when he
'defected' and has since been subjected to harassment by
the Special Branch. Significantly, he, along with several
white colleagues who joined him, is entirely scornful of
the suggestion that multi-racial rugby is now on its way
in under SARB's direction: the changes are 'just a lot of
window dressing', he says. (16)

Harassment and intimidation meted out against genuinely
non-racial sport contrasts markedly with the rewards given
to those few blacks who do allow themselves to be accommo-
dated by the white bodies. Besides being given the
opportunity to tour abroad which their fellow Blacks have
always been denied, these 'collaborators' are often given
secure jobs as individuals, and offered financial inducements to improve their club and organisational facilities.
Such inducements are naturally most attractive, given the
abysmal level of facilities available to Blacks and given
the fact that the government spends five times as much
money on white sport as it does on black sport – a
disparity compounded by the fact that Blacks outnumber
Whites by 4 to 1.

The strategy of co-opting certain Blacks and controlling
those who dissent is part of a total strategy by the Whites.
They now recognise that the old approach of brazen
apartheid is not viable socially. It is also restrictive
economically because an economy which has been, and still
is, industrialising and growing as fast as South Africa's,
requires a large pool of skilled labour, which in turn
requires racial barriers in the labour market to be
reduced. And so, the Whites have sought deliberately to
cultivate and co-opt a black urban middle class, offering the
prospect of jobs to more skilled black workers and relaxing
aspects of so-called 'petty apartheid' such as segregated
park benches. Even recent initiatives to legitimise
certain black trade unions can be seen as a method of
co-opting and thereby bringing within an orderly bargaining
framework, previously unruly and militant action by black
workers. Although there are factors peculiar to sport
which have forced changes within it, nevertheless such
changes should be set against the background of the
general programme of South Africa's white ruling class.
And because sport plays such a pivotal role in the
society, because it has been the target of such successful
international pressure, sport is now one of the major
ideological battlegrounds upon which the country's future
is being fought.

CONCLUSION

Meanwhile, the past decade has proved conclusively that only an uncompromising boycott strategy by opponents of sports apartheid produces results. As has now been conceded by the heart transplant surgeon, Professor Christian Barnard, and by white South Africa's rugby supremo, Danie Craven, isolation *has* worked: the protest campaigns have done more than anything else to force changes. (In the past both men have been fierce critics of such campaigns.) The former England cricket captain, Mike Brearley, put it succinctly when he argued: 'Any achievements in multi-racial sport over there have been obtained through South Africa being isolated.' (17)

That isolation should remain until sports apartheid has been entirely abolished (see the appendix to this chapter for a list of conditions to be fulfilled to meet this). Despite the growing clamour for South Africa's readmission to the world arena, the reality is that Whites will only change further beyond the present cosmetic level if they have the incentive to do so. If the boycotts are eased that incentive will disappear. On the other hand, if they are maintained, there is every prospect of an acceleration of the pace of change – in which case, not only could the hopes of black sportsmen and women rise dramatically, but the consequences should reverberate through the wider fabric of apartheid.

REFERENCES

1 Speech by Denis Thatcher to the London Society of Rugby Football Referees, 6 December 1979.
2 Letter from the Prime Minister, Mrs Thatcher, to the Chairman of the British Olympic Association, 19 February 1980.
3 'Guardian', 24 December 1973.
4 See Richard D. Mandell, 'The Nazi Olympics', London, Souvenir Press, 1972; and Judith Holmes, 'Olympiad 1936', New York, Ballantine Books, 1971.
5 See also Mandell, op. cit., and Holmes, op. cit., and Arthur D. Morse, 'While 6 Million Died', New York, Ace Books, 1967, for a revealing analysis of the sports world's reaction to pressure over the Berlin Olympics and its rationalisation of Nazi ideologies and atrocities.
6 'Guardian', 28 July 1976.
7 'Sports Illustrated', USA, June 1968.
8 Harry Edwards, 'The Revolt of the Black Athlete', New York, Free Press, 1969.

9   Ibid., p.138.
10 See my 'Don't Play with Apartheid', London, Allen &
    Unwin, 1971, pp.49-59. Also Richard E. Lapchick,
    'The Politics of Race and International Sport: A
    case study of South Africa', Westport, Connecticutt,
    Greenwood Press, 1975.
11 Richard Thompson, 'Race and Sport', Oxford University
    Press, 1964, and 'Retreat from Apartheid', Wellington,
    Oxford University Press, 1975.
12 Basil D'Oliveira, 'The D'Oliveira Affair', Glasgow,
    Collins, 1969.
13 'Don't Play with Apartheid', op.cit., and my Direct
    action and the Springbok tours, in R. Benewick and
    T. Smith (eds), 'Direct Action and Democratic Politics',
    London, Allen & Unwin, 1972, pp.192.202.
14 See Stewart Harris, 'Political Football', Melbourne,
    Gold Star, 1972.
15 See Joan Brickhill, 'Race Against Race', International
    Defence & Aid Fund, 1976, for an analysis of the
    multi-national sports policy.
16 BBC, 'The World at One', 28 August 1979.
17 'Daily Mirror', 20 August 1979.

APPENDIX

Extract from a Memorandum submitted to the British Sports
Council by the Stop All Racist Tours Committee in January
1980.

PROPOSED CONDITIONS TO BE FULLY SATISFIED IF SOUTH AFRICA
IS TO BE CONSIDERED FOR RE-ADMISSION TO WORLD SPORT
    1 Both the South African Government and all
internationally recognised South African sports organisations should publicly commit themselves to a fully
integrated, truly non-racial sports system.
    2 An Act of Parliament should be introduced specifi-
cally exempting all aspects of sport from the apartheid
laws and regulations which at present restrict it: the
Group Areas Act, Separate Amenities Act, Urban Areas Act,
Liquor Act, Pass Laws, permits regulations, etc.
    3 Part of that Act should expressly forbid the
constitution of any sports club or federation to contain
racially exclusive rules or conditions of membership.
    4 All players, spectators, trainers, etc. should have
the same rights of access to all sporting clubs and ground
facilities throughout the territory of South Africa.
    5 The organisation of each and every sport should be
entirely integrated on a non-racial basis.

6   Within the educational system all sport should be integrated on a non-racial basis.

7   The Government should plan and put into action a sports development programme which will raise black sport as a whole to the level of all sport in South Africa, with each citizen enjoying an equal proportion of the state funds devoted to sport.

8   All restrictions (banning orders, the confiscation of passports, refusal of exit visas, etc.) regarding the representatives of non-racial sport should be lifted, and police harassment of the non-racial officials and players ended.

The above conditions having been fulfilled, an international sports commission should go to South Africa to establish whether a basis exists for re-admission to world competition.

Index